Black Baltimore A New Theory of Community

Children in the daycare center operated by Union Temple Baptist Church in Upton play under the watchful eye of their pastor, Reverend Vernon Dobson.

Black Baltimore

A New Theory of Community

HAROLD A. McDOUGALL

Temple University Press Philadelphia

Temple University Press, Philadelphia 19122
Copyright © 1993 by Temple University. All rights reserved
Published 1993
Printed in the United States of America

⊗ The paper used in this publication meets the minimum requirements
of American National Standard for Information Sciences—Permanence
of Paper for Printed Library Materials, ANSI Z39.48-1984

Library of Congress Cataloging-in-Publication Data
McDougall, Harold A. (Harold Augustus), 1945–
    Black Baltimore : a new theory of community / Harold A. McDougall.
    p.   cm.
    Includes bibliographical references and index.
    ISBN 1-56639-037-0 (cloth)
    1. Afro-Americans—Maryland—Baltimore.   2. Baltimore (Md.)—
Social conditions.   3. Baltimore (Md.)—Politics and government.
I. Title.
F189.B19N45   1993
305.896′073′097526—dc20   92-32548

For my wife, Beverly,
my daughter, Emily Nadja,
and my sons,
Miné, Masai, and Jonathon

Contents

Acknowledgments

THIS IS my first book. I believe I am permitted to use these first pages as a public acknowledgment of the many people who have influenced, directed, and nurtured me over the years. Of course, my mother and father, Olga and Harold McDougall, and my grandparents, Dorothy Jumper and Clifford Cheltenham (both now deceased), top the list. But in what I consider my professional life, beginning more than twenty-five years ago, there have been many, many such people: Margo Adair, Allan Axelrod, Suzanne Berger, Max Bond, Joseph Brooks, Bob Brown, Robert S. Browne, Haywood Burns, Guido Calabresi, Carl Callendar, the late Denise Carty-Bennia, Leroy Clark, Rhonda Copelon, Martha Derthick, Charlie Halperin, Jill Hamberg, Charlie Inniss, Carl Johnson, Bud Kanitz, Duncan Kennedy, Arthur Kinoy, the late Arthur Leff, Howard Lesnick, Jim Lowry, Frank Michelman, Rich Rubenstein, Sheila Rush, Richard Sennett, Bill Strickland, and Claude Weaver, to name a few.

Then there are the people who contributed directly to the book itself. First and foremost are my colleagues at the Catholic University Law School, who individually and collectively have provided me with the kind of supportive environment in which writing takes place. Father David Granfield, Ray Marcin, and Bill Wagner have been especially helpful in the areas of philosophy and religion. I commend also our superb (computerized) research librarians, Brian Baker, Diana Botluk, and Mark Hammond. There are my research assistants, Kelly Breuer, Rosalie Charpentier, Kathy Doan, Allen Douglas, Bonnie Glenn, Lisa Grattan, David Lisi, and Flair Mills, all of whom were creative and energetic, some of whom wrote first drafts of historical and background material. There are the students in my housing and related seminars at the Catholic University and Cornell law schools, many of whom made similar contributions.

Colleagues from other law schools played important roles as well. Frank Michelman of Harvard, as on so many previous occasions, provided pivotal criticism and suggestions. Greg Alexander of Cornell demolished a lumbering first draft and forced me to get the manuscript into fighting shape before I sent it into the ring with him for a second round. Myres McDougal, more mentor than colleague, started me on this project years ago when he elicited my assistance in a redraft of his landmark book, *Property, Wealth, and Land* (with David Haber), and expressed his belief that I might "cut deeper than Charlie Reich did." The entire Cornell law faculty grilled me at a lunch, appropriately styled, for "half-baked" ideas.

Many Baltimoreans provided first-hand information and criticism as well as intense, often poignant insights: Ameen Bahar, Barbara Bezdek, Bonnie Birker, Joe Green Bishop, Paul Coates, Ruth Crystal, Vernon Dobson, Rona Feit, Carl Gabel, Sue Goehring, Mark Gornik, Arnie Graf, Bernita Holsey, Ella Johnson, Dennis Livingston, Glen McNatt, Awilda Marquez, Linda Meade, Arthur Murphy, William Murphy, Sr., Daki Napata, Jackie Philson, Darnell Ridgley, Gary Rodwell, William Shahid, Allan Tibbels, Elva Tillman, Albert Vaughn, and Athena Young only begin the list.

Finally, there are my guardian angels at Temple University Press—Jane Cullen, who believed in my ability to do this, and provided me with a sounding board over several years, and Doris Braendel, who took charge with a real understanding of what I was trying to say, and provided me with the essential discipline, direction, and inspiration that was necessary to bring the project to a close.

Harold McDougall
Silver Spring, Maryland

Black Baltimore A New Theory of Community

Prologue

"Don't lament lost opportunities.
When God opens a new one for you,
give it all your allegiance."

—Reverend Albert Vaughn,
pastor, Sharon Baptist Church of Baltimore

PARTLY AS a result of its history—a paradoxical mixture of slavery, commerce, industry, and suburbanization—Baltimore today combines aspects of urban living that can be found only in isolation in other cities of the eastern seaboard and the Midwest. For example, Baltimore is predominantly black, like Washington, D.C., yet it also has a significant white ethnic population, like New York, Boston, Philadelphia, and Chicago. In fact, enclaves of ethnic Europeans remain within the city's urban core, giving the city a unique flavor. Baltimore is the southernmost city of the North, and the northernmost city of the South, its population and physical structure marked by the slave plantation, the merchant ship, and the factory. A leading site for the importation of African slaves, Baltimore's participation in the slave trade reached a peak at the same time that the city emerged as a regional commercial metropolis because of the grain and iron brought in from the Midwest via the Baltimore & Ohio Railroad. Having developed at the crossroads of the different cultures that have shaped America—part slave, part free; part "native" white, part immigrant; part southern, part northern, and part midwestern—Baltimore is rich in the social, civic, and cultural organizations produced by all these strains. Today Baltimore is predominantly black, and it is that culture which is the principal focus of this book.

I begin with my paternal great-grandfather, William McDougall, who entered this country in the late 1870s through the port of Bal-

1

timore. He came from the Caribbean island of St. Croix. His father was an Irish merchant seaman, his mother an African woman who lived on the island. As my grandfather (deceased at ninety) told the story, my great-grandfather got off the boat and walked toward the city. A white man (who may have thought my great-grand father was white also) came up to him and asked if he had voted for mayor yet.

"No," my great-grandfather answered.

"Here's a dollar," said the man. "Go vote for so-and-so."

And that was the first dollar my great-grandfather made in this country.

William came to Baltimore, like many other people of African descent, because he had heard that it was a place of great opportunity. A strong and vibrant "vernacular" black culture in the city provided a context for many forms of organization. The term "vernacular," from a Latin word meaning "native to a place," has been used in English primarily to designate a native language.[1] Ivan Illich, in his book *Gender*, gives the term a broader meaning, however, and portrays the vernacular as an entire culture, "home-made, homespun, home-grown," developing gender roles, home life, and gossip as well as community institutions such as churches and civic associations.[2] Blacks' participation in Baltimore's government and economy has been enhanced by their vernacular culture—styles of speech, techniques for building relationships, and modes of organization and networking. Despite many setbacks, this vernacular culture provided a springboard for upwardly mobile members of the black community who strove to break out of segregated inner-city neighborhoods. Some succeeded at the cost of the very culture that was their means of escape.

Bernita Holsey, a feisty, middle-aged black woman with an improbable—and compelling—combination of class and street smarts, is a specialist in preparing disadvantaged people to start small businesses. She and her family typify Baltimore black upward mobility. Her father, a United Methodist minister, moved his family to Baltimore from Maryland's eastern shore, settling in a neighborhood known as Sandtown. "It was called that because it was so sandy," Holsey explained. "I remember in the basements of some of the older buildings, particularly the churches, you could still see the sand." But as an upwardly mobile family, they moved on, first to "Sugar Hill," as Druid Heights was then called (does every black neighborhood in the United States have a Sugar Hill?). As segregation barriers fell, they kept moving north and west, finally settling in tree-lined Forest Park, just inside the city limits.

Holsey recalled in an interview the mixed blessings that integration brought. Working in the Baltimore public school system immediately after the end of segregation, she witnessed confrontations between black parents and white teachers over the latter's racist remarks in class. The civil rights movement had opened up new opportunities for black teachers, many of whom left the system. Many of the white teachers, despite their antipathy toward their new black students, stayed in the school system because they had job security. Holsey has concluded, moreover, that the political gains made during the 1960s and 1970s, when many "first" blacks were appointed or elected to various offices, were often symbolic rather than tangible advances that black people could comprehend or that made a difference in their lives. Some of these newly minted officials treated black citizens cavalierly, as if they had "crossed over," leaving the less fortunate members of the vernacular community behind. It was hard, she recalls, to accept public pronouncements from these same people that blacks should "stick together" come election time.

The civil rights movement, a boon to the upwardly mobile black middle class, failed to advance the black community as a whole. As the "talented tenth" (W. E. B. DuBois' term) left the black community, seeking suburban lifestyles and more universal middle-class status, black vernacular culture was assimilated and dispersed, and its roots began to wither. Community activists remaining in black Baltimore began building institutions designed to fill the growing gap between the social functions the weakened vernacular community could no longer perform and the social functions that government was increasingly unwilling or unable to perform. Such "paragovernmental" activity was often thwarted or corrupted by powerful white elected officials, leading community activists to conclude that electoral power was a *sine qua non* for reconstructing the black community. Like the civil rights movement, this new thrust was also led by the upwardly mobile leadership class of the black community; the great majority of working-class and poor black residents of Baltimore were relegated to the role of consumer, rather than participant, in the growth of political power.

But that does not mean that people in these forgotten neighborhoods are not ready to get involved. At the northern end of Holsey's old neighborhood of Sandtown, now a deteriorating black community dotted with arid, vacant lots, Athena Young's little son watered the plants that filled her apartment. Her daughter read aloud from *The Berenstain Bears* and proudly showed her first-grade report card. They were both filled with their mother's energy and light. "God's Gift," said a poster on the door to the kitchen, depicting three smiling black children.

"We don't have control over the forces of evil," Young said, "even if we're good at heart, even if we organize the whole country. All we can do is fight what may be a series of losing battles, hoping that we'll win the war. Like the slaves, who worked from 'can see in the morning' until 'can't see at night.' They hung in there and eventually were freed.

"Spiritually, you know whether what you're doing is right or wrong. We've been physically released from slavery but our minds haven't been freed yet. Once you have kids, though, you can't just sit back. You have to do more than just try to save your own butt. You've got to help save the community your kids are going to come up in.

"It can even be fun," she added, with a broad grin.

Jackie Turner is from Harlem Park, adjacent to and in many ways similar to Young's neighborhood of Sandtown. She insisted that the negative and antisocial behavior she sees in her own community has to be met in a neighborly way. "Don't put people down. If you see some kids who look like they're doing drugs or dealing drugs, you have to speak to them. 'I know your Mom, she put a lot of love into you,' I tell them. They call me 'Auntie' and they respect me and listen to what I say. The newspapers and the T.V. give us a lot of negative attention, but they're not interested when anything positive happens. Maybe 10 percent of the people use drugs, don't take care of their homes, let trash pile up in front of their door."

To illustrate just how bad things can get in her neighborhood, Turner told me about a police lynching of a black man suspected of raping and murdering two white girl children in suburban Glen Burnie. The young man, known as "Tony" to his neighbors on Turner's block, was seen as a friendly person who played with neighborhood children. An informant had told the police in Glen Burnie, where Tony worked with a foster parent agency, that Tony was the perpetrator of the crime.

"The FBI and the police came, dozens of them. They had no intention of taking him alive; when they got out of their cruisers there wasn't a nightstick in sight, only guns. My kids were sitting on the front steps when the shooting started. They asked me, 'Why did they do it, Ma? Why did they kill him?' When Tony died, he told the people near him, 'I didn't do anything. Tell my mother and sister I love them.' He laid on the ground for hours. The police didn't even cover him up."

Turner expressed concern that neighborhood children have started to think it is normal for someone to be lying in his own blood. But how do you explain something like this without making the child afraid for his own life? "Is the only way to teach them to be submissive to white people?" Jackie asked, opening her hands in a gesture of pure frustration. "Even when the white people are wrong? We need to get the 90 percent in Harlem Park together to fight to save the other 10 percent."

Ameen Bahar, from Upton, another adjacent neighborhood in West Baltimore, is forty, older than Turner and Young, who are in their mid-twenties. He is the youngest of a family of eight children, all of whom have been Muslims and all of whom took the same last name. Originally a Christian, Bahar was a member of the Muslim Masjid Al-Haqq in Upton from 1975 to 1985, from the time Warith Muhammad took over the Nation of Islam to the time a faction of the masjid split off and relocated in Liberty Heights. A year after he left the Muslims, Bahar became a Buddhist. He was very depressed, sitting in a park with a pistol in a paper bag, contemplating killing himself, his wife, and their infant son. A man walked by and said, "You look mighty upset, brother." Bahar agreed, telling him what he planned to do. The man was a Buddhist. "Listen, why don't you come with me to this meeting. After that, if you still feel like going ahead with your plans, feel free." Bahar went with him. "I've been chanting ever since," Bahar said, grinning. "He saved my life."

Bahar's greatest talent is jazz singing. He sang in clubs in the American Southwest, while doing room service in hotels as a day job. He knows lots of musicians and wants to open a restaurant, with entertainment. His father has an after-hours social club; his brother Abdel, a very successful Muslim, is acquainted with Muhammad Ali. "I want to create value from my life," Bahar said thoughtfully. "I want to be part of something positive in this life, even a small thing and a small part, just to add something to the peace of the world. So many people have no self-esteem. The negative is always reinforced, never the positive. World Peace, what the Buddhists call 'Kosen Ufa,' is everybody's dream, but the only way you'll get it is if everyone changes from within. All the poison out there, all the hatred. Black on white, gay on straight, skinny on fat."

"People have to learn how to accept themselves before they can learn to accept other people. It's a sad situation, the way we are now. Every neighborhood in West Baltimore, things are really bad, especially for the kids. Don't give the kids your prejudices, don't poison them with the stuff you've been poisoned with. This is as much for my son as it is for me. We've got to do something for the youth. If we don't affect them, what's going on around us now will be the future. Bleak, as far as you can see."

Black clergy, members of Baltimore's Interfaith Ministerial Alliance and its offshoot, Baltimoreans United in Leadership Development (BUILD), a citywide coalition of churches, community-based organizations, and labor unions, have organized to address the problems of Baltimore's inner-city poor. BUILD has prodded the city's elected black leadership to lend funding, staff, and planning resources to a joint "community-building in partnership" effort in Sandtown, which has the potential to develop the neighborhood as a national showpiece of participatory democracy, human development, and neighborhood renovation.

Sharon Baptist Church in Sandtown is a new member congregation in BUILD. As I waited for my appointment to interview the Reverend Alfred Vaughn of Sharon Baptist, he was taking care of a number of ongoing matters. A state senator was waiting to get his advice. Two or three glamorous, formidable-looking elderly black women had several questions about how their committees were running. While I waited, they laughed and joked with me.

Reverend Vaughn's easy, confident manner is pure vernacular, and reminded me of what the old folks in the South call "home training"—the social skills, taught at home, that form a foundation which gives a person tremendous advantages in the world of human affairs. Reverend Vaughn has more than home training, though. He has *church* training, *institutional* training, a level of vernacular preparation available only to a few. Vaughn's family has been a part of Sharon Baptist Church since his grandmother was baptized into the congregation by its founder, Reverend Alexander, who also founded the city's premier black newspaper, the *Baltimore Afro-American*. Vaughn has learned the history of his church and of his community from the elders of Sharon Baptist. "Sharon Baptist was founded in 1885 and has been in its present building since 1914," he told me.

"We've always been a part of this community. Trolleys used to run right beside the church."

Vaughn's unusually high level of vernacular training had a purpose: to prepare him for leadership. He has learned to manage, in a seemingly effortless, reflexive manner, the cross-currents of human relationships involving not five or six people, as in a family, but hundreds—in some cases, a thousand people, the size of some of the churches in West Baltimore.

"I owe my whole development to this church, to the people of Sandtown. They've been my inspiration, they saw in me a spark and ignited it. It's my responsibility to pass it on to those who come later. Our ministry is based on Luke—heal the brokenhearted, set the captive free. Sandtown is a very fertile area for that particular gospel. All the needs in the world are here, and the churches of Sandtown are beginning to address them—soup kitchens, food banks, all financed by our own congregations. It's about giving a hundred dollars to keep a single mother's water from being turned off. The needs of the people in our community are *real*; you have to be here, to walk out in the streets to see it, to understand.

"We can't miss a whole generation of people desperately in need of help. Our business is always to be in the marketplace where the people are. Some of their worldly cares may rub off on us, but some of their grace may also.

"Death is the great equalizer. Each of us has a golden opportunity to find out what God intends for us and to be about that business. Don't lament lost opportunities. When God opens a new one for you, give it all your allegiance."

Even the highly developed vernacular leadership of Sandtown's churches can fail, however, if they cannot make an adjustment to the newer, more democratic forms of community participation that are needed to reach the community's forgotten poor and working people and involve them directly in their own development. Small social action units, more flexible and closer to the grassroots even than the community organizations that have allied themselves with clergy in BUILD, will be necessary for this work. Such "base communities" are small peer groups of perhaps a dozen or two dozen people who share a similar philosophy, life condition, and social objective. First seen in the liberation theology movement of Latin America, base communities are important networking and empowering devices by which development—economic, political, and social—can be rooted deep in the community. Base communities need to be found and encouraged where they exist, and organized where they do not. Base communities can be formed by churches building peer groups within their congregations, by community-based organizers, even by social workers among their clientele.

A network of such base communities, existing at the neighborhood level and reaching up into the ranks of black and white civic leaders, could weave a new kind of community, capable of handling some of our especially intractable and difficult social choices, providing a communitarian, consensus-driven form of dispute resolution to complement present majoritarian techniques. I see the foundations of such a New Community in Baltimore being created as community-spirited organizers, clergy, public interest advocates, businesspeople, and government workers interact, network, and build relationships through which more and more of Baltimore's urban agenda is being developed and carried out.

Chapter One
Civil Rights and
the New Property

There is nothing wrong with poor people having power.

—Darnell Ridgley, Baltimore community organizer

EVER SINCE the New Deal, declared Charles Reich in his 1964 article "The New Property," the wealth of more and more U.S. citizens has come to depend not on their ownership of private property, but rather on their relationship to government and their receipt of "government largess," such as social security, public insurance and compensation, licenses, franchises, benefits, subsidies, use of public resources, and government contracts. Reich argued that when such government largess determined safety and status, it should be held as of right and granted the same protections from government interference enjoyed by private wealth. Thus, government largess would become the New Property.[1] For me, "New Property" has a broader connotation, evoking the "public interest," regulatory approach of the Democratic party from the New Deal to the Viet Nam War, including the full range of civil rights protections and programs developed during that time. Yet the public interest—in pursuance of which government regulation takes place—is often difficult to define. This problem has become increasingly important as the public becomes less and less a community and more and more a mass of alienated individuals, unable to effectively assert their "interest."

My reason for studying Baltimore is to examine the themes of participatory democracy and community empowerment illustrated by self-help efforts in the city's vernacular black community, and to consider how participatory democracy and community empowerment might help to better define the public interest, as well as furnish social approaches that are useful, and often necessary, complements to public interest regulation. The struggles of the black community of

9

West Baltimore through succeeding stages of American social and political history reveal a tension between the institutions of community and the institutions of government that has significance for the American citizenry as a whole. That significance is thrown into sharp relief by the particularly intense stresses and strains the black population has experienced in dealing with both sets of institutions.

The Conflict Between Rights and Community

The legislative and litigation-oriented agenda of the modern civil rights movement, like the liberal Democratic agenda with which it is allied, has neglected the need for community. While achieving great rewards for individual African-Americans, the modern civil rights movement has undermined not only a sense of community among black people but also some of our strongest institutions, particularly those rooted in the vernacular. In this respect the civil rights movement reflects U.S. constitutional and legal traditions as a whole, in which "democracy" has traditionally meant representative, pluralistic government, secured by national election, by which the sovereign people delegate to representatives their primary right to govern, giving up civic activity and civic responsibility in the bargain.[2] This view, rooted in the liberal democratic traditions of the Federalists, sought to restrict the involvement of the people in governance and to secure democracy through "representation, privacy, individualism, and rights."[3] The Federalists were apprehensive about widespread popular participation in government after the Revolution, seeing in it the danger of factionalized dispute and the possibility that a popular majority might vote to repudiate debts, interfere with property rights, or otherwise trample upon liberal values.[4] They sought to protect these values from majority factions by devices such as representation, separation of powers, and judicial review.[5] Thomas Jefferson's Anti-Federalist, "civic republican" approach of direct democracy was thus tempered to the "realities of governing in a large-scale nation-state," entailing an enormous reduction in participation and active citizenship.[6] In the federalist tradition, the engagement with community associated with the civic republican approach is sacrificed for "rights," which create power only when they disempower someone else.

John Locke hypothesized a "political society," that would be "intermediate between an anarchic state of nature and the emergence of formal, specialized government.[7] Political society is constituted when men agree to "join and unite into a community for their comfortable, safe, and peaceable living one amongst another, in a secure enjoyment of their properties and a greater security against any that are not of it."[8] Alexis deTocqueville, in his travels in the United States, observed such phenomena as well: "If a stoppage occurs in a thoroughfare and the circulation of vehicles is hindered, the neighbors immediately form themselves into a deliberative body; and this extemporaneous assembly gives rise to an executive power which remedies the inconvenience before anybody has thought of recurring to a preexisting authority superior to that of the persons immediately concerned."[9] Political society is also observable in barn raisings and the rotating cooperative harvesting of fields in rural areas.

Locke observed that political society, the diffused capacity of the people to organize their own affairs, continues to exist as a backup for government itself. It reemerges when the effectiveness of government is suspended, when "government visibly ceases and the people become a confused multitude, without order or connection."[10] Political society is to be distinguished from government, which has a monopoly on the legitimate use of force and which undergirds the positive law that organizes what I will call "governmental" society.[11]

Political society should be distinguished not only from social life organized by government, but also from social life organized by "paragovernmental" bodies such as special interest and public interest groups, trade associations, community-based organizations, and social movements, "whose functions and structures may be analogous to those of the larger political system but whose powers and responsibilities are narrower in scope."[12] In this "paragovernmental" society, citizens in voluntary association seek either to affect the way government operates or to assume some of its functions, in neither event receiving any increment of the government's monopoly on the legitimate use of force. Paragovernmental activity has two distinct dimensions. One is the politics of intervention, which encompasses the activity of special interest groups, protest movements, and public interest organizations, attempting to affect government policy and its implementation. The other is the politics of parallelism, in which self-help organizations pull themselves together to fill vacuums created by the inability or unwillingness of government to provide or create the essential conditions of social life—housing, employment, education,

public safety, civic guidance. As our society's representative government has become alienated and distant, and proven less able to organize production, manage conflict, or rationalize social life, both intervention and parallelism have increased.

"Booker T. and W. E. B."

The conflict between liberals and conservatives *within* the African-
American community over the nomination of Judge Clarence Thomas
to the Supreme Court signaled a growing diversity of opinion among
African-Americans as to how to proceed into the future. Specifically,
should (conservative) strategies of parallelism or (liberal) strategies of
intervention predominate? This debate goes back at least as far as the
historic conflict waged at the turn of the century between the conservative Booker T. Washington, an advocate of the strength of vernacular institutions (parallelism), and the liberal W. E. B. DuBois, a
proponent of "rights-based" protest (intervention). Washington was
concerned with the role of mediating institutions, those social units of
lesser scope and coercive power than the state which have a strong
hand in shaping social life and which are deeply rooted in the vernacular community: family, church, university, small business, fraternal
association, civic association, and the like.[13] DuBois, younger and a
radical, claimed that Washington's emphasis was misdirected and
that social and political strategy should focus on confrontation with
the racist state, on protest and agitation for reform. These two distinct
lines of thought—concerning the creation of parallel, "mediating" institutions in the black community (Washington) and the mounting of
vigorous protest and critique of objectionable state actions and omis-
sions (DuBois)—evolved separately. Washington's approach has surfaced not only among modern black conservatives like Thomas Sowell
and Glen Loury, but also among black nationalists, beginning with
Marcus Garvey and continuing through Elijah Muhammad, Malcolm
X, and Louis Farrakhan. Especially in its "nationalist" incarnation,
Washingtonianism has been a expressed in large measure in the black
vernacular, and is thus a philosophy particularly attractive to the
black working and lower classes, who remain steeped in that tradition. DuBois' approach is seen most directly in the National Association for the Advancement of Colored People (NAACP), which he
helped to found. It focused on the upwardly mobile, middle-class,
elite, the "talented tenth" of the community, and particularly the

northern black intellectuals, who later became more and more estranged from the vernacular community.

The protest politics of W. E. B. DuBois or the communitarian economics and civic self-help of Booker T. Washington? Or some combination of the two? It is a consistent question among African-Americans, evoked in poetry in 1968 by Dudley Randall, a DuBoisian:[14]

Booker T. and W. E. B.

"It seems to me," said Booker T.,
"It shows a mighty lot of cheek
To study chemistry and Greek
When Mister Charlie needs a hand
To hoe the cotton on his land,
And when Miss Ann looks for a cook,
Why stick your nose inside a book?"

"I don't agree," said W.E.B.
"If I should have the drive to seek
Knowledge of chemistry or Greek,
I'll do it. Charles and Miss can look
Another place for hand or cook.
Some men rejoice in skill of hand,
And some in cultivating land,
But there are others who maintain
The right to cultivate the brain."

"It seems to me," said Booker T.,
"That all you folks have missed the boat
Who shout about the right to vote,
And spend vain days and sleepless nights
In uproar over civil rights.
Just keep your mouths shut, do not grouse,
But work, and save, and buy a house."

"I don't agree," said W. E. B.,
"For what can property avail
If dignity and justice fail?
Unless you help to make the laws,
They'll steal your house with trumped-up clause.

A rope's as tight, a fire as hot,
No matter how much cash you've got.

Speak soft, and try your little plan,
But as for me, I'll be a man."

"It seems to me," said Booker T.—

"I don't agree,"
Said W. E. B.

As we today ponder the question "Booker T. or W. E. B.?" we
must frame our answers in terms of how much we should, or need to,
rely on formally constituted political institutions to organize our community life. What functions can be carried on by other sorts of institutions, such as churches, civic groups, and economic associations,
particularly those rooted in the vernacular?[15] Which functions can be
handled by social cooperation, and which require institutional management?

Matthew Crenson in his book *Neighborhood Politics* notes the occasional reemergence of elementary political society in Baltimore
neighborhoods where the atrophy of municipal functions had left a
vacuum. Crenson sees the neighborhood as a miniature "public," society's "near-compulsory voluntary association."[16] For him the neighborhood is a "polity. . . . neither a government nor a private group
but something in between, [deriving] its political status both from the
functions it performs and from the public nature of the constituency it
serves."[17] In this exploration of black Baltimore, however, we shall
not focus on neighborhoods as polities. This book is concerned instead with voluntary organizations operating at the neighborhood
level, and with the powerful dialectic such organizations have created
between parallelism and intervention. Working through the citywide
BUILD coalition, for example, parallel organizations in black Baltimore
neighborhoods have achieved a much more decisive interventionary
power than could any organization that operates by intervention alone.

The New Deal and the New Property

Parallelism and intervention both have a long history in Baltimore.
Between the Great Depression and the Viet Nam War, parallelism
lost ground steadily. Under the New Deal, government began to displace many traditional, vernacular techniques of caring for elders and
children, feeding the hungry, sheltering the poor, and organizing
civic life—not only in the black community, but in communities all

over the United States. The Depression itself had already delivered a great blow to the image of the Republican business leadership of the city of Baltimore, with which the "privatization" of Washingtonianism was associated, since the crash was widely viewed as the result of manipulation by business titans. Yet the more the pre–New Deal government became involved in bailing out the business sector, the more the average Baltimorean saw the hard times as the government's fault. The imposition of a tariff on trade in manufactured goods favored industry but hurt shipping, and government was blamed even though it was industry that benefited.[18]

When the New Deal began, the people of Baltimore—even working people—were reluctant to support it, so suspicious of government had they become. They were much more willing to accept the leadership of a powerful president than the services of an enlarged bureaucracy. They were angry at government workers with guaranteed jobs and were anxiously critical of their performance. But as the Depression got worse, they had to change their tune.[19]

The principal role for government, thought the average Baltimorean of the period, was to organize into a smoothly running mechanism the different factions of society that had fallen out, increasingly along class lines, to compete for scraps of economic security. In this respect they recalled the unity forged during World War I but remained suspicious of the kind of regimentation they saw developing in the Soviet Union. Civilian Conservation work camps were seen as similar to Wartime training camps, for example, and were hence acceptable. The nexus between war and domestic development as alternative Keynesian job-creating techniques could not have been more apparent. Throughout the New Deal Baltimoreans would vacillate between approval of warlike mobilization to "fight" the Depression and fear of centralized government.[20] Perhaps they, like other Americans before and since, understand war, but not domestic social needs in peacetime, as reasons for large-scale economic mobilizations.

As time went on, Baltimoreans began to accept the fact that their well-being had come to depend more on their relationship to government and their receipt of government benefits than on their ownership of or access to private wealth: Reich's "New Property." The availability of this New Property, however, depended upon the ability and inclination of the public interest/regulatory state erected by the New Deal to dispense government largess. This ability and inclination were, in turn, lodged in the liberal New Deal coalition of the Democratic party, whose influence came to rest on U.S. military and economic leadership of the post–World War II international system. That leadership promoted trade and maintained open access to markets, raw materials, cheap labor, and investment opportunities for U.S. industry. U.S. industry, for its part, formed multinational enterprises that farmed out various stages of production to Third World countries, where labor was cheap. The U.S. government protected such investments with military power, high-tech military and intelligence apparatus, and a veneer of foreign aid.

Under the sustained prosperity of the postwar era, a business-labor accord arose in which unions, affiliated with the Democratic party, not only maintained the advantages of the New Deal (chief among them the New Property) but also received concessions in wages and working conditions. After the civil rights and urban renewal struggles of the 1950s and 1960s, minorities were brought into the accord as well, and business began making donations to minority improvement efforts and supporting civil rights and economic opportunity legislation.[21] All these gains added to the government largess Reich thought was so important.

The government largess associated with the New Deal and Lyndon Johnson's Great Society finally gave liberal, representative democracy a communitarian face. Post–New Deal liberals like Reich argued that such awards should become entitlements however, protected not by the community, but by a regime of individual rights. Reich felt that to preserve liberal, representative democracy, the role of government must increase, albeit within the framework of checks and balances. For Reich, the autonomy of people "inside" the system—supported by and dependent upon institutions such as corporations and government agencies—would be compromised without government (primarily judicial) protection. He saw people "outside" the system, while free from institutional control, as even more vulnerable. Most employment is found "inside," in the system's institutions; as most wealth derives from them, they constitute society's primary source of economic support.[22] The behavior of such institutions also has a profound impact on the social and natural environment, and thus significantly shapes the lives of "outsiders" as well as "insiders."[23] Race relations, environmental balance, health, education, and the quality of urban life are features of the "ecology" in which we live and which is subject to disturbance by the actions of institutions in the organized or bureaucratic sector of society. Thus, community-building cannot be left to cooperation, but must be created by rights and administration. This is a logical extension of the New Deal approach.

Electoral Politics and the Decline of the Public Interest/Regulatory State

Depending upon state power to check state power, though this is central to the idea of checks and balances, is, at bottom, a circular proposition.[24] Protected recipients of "government largess" can easily become—or at least come to be perceived as—"special interests," whose life enhancement through regulation invariably compromises that of others, often in ways that are arguably unfair.[25] The regulatory system rationalized by the New Property can easily wind up serving special interests rather than the public interest, in an increasingly privatized political process. Special interests have come to dominate both election and governance, that function having been abdicated by both the political parties and the people.[26]

Without real leadership from either party, the media set the public policy agenda. The media tend to present news in dramatic and personalized form, focusing on individuals and their personalities rather than on the political, economic, and historical processes at work.[27] Absent a background in public affairs, the news "consumer" comes to view events as carried on by super-personalities, reinforcing his or her own feelings of powerlessness and disengagement.[28] The media also regard longstanding policy problems such as excessive defense spending, the problems of savings and loan institutions, poverty, and the lack of adequate health care and housing as unworthy of coverage until they reach crisis proportions, further reinforcing the consumer's sense of powerlessness.[29] Finally, the media package events and personalities to conform to media personnel's perception of what the consumer will "buy." Official versions of events are sought out, giving government officials and successful businesspeople inordinate deference, while the views of deviants such as strikers, demonstrators, racial minorities, and members of minor political parties are undercut, minimalized, or discredited.[30] Campaign specialists focusing on media coverage, advertising, and packaging organize election campaigns. Political Action Committees (PACs) raise the funds necessary to wage political warfare at the end of the twentieth century—high-tech, slick, and media-centered. Voter mobilization, electoral politics, and policy implementation are no longer linked into a single network of political influence.[31] Instead, numerous special interests compete for shares in policy making, confined only by the broad and general limits that the results of elections impose.[32]

On the federal level, for example, transportation magnates have been treated to barriers that restrict the entry of newcomers into their economic field, creating publicly supported cartels. Banks have been treated to a free ride on taxpayer-insured deposits. Developers have been allowed to play fast and loose with government money designed to house the poor. Reich's program, then, does not ultimately point to forms of social organization that we can trust to exercise power in our own favor, much less in someone else's.

Indeed, the most defenseless in our society, for whom Reich professed some concern, have had an even less encouraging experience with the public interest/regulatory state. Reich attacked the early New Deal vision of public assistance (which was based on the expertise of the social workers who operated the welfare system), but William Simon argued in 1985 that it was better than the rights-based, formalized system that Reich's article lauded in its stead.[33] Simon perceived the overall social welfare vision of the early New Deal as that of a state administration manned by sympathetic/empathetic professionals, who used their expertise in tailored and targeted ways to increase, rather than decrease, the autonomy of recipients of government largess. This is a vision of a benevolent state bureaucracy that seeks to help rather than to harm or disempower us.

How well do these competing visions apply to Baltimore? To the black poor of Baltimore, neither welfare bureaucrats nor judges appear benevolent; rather, both are viewed as instruments of social control, part of a force of occupation. Many of the women I met in Baltimore who were leaving welfare for small business endeavors first developed their networking skills while trying to get welfare workers to do their jobs. And there are ironic parallels between the self-help efforts of black women on welfare to free themselves from "the system" (as they themselves call it), and the parallel efforts of some of their male friends and husbands to network themselves out of prison. The bottom line here is that for those outside the legitimate "system" both Simon and Reich value, there is another: welfare for the women, prison for the men. Those who must live within this other system see themselves as captives. Darnell Ridgley, a community organizer in Baltimore, wants to get people away from the "junkie syndrome," which hooks people on government largess, making them dependent and resentful. "There is nothing wrong with poor people having power," she says. "People keep trying to keep them under control; that's why poor people don't know how to do anything."

Moreover, liberal democracy, which encourages private but not public life, seems to have produced an unequal society that, as the New Deal liberal Democratic coalition discovered, can be maintained only at an escalating cost and with increasing difficulty. The economic and social costs of the Viet Nam War sent the United States into a period of stagnation and inflation, eroding its dominance and undercutting the rationale for the public interest state. With these reversals in the political and economic fortunes of the United States, the role of government in organizing social life began to recede. Simon's vision of the welfare state has been as surely undermined by the economic and political reversals of the post–World War II era as Reich's has been. Like Reich's paradigm, Simon's must operate in the context of a representative government grown increasingly alien and distant, with the people's means of insuring accountability limited to closely managed elections.[34] Clearly, we do not increase our autonomy by use of the impersonal, rights-based regime derived from the New Property, but neither do we increase it through a benevolent, respectful welfare state. Reich's rights-based regime increases the power of judges and lawyers. Simon's benevolent welfare state increases the power of legislators and social welfare bureaucrats.[35] Properly designed programs can play a crucial role in improving the long-term prospects for the nation's poor, but those efforts that made some progress in breaking the cycle of disadvantage, such as Head Start, Volunteers in Service to America (VISTA), and the Job Corps, have been greatly reduced or completely abandoned.

The Shortcomings of the Civil Rights Movement

Interventionist politics came to dominate African-American social strategies after the New Deal, as the activities of the state became more and more the focus of everyday life. As had Americans of all races and creeds before them, African-Americans signaled the acquisition of the middle-class status needed for successful intervention by relinquishing their ethnic communitarian or vernacular traditions.[36] Increasingly, the mass media displaced many of the vernacular means of communication and sharing ideas in the African-American experience—especially ethnic and neighborhood newspapers, but also meetings of various types.

The civil rights boycotts and demonstrations of the 1950s led to political organization in the 1960s, and middle-class blacks began to win a share of government jobs and jobs with contractors serving the government in Baltimore. Government power increased as it was called upon to defend the individual against "the old tyrannies of hierarchy, tradition, status, [and] superstition" associated with the vernacular community.[37] This defense was carried out by emphasizing *rights* (the DuBoisian strategy); ironically, it isolated individuals not only from the abuses of state power but also from one another, damaging the human networks that were the positive side of the old, vernacular community. Booker T. Washington had seen the value in these human networks, and focused his attention on the mediating institutions in which they tended to be nourished and supported—church, fraternal association, small business. In contrast, the civil rights movement severed the bond between the upwardly mobile black middle class, in search of more universal middle-class status and suburban life, and the black vernacular culture.[38]

As the New Deal and its progeny of social programs faltered after the Viet Nam War, civil rights–oriented intervention and protest activity began to lose its compass, appearing more and more unreasonable the less there was it could achieve. The alienated middle-class black citizen, shorn of roots and vernacular techniques for self-help, was stuck in the politics of intervention. After the civil rights movement peaked, however, parallel activity in the old vernacular neighborhoods of black Baltimore began to increase. Abandoned by the middle class, working-class and poor black people turned to traditional coping and support techniques, creating parallel rather than interventionist modes of handling the crisis. The church, repository for the vernacular culture of the black community, played as important a role in this endeavor as it had in focusing middle-class protest in the civil rights movement.

Black community activists in Baltimore struggled to patch up the gaps left by the departure of the middle class, the inability of the vernacular community to perform its old social functions, and the unwillingness of government to meet its commitments. As their parallel activity collided with the intransigence of elected officials, many community activists came to the conclusion that electoral power (intervention at the highest level) was required for reconstruction of the black community. As with the civil rights movement, however, the leaders and beneficiaries of this new thrust came from the relatively affluent leadership class of the black community. As noted in the Prologue, the great majority of working-class and poor black residents of Baltimore became consumers of, rather than participants in, the process of political empowerment.

A tentative answer to the question "W. E. B. or Booker T.?" seems to be, "Both." Strong arguments can be made that the relationship between the two strategies is not dichotomous but dialectical. The "civic republican" and communitarian tradition (in which Washington might be placed) and the "liberal-individualistic" tradition (in which DuBois might be placed) can be synthesized into a "third way," exemplified by community-based organizations that engage in both parallelism and intervention. These organizations in fact perform the traditional role of communitarian mediating institutions, but they have also begun to advocate for individuals (generally their members) vis-à-vis the state. That is, the mediating "community" institutions with which Washington was concerned have become essential power bases for engaging in political dialogue, in government arenas, over the kinds of public benefits and public protections that were primary for DuBois. Individual rights are thus enhanced by participation through "mediating" institutions in the larger political scene. This process was perhaps first demonstrated by the activities of labor unions, upon which Saul Alinsky's community organizing model was originally based. It is illustrated in this book by the activities of the black church in Baltimore, a vernacular, mediating institution that has not only engaged in parallelist provision of needed social services for the black community but has also, again and again, furnished the launching ground for all manner of electoral and protest campaigns.[39]

Even well-intentioned "third way" efforts, however, often do not reach deeply enough into the black community's forgotten poor and working class to involve them directly in their own development. Further, as such mediating institutions engage in advocacy for their individual members in the "corridors of power," they become more like their opponents, reflecting the hierarchical tendencies they critique, using "representative democracy" rather than "participatory democracy" for their accountability and legitimacy. This problem can perhaps be alleviated by developing smaller, more informal "base communities" that can be spun off from mediating institutions or, in some cases, can stand on their own.

The Role of Base Communities in Rebuilding the Black Community

To have civil rights, it seems, is not a condition, but a vocation. As Harry Boyte's work demonstrates, full citizenship requires something more: the employment of one's civil rights to build a public identity, a place at the table, a share in the public goods that society collectively produces in the arena of political action. This type of citizenship cannot be legislated; it is and must be created and re-created day after day, in the rough-and-tumble, morally ambiguous arena of public affairs. The exhortation in morally polarized terms associated with the protest movements of the 1960s (DuBois' intellectual descendants) today appears as so much childish posturing. Retreat to parallel institutions with no thought to the state machinery that is poised to crush them at any time is as foolhardy now as it was in Washington's time. But the mediating institutions Washington cherished, many of which he helped to build, intervening together in public discourse on behalf of the entire black community—now, that's real power.

While Harry Boyte and his intellectual mentor, Saul Alinsky, would certainly disagree, however, it seems to me that, in these difficult times, power is at best a necessary evil. In Baltimore, as elsewhere, struggling with the hierarchical public and private organizations that wield power in our society induces comparable tendencies toward hierarchy in even the most idealistic of groups. Within and between Baltimore's interventionist and parallel organizations something more hopeful is occurring: people are bonding together in relationships intermediate to something that I call the New Community in conscious juxtaposition to the metaphor of the New Property.[40] Base communities of the type first seen in the liberation theology movements of Latin America have an important role to play in building this New Community.

"Base communities" provide a small, intimate social action unit that serves to supplement rather than replace the mediating institutions of community or the political mechanisms of government in their respective imperfect roles. Base communities provide a nonhierarchical "home base" of support and direction for individuals engaging with political and mediating institutions in public life. Base communities can facilitate the work of mediating institutions by rooting that work deeper into the community, and by providing participants with a private, more intimate form of social activity to complement the more contentious public side as Boyte notes. They can also develop among people who are directly attempting to influence the activities of the state, sometimes without reference to work with a mediating institution. (Some civil rights and poverty lobbying groups immediately come to mind.)

A network of base communities can weave a new social fabric. Already such a network is being created in Baltimore by community-spirited organizers, clergy, public interest advocates, business people, and government workers, whose commitment to a New Community is demonstrated by their determination to overcome social dichotomies among themselves, to achieve economic autonomy, and make decisions through consensus, rendering government's monopoly of coercive power less and less relevant. This New Community grows from the positive roots of the Old, or vernacular, Community, using the same type of human networks and often similar or even "renovated" vernacular communication techniques. Yet it self-consciously avoids the parochialism and narrowmindedness we often associate with the old ways, chiefly by resort to the tolerance and vision that are the most positive legacy of the civil rights movement.

Clearly, there is some tension here. How much can and should we do for ourselves through this New Community? We pay taxes, we should not let government off the hook. But how much energy should we divert from the social welfare values we *can* create by ourselves to a possibly vain program of exhortation and protest, particularly when directed toward a state that is economically, and perhaps politically, bankrupt? Regardless of how we answer these questions, it seems indisputable that at this point in history base communities can help us to check, facilitate, and supplement the patterning of social life now being undertaken both by government and by mediating institutions.

We cannot do without the government, which protects us from the abuses of power associated with the Old Community, the oppressive and parochial face of the vernacular. At the same time, we need the positive networking strength of the Old Community to protect us from the excesses of government. In the middle of this dialectic (not dichotomy) stands the base community. The base community is small and informal enough to remain nonhierarchical, unlike most larger institutions, even those engaging in social protest, as they operate in the arenas of power. At the same time, it saves us from the need to reduce ourselves to lone, alienated, isolated individuals to avoid hierarchy (a conservative or perhaps libertarian position). Base communities, of up to two dozen people, can provide us with support both in terms of human relationships (their private or paedic dimension) and in terms of social action (their public or imperial dimension).[41]

The New Property I define to include the whole panoply of government benefits and protections associated with the post–New Deal, liberal Democratic political coalition and with the public interest regulatory state. Participatory democracy can help better define the "public interest" that such a state is designed to serve. Community empowerment can also build mediating institutions, which are a necessary complement to both public interest regulation and participatory democracy. We shall use the black community of Baltimore and its struggle for civil, political, and social advancement to illustrate this point, concentrating on four neighborhoods on the city's West Side. Upton is the oldest and now most deteriorated. Park Heights is the newest and most upwardly mobile. Harlem Park was one of the first areas of experimentation in urban redevelopment in Baltimore, while Sandtown is the most recent venue of such experiments, the Community Building in Partnership effort of the city of Baltimore, the Enterprise Foundation, Baltimoreans United in Leadership Development (BUILD), and the Sandtown-Winchester Improvement Association.

Chapter Two
Baltimore's Vernacular Black Community

The black community has very little experience
with power and money and influence
that has lasted more than a generation.
—Arthur Murphy, scion of one of Baltimore's
most prominent black families

SLAVERY flourished in the rural east and south of Maryland, but in Baltimore a small community of free blacks had been established by the early 1800s through manumission and the "hiring out" system. Slaves in the city were permitted in some instances to hire themselves out to employers, paying their master a percentage of their earnings and sometimes even maintaining their own homes and families. Partly as a result, the city was ambivalent about slavery, though as a municipality it remained under the thumb of the plantation owners who dominated the state legislature and, despite strong abolitionist activity in Baltimore, continued to defeat abolition bills. Until 1817, blacks convicted of petty crimes could be sold as slaves outside the state — "sold South" as it were. The criminal justice system and the penitentiary system continued as a means of repressing blacks, free or otherwise. The plantation owners were particularly concerned that Baltimore not become a haven for runaway slaves.

It was about 1827 when William Lloyd Garrison arrived in Baltimore. He came to assist in editing the *Genius of Universal Emancipation*, the nationally circulated newspaper of the Baltimore Anti-Slavery Society (organized in 1825), which was edited by Benjamin Lundy.[1] Slave traders were their primary target. Abolitionist forces in Baltimore received a setback in 1831 as terror spread throughout the southern white population after Nat Turner's rebellion in Virginia. Maryland passed legislation severely limiting manumissions. Owners

25

who wished to manumit slaves were encouraged to require the manumitted slave to "repatriate" to Liberia. Free blacks were discouraged from entering (or returning to) the state; the penalty was enslavement. A white person had to be present at most black assemblies—again the punishment for an infraction was being sold back into slavery.

Caught between their own antislavery forces and the proslavery state legislature, Baltimore citizens began more and more to look to recolonization as the answer. Mob violence increased against blacks, who were disabled from charging their attackers in court by whites-only testimony laws. Slave traders, encouraged by these developments, sold many blacks "South" (including free blacks who had been imprisoned or simply abducted) from the 1840s until the Civil War. So-called Jacob's Laws, designed to eliminate free blacks from the state entirely, were debated in the state legislature in 1855. Thus, "the possibility of re-enslavement, discriminatory legislation, and social mistreatment negated much of the free Negro's legal and economic freedom."[2] Yet even in this precarious environment, free blacks created their own schools, learned trades, bought their freedom, and, where necessary, litigated to keep it. As a result of their efforts against great odds, Baltimore boasted the largest number of freed blacks of any city in the nation on the eve of Emancipation. These freed blacks formed the core of Baltimore's vernacular black community.

After slavery was banned in the United States, former slave owners reestablished a quasi-slave system in various parts of Maryland by manipulating the state's apprenticeship laws. In December 1865 a convention organized by black church leaders called for an end to such abuses. Judge Hugh L. Bond, a white Baltimore criminal court judge who had assisted in the formation of the Baltimore Association for the Moral and Educational Improvement of Colored People, repeatedly honored parents' requests for writs of habeas corpus to secure the release of children held illegally in other parts of the state.

The abolition of slavery, and eventually of the apprenticeship system, underscored the need to provide educational facilities for black children. By 1865, seven schools had been established by the Association to educate approximately three thousand black children. In 1867, when the Association's survival was threatened by a lack of funds, a Maryland state constitutional convention ordered the founding of black schools statewide. There were to be two separate school systems, each financed by taxes raised from the respective communities. The results, of course, was that schools for whites were much better funded than those serving black children. In addition, the Baltimore school board refused to hire blacks to teach in the schools. It was not until 1888, after nearly two decades of public protest and numerous petitions to the school board, that the city passed an ordinance authorizing the hiring of black teachers.[3]

The Rise of the Black Church

The black church was of particular importance in the vernacular black community of Baltimore, both before and after Emancipation. It has always been the hub of the community's social, political, and cultural life. Baptists, the largest congregation in Baltimore's black community today, date from 1837. (Union Baptist, the first independently organized black Baptist church in the city, was founded in 1852.[4]) The oldest congregation in the black community, dating well before the Revolutionary War, was Episcopalian. This was the Anglican religion of most slave owners, and blacks attending Episcopal church services were segregated from the white parishioners. The first all-black Episcopal congregation, the St. James First African Protestant Episcopal Church, was founded in 1824. St. James was Baltimore's third black church, two black Methodist churches having been started earlier.

In 1831, Pope Gregory XVI commissioned the Oblate Sisters of Providence, a group of black nuns originally from Cuba and Santo Domingo who had begun educating poor black children in Baltimore.[5] In 1857, the order, then occupying the basement of St. Ignatius Church, founded a black congregation called the Chapel of the Blessed Peter Claver. The congregation moved in 1864 to a recently purchased Universalist church, which it dedicated as the Church of St. Francis Xavier, the first black Catholic parish in the United States.[6] Yet black Catholic congregations continued to be led by white priests. Because of this, and because of Catholicism's identification with the Irish and German immigrants with whom blacks later had so much difficulty, the Catholic Church never gained the same following in the black community that it enjoyed among white ethnics. Still, there are more black Catholics in Baltimore than any other city in the United States except New Orleans.

The Methodists were the first denomination after the Episcopalians to gain a strong following in the black community, winning numerous black converts before the Revolutionary War because of their evangelizing among slaves and free blacks, and their policy of holding integrated services. Dr. Thomas Cole, a Methodist cleric from Wales, led an antislavery crusade in Baltimore in 1785.[7] This policy proved short-lived however, and after the Revolution the Methodists succumbed to peer pressure and hardened racial lines within the denomination. This was the beginning of the black church in Baltimore as we think of it today, churches associated with collective action by blacks to create a community in which they could pursue their wholeness as a people, in economic and political as well as in spiritual terms.

Spurred by Methodist backsliding, a group of black Methodists, led by Richard Allen and Absalom Jones, formed the Free African Society in Philadelphia in 1787.[8] Methodist abolitionists in Baltimore gave black parishioners a building on Sharp Street for a church. This was the origin of the Sharp Street United Methodist Church, the oldest black congregation in Baltimore and by 1830 one of the principal black churches there.[9] In 1802 a group of militant black parishioners from Sharp Street split off to form an African Methodist Episcopal (A.M.E.) congregation, which became a separate denomination with its own hierarchy. The A.M.E. denomination took root nationally at a convention of like-minded individuals held in Philadelphia in 1816. In 1817, the Bethel A.M.E Church was founded on Fish Street in Baltimore with a congregation of six hundred, the second-oldest black church in Baltimore. By 1860, Bethel had fourteen hundred members. Throughout the history of black Baltimore, parishioners of Bethel and similar churches have ministered to the needs of the black community, taking the lead in organizing their fellow blacks in labor unions, civil rights demonstrations, political action, economic development, and spiritual renewal.

Vernacular Communities in Conflict:
Blacks and Immigrants

Baltimore was the most significant commercial-industrial city to be populated by large numbers of both blacks and immigrants, living and working in some degree of proximity to one another.[10] Between 1740 and 1820, the number of immigrants coming to Baltimore was small, but this trend reversed itself dramatically in the ensuing decades. Between 1820 and 1830 there was a more than fivefold increase: 55,000 arrived in 1830, as compared with 10,000 in 1820. Between

1840 and 1850, social and economic upheaval in Germany, Austria, and Ireland drove large numbers to the United States. During 1850 almost one hundred thousand immigrants entered Baltimore harbor, and the city's foreign-born population increased by nearly 50 percent in that decade.[11] The majority of the new arrivals were from Germany and Ireland.

Before the 1850s "native" whites dominated the skilled trades; semiskilled trades were divided about evenly between free blacks, native whites, and immigrants, and the free blacks dominated the unskilled jobs. In the 1850s, as Baltimore grew in stature as a commercial city and the number of Irish and German immigrants increased, the blacks in Baltimore's population began to be outnumbered. Almost immediately the German and Irish immigrants clashed with each other over unskilled jobs. Even before the influx of Irish beginning in the 1840s, ethnic rivalries between Germans and Irish had led to violent confrontations in the workplace. On August 11, 1839, one hundred Irish laborers reportedly assaulted German contractors and their employees. A German priest gave the names of the Irish involved to the management. Federal troops killed eight workers and arrested twenty-six others. Immigrant whites also began to harass blacks as economic competition between them increased. Tensions were exacerbated in the late 1850s when a downturn in economic conditions led employers to cut wages, pitting those willing to work for the new wages against those who demanded the old pay. Eventually, the immigrants drove the blacks out of skilled and unskilled jobs with a combination of sharp competitive practices and physical violence.[12] The Irish were particularly hostile.[13]

Black stevedores, dockworkers, and caulkers in Fells Point were prime targets.[14] Prior to 1850 there were virtually no white ship's caulkers in Baltimore. (The young Frederick Douglass worked as a caulker.) The black caulkers at the Baltimore port established a reputation for fine workmanship and efficiency, and formed a labor association to protect their control of the profession. They had begun to negotiate for higher wages and better working conditions when the return of men from the Civil War, coupled with a drop in demand in the war's aftermath, led to a labor surplus. Immigrant white caulkers from South Baltimore strove to drive black caulkers out of Fells Point.[15]

Riots between blacks and the white immigrants vying for their caulking jobs were frequent. At one point two alley homes in Fells Point "accidentally" burned on the same day. Then, in September

1865, the white caulkers persuaded white joiners and carpenters to go on strike to protest against the presence of the black caulkers. Anyone who defied the ban on working with blacks was subject to a twenty-five-dollar fine. That winter employers began to capitulate to the strikers' demands, firing black workers and replacing them with whites. Thousands of free black males left the city in search of employment, fragmenting black families.[16]

The resulting disruption of the black community was used by former slaveholders from the eastern shore as ammunition for the argument that blacks could not exist outside of slavery, that they were "shiftless, lazy, and idle." They pressed in the state legislature for vagrancy and other laws ("Black codes") designed to herd blacks back into semislavery.[17] Free blacks had acquitted themselves creditably vis-à-vis native whites during the early part of the nineteenth century, occupying those lower-status jobs that native whites disdained, and building an economy and a society on those foundations. Now in their violent quest to eliminate the free black from labor competition, the immigrant whites were aided by former slaveholders who had hired out their slaves and who considered the free black a competitor. Baltimore's black community thus had to withstand not only the impact of slavery and segregation typically visited upon southern black populations, but also the racism and violence characteristic of northern cities where immigrant whites competed with free blacks for jobs. Their achievements are thus doubly impressive. Through these trials, the black church was a focal point for the activities that kept the community strong.

Washingtonianism in Baltimore: Mediating Institutions and Small Businesses

Disappointed with their status in the public sector during the immediate post-Emancipation period, blacks turned to self-help. Black churches in Baltimore accumulated property valued at approximately half a million dollars and generated an estimated one hundred thousand dollars in annual tithes. The black community at large supported seventy-nine beneficial societies with an average of eighty members each. In addition to free neighborhood elementary schools, the black community raised funds for a high school, a seminary, and a teacher's college, as well as an orphanage and a home for aged black women.

As it became increasingly clear that Emancipation had not brought an end to discrimination and segregation in the workplace any more than in other arenas of social life, black leaders in Baltimore encouraged black workers to organize their own unions. In July 1869 Isaac Myers, a leading parishioner at the Bethel A.M.E. Church, organized a meeting of various skilled and semiskilled workers at the Douglass Institute in Baltimore. Twenty-three crafts were represented, including molders, engineers, painters, brickmakers, and longshoremen. The Douglass Institute was the natural site for the gathering. Named after Frederick Douglass, it was intended to provide a central meeting place for blacks throughout the city and state. At its dedication ceremony, Douglass publicly announced that he had modified his opinions on the merits of black associations and institutions: previously concerned that they might inhibit black assimilation to white society, he now affirmed the important role they could serve in expressing black solidarity and pride.

As time went on, the labor movement in Baltimore continued to polarize along racial lines. The Knights of Labor recruited blacks beginning in 1880, but encouraged them to form their own assemblies. Blacks formed assemblies for such semiskilled trades as the brickmakers, wagoners, and stevedores, boasting sixty thousand members by 1886.[18] The Knights began to decline in 1886, however, after the Haymarket Square riot in Chicago, and they were essentially defunct by the early 1890s. Their passing eliminated from the labor scene the only proponent of any modicum of racial understanding among the working classes. The American Federation of Labor, which next gained ascendance, was composed solely of skilled craftsmen and limited to whites. During the movement for an eight-hour day, however, white AFL unions tried to bolster their bargaining position with employers by recruiting blacks to join them. For the black community, this was too little and too late. In a speech at a Methodist church, a black attorney urged what proved to be a short-sighted strategy, advising black workers to resist the call of white unionists for assistance in their struggle, and arguing that the more trouble whites made for their employers, the more attractive black laborers would become. For his part, Myers organized a Colored State Industrial Fair to promote black labor and urged black workers to declare their allegiance to the Republican party.

These Washingtonian strategies failed to challenge the traditional racist posture of the white unions, and isolated black laborers became even more vulnerable to Baltimore's recurring economic crises. When the city prospered, black workers made incremental gains, but during each period of high unemployment, it was the unskilled blacks who were the first ones out of a job. Through their unions, whites had access to apprenticeship programs that enabled them to gain skills and advance economically. Blacks, barred from union membership, had no comparable way to gain the skills needed to secure positions in the various crafts, and the number of skilled black workers steadily declined. By 1911, the black population in Baltimore, except for a small professional class, was confined largely to unskilled, low-paying jobs, with most white businesses refusing to hire blacks for anything but manual labor.

Baltimore's consumer markets provided some opportunities for black self-employment, beginning a tradition carried on in the city today by "Arabbers," who have for generations sold produce in the black community from horse-drawn carts: "Many present day black small settlements in the metropolitan area made the transition in the 60's and 70's from slave quarters to dirt road villages by gardening and marketing the produce. . . . By building a boat, wagon or cart, and buying a mule or horse, a man could develop considerable flexibility; he could carry his own produce to market, he could fish, he could work as a market man. . . . A web of personal connections allowed black entrepreneurs in several sectors to reinforce each other."[19]

In a larger-scale business venture under Myers' leadership, black caulkers and members of the black business community organized a cooperative stock company, leased a lot for $40,000, and launched the Chesapeake Marine Railway and Dry Dock Company in 1866. Within four months they had raised $10,000 from the black community by selling five-dollar shares. The Dry Dock Company stayed afloat for twenty years, and provided blacks in other parts of the country with an example of the advantages of founding their own businesses.[20] Many of those involved in the Dry Dock and similar ventures, including Myers himself, were members of the Bethel A.M.E. Church. "Bethelites" played an important role in organizing the black community and raising funds for charitable endeavors.

By the 1880s a number of important postwar black enterprises had failed, including the Dry Dock Company and a steamship company. In 1894 the Northwestern Family Supply Company opened, the largest black-owned cooperative since the Dry Dock Company. It offered a large variety of groceries, clothing and household goods. Two years later, the business collapsed. In 1895 the black-owned Lexington Savings Bank was founded, offering interest rates that were higher than those available at white-owned banks. Two years later the bank went into receivership. Other business failures in the 1890s included a cooperative furniture store, a cooperative shirt factory, a cooperative machine shop, and a savings and loan association. This pattern of failure persisted into the new century. Between 1902 and 1910, a black-owned shoe company, department store, and bank came and went.

Black-owned businesses failed for a variety of reasons, including questionable business practices and poorly trained staff, but the two most important were a lack of black customers and insufficient capital. No business, no matter how well run it was, could survive without the patronage of the black community.

> The preference of Negro residents for purchasing goods and services from whites rather than "buying black" was noted often by contemporaries, especially during the 1890s when the former fluid pattern of race relations began to change, thus making the habit more objectionable. Observers lamented the fact that most Negroes in the city traditionally purchased their groceries and household items from white rather than black merchants; that whites, not Negro artisans, printed the sermons of Negro clergymen. . . . In addition, critics noted that financial resources that might otherwise be used to help sponsor a Negro drugstore, an insurance company, [etc.] were generally directed elsewhere. The collective financial resources of individual Negroes, Negro organizations and Negro churches were invested in real estate, white building and loan associations or deposited in white owned banks.[21]

While certainly not advocating a return to the repressive atmosphere of the 1860s, the *Afro-American Ledger* argued in several editorials during this era that a more racially polarized environment actually had certain advantages. The ease with which blacks had obtained access to white goods and services during preceding decades had hurt the community in the long run, the editors said, by taking away an incentive for economic self-sufficiency.

Black self-help strategies were least successful in the arena of housing, perhaps because this was an area in which a complementary, "rights-based" DuBoisian strategy was sorely needed. Though the black community had organized numerous beneficial societies and unions by the turn of the century, they had only one building and loan society. In contrast to the Germans and other ethnic groups, who developed such institutions, the black community had virtually no access to the credit needed to build new homes. There were only a handful of black homeowners during this period, and the chronic housing shortage was exacerbated by an influx of rural blacks from the eastern shore of Maryland and from states farther south. Before 1850, most blacks lived in the central, southern, and eastern sections of the city, but there was no predominantly black area. Blacks and native whites lived side by side throughout most of the city in the "southern" pattern. After the Civil War, German and Irish immigrants began to change this residential matrix, especially as they increased in wealth and status, developing neighborhoods in north Baltimore that tended to be all-white in the "northern" and "midwestern" pattern.[22] The more successful native whites left the city entirely, commuting to work from bedroom suburbs by foot, buggy, and omnibus. At the turn of the century, the upwardly mobile members of Baltimore's black community—about two hundred and fifty black professionals, mainly doctors and lawyers—further shifted Baltimore's residential patterns as they began to move north and west, into "secondhand" neighborhoods formerly populated by immigrant groups that could now afford to build homes elsewhere in the city. These secondhand neighborhoods were often locations that had permitted the establishment of prestigious black institutions, such as the older churches, but that heretofore had resisted residential incursions. Later, black middle-class parishioners began to move into the neighborhoods in which their churches were located.

DuBoisianism in Baltimore: Early Black Political Power

Although blacks were virtually prohibited from voting in Maryland until 1870, a number of black residents of Baltimore participated in the Border States Convention of Republicans, held in the city on September 13, 1867. The purpose of the convention was to support civil and political rights for all citizens. By the next fall, however, relations between black Republicans and state party officials had deteriorated. In May 1868, the State Central Committee, reversing a previous decision, denied admittance to delegates elected by blacks, allegedly because the electors had not followed proper voting procedures. After being rebuffed at the convention, 500 black Republicans held a mass meeting at the Douglass Institute to discuss future relations between blacks and the Republican party. A resolution was passed supporting the radical faction of the party, which had been the most sympathetic to black concerns.

In August 1868 blacks in Baltimore organized a Colored Border States Convention and later participated in a National Border States Convention. Isaac Myers, in addition to his numerous activities on behalf of Baltimore's black community, was also a prominent national Republican politician, and served in a number of capacities at the federal government level. In the aftermath of the Republican victory in 1870, Myers sent a letter to President Grant, "requesting him to acknowledge the part played by black Republicans in his victory and give them their share of the spoils."[23] In 1871 Myers presided over a national gathering of blacks that urged black communities across the country to resist the efforts of some groups, particularly white labor unions, to woo them away from the Republican party. In December 1873 blacks met to elect delegates to the National Civil Rights Convention in Washington, D.C., which had been called to put pressure on Republican congressmen to support civil rights legislation. Myers suggested that in addition to trying to influence the Republican-controlled Senate, efforts should be made to pressure the Democratic-controlled Maryland legislature to pass civil rights laws. This suggestion gained support in the form of a resolution asking the national meeting to draft a petition to the Maryland legislature.

Despite Myers' efforts, by the end of the 1870s black Republicans in Baltimore expressed increasing dissatisfaction with their treatment by Republican leaders, complaining that they were not being given an adequate share of the party's patronage appointments.[24] Some black community leaders urged blacks to stick with the party as their best hope; others publicly questioned whether it was prudent for the black community to link its fortunes exclusively to one party. At a meeting of black Republicans in 1879, "the blacks said it was time the local party gave due recognition to two-thirds of its members—its black voters—as Democrats recognized [their] regular Irish and German voters. The lack of black participation in the machinery, none on the City Executive Committee, and only three on the State Central Committee, was another complaint. Reluctantly, blacks acknowledged they had been used by white Republicans to get themselves elected or appointed to office."[25] In 1880 black Republicans in Baltimore held a conference to form the Equal Rights League, secure more patronage for black Republicans, and force the city to hire black teachers and permit blacks to serve on juries. In March 1880 the League achieved the last goal when the city agreed to place the names of blacks on its jury rolls.

Preparations for the 1880 presidential election highlighted the growing rift between black Republican leaders who continued to support the party despite its unequal treatment of blacks, and those who advocated withdrawing support from the national candidates as an act of protest. Advocates of a splinter party charged that the existing local black party leadership was too deferential toward the larger Republican organization. Despite the dissension among their leaders in Baltimore, and even though black voters supported an independent slate of candidates for a number of local offices in the 1880s, the majority of blacks remained loyal to the party.

The black churches in Baltimore also played an important role in organizing the struggle for equal treatment through the ballot. In 1882 a conference of black ministers discussed the community's problems and formed the Brotherhood of Liberty. Efforts by this group and others led the Supreme Court of Baltimore City in 1885 to recognize the right of black lawyers to practice before it.[26] The ministers were also instrumental in getting blacks to vote and were involved in the struggle to wrest more patronage from the Republican party.

As the Reconstruction period drew to a close, the Republican party, which had dominated southern politics since the end of the Civil War, turned its attention elsewhere, abandoning its black supporters. The Democrats began to reassert control of southern legislatures. Between 1890 and 1910, southern state governments passed a series of laws imposing literacy tests, poll taxes, and other requirements that, when "creatively" administered, disenfranchised most blacks. At the same time, though blacks in the North retained the right to vote, they lacked sufficient numbers to elect many blacks to office. As a result, from 1890 to the 1930s fewer blacks occupied elected office nationwide than at any time between the Civil War and the present. Yet, during this same period, the political influence of Baltimore's black community continued almost unabated. Like a northern state, Maryland rejected Democratic efforts to disenfranchise blacks. The Maryland legislature passed disenfranchisement amendments, in 1904, 1908, and 1911, but these efforts to exclude blacks from the polls were defeated in statewide referendums. Like a southern city, however, Baltimore had a large number of black residents. These two factors, combined with the high-level, church-centered organization of Baltimore's black community, account for a degree of black electoral achievement that was unmatched anywhere else in the country. Between 1890 and 1931, six black Republicans held seats on the Baltimore City Council, winning thirteen out of eighteen elections during this period.[27]

Blacks on the Baltimore City Council, despite their small numbers, were not only an important voice for the black community in their own city, but spokesmen for blacks all over the country. In addition to working to secure legislation favorable to their own constituents, Baltimore's black councilmen were in a position to extend courtesies to black organizations that were available in few other cities. Several times between 1907 and 1913 these councilmen introduced resolutions inviting various national black organizations to hold their annual conventions in Baltimore, giving them the same access to certain public facilities that white groups enjoyed.

A prominent figure among Baltimore's black city councilmen was Harry S. Cummings, the first black elected to the council, who began his tenure in 1890. Cummings, the grandson of slaves, grew up the son of free blacks in Baltimore. In 1899 he was one of the first two black students to graduate from law school at the University of Maryland, and was admitted to the Baltimore bar that same year. The second black to hold City Council office, John Marcus Cargill, was a physician and minister. He eventually gave up politics to practice medicine full time, inventing and patenting several medicines. Hiram Watty, who served on the City Council from 1899 to 1905, was one of the few blacks in Baltimore to benefit from Republican party patronage, and held positions in the Customs House and the Baltimore office of the U.S. Treasury.

In 1895, Democrats, angered by Republican victories in the gubernatorial and Baltimore mayoral races, stepped up their efforts to disenfranchise blacks. By 1900, the Democratic party was making openly racist appeals for segregation laws and disenfranchisement legislation. By 1901, the Republican party was insisting that blacks and whites be seated separately at party functions. From that year until 1911, when the last of three amendments designed to eliminate blacks from the voter rolls was defeated, black members of the City Council, as well as other black leaders in Baltimore, were constantly having to devise ways to outmaneuver Democrats bent on destroying the power of the local Republican party, while fighting against backsliding in their own party.

Segregation and Municipal Land Use Control

Throughout the 1870s and 1880s, race relations were relatively fluid in Baltimore, with a fair amount of intermingling between blacks and whites in public gathering places. At the same time that industrialization drew southern and eastern Europeans to Baltimore, however, large numbers of rural southern blacks also arrived, pulled by the same promise of jobs, but pushed by racism and the decline of the cotton crop rather than European factionalism. The blacks who migrated to Baltimore in the 1880s and 1890s were different from the free population established there before the Civil War. These "new" blacks were rural, unskilled, and too poor to live in other than abject conditions. After their arrival, rigid patterns of racial and class/ethnic segregation developed in Baltimore for the first time. By the turn of the twentieth century, blacks of all classes were increasingly being made to feel unwelcome in the city's parks, hotels, theaters, and restaurants.

The new black Baltimoreans crowded into the first black ghetto, an area known as Pig Town. White immigrants and blacks who were better off moved as far away from Pig Town as possible, proceeding north and west from the central and eastern districts in which they had lived, but the poorer blacks followed close behind. As whites abandoned their new northwestern neighborhoods to affluent blacks, and as poorer blacks crowded in after them, the black slums expanded. Overcrowding and disease increased in black neighborhoods, and wealthy white property owners lobbied for an ordinance that would confine all blacks, regardless of economic station, to ghetto areas.[28] The resulting law further increased overcrowding in the black areas, transforming them into incubators for a level of crime and disease that threatened the entire city.[29]

Wealthy, "native" whites (generally Anglo-Saxon Protestants) employed land-use controls to regulate the housing market in order to create exclusive communities that shut out not only blacks, but even "undesirable" (read "ethnic") whites. In 1899, this white elite launched Baltimore's City Beautiful movement by founding the Municipal Art Society, which developed the first city plan in 1906. As part of the background work for the new plan, the Municipal Art Society commissioned a study of housing conditions in the poorer, more crowded areas of the city. Two of the four districts surveyed were "tenement districts," so called because they contained a large number of houses that were occupied by more than three families. One of the tenement districts was made up primarily of Russian Jews, with a small number of Italians; the second was composed almost exclusively of Poles. The study found that 40 percent of the 250 houses surveyed in these two districts were home to more than three families, and that single-family homes were increasingly being subdivided into smaller and smaller dwelling units, housing an increasing number of families. The other two areas surveyed were "alley districts." Alley housing consisted of one-story shacks, typically containing no more than 700 feet of living space. The majority of alley dwellers were black. One of the alleys studied was the infamous "Biddle Alley," which had the highest rate of tuberculosis in the city; the other was located in South Baltimore. Not only were the alley districts overcrowded; they lacked even basic sanitation.

Like many of their fellow reformers, the authors of the report expressed openly racist attitudes toward blacks. While the report is not a "study of social conditions," they stated they found it impossible to observe the "gregarious, light-hearted, shiftless, irresponsible" alley dwellers without wondering how much the residents themselves were to blame for their horrible living conditions. (The report contains no such disparaging commentary about the immigrant tenement population.) Further evidence of the reformers' indifference to helping the black community is found in the report's "Recommendations for Remedial Action." This section is devoted almost exclusively to suggestions for bettering conditions in the tenements; except for urging the city to provide regular sanitation inspections of the alleys, the report is silent on what could be done to improve housing conditions there.[30]

Middle-class proponents of zoning in Baltimore said that it would "bring order out of chaos. . . . [Without zoning] no city [can] properly promote greater economy, convenience, safety, health and comfort in industrial, business or living conditions; or make the city more beautiful and attractive."[31] Beyond the progressive rhetoric, there was a darker side of the zoning movement. The author of a 1920 article entitled "Unwalled Towns" wrote that city planners and zoning experts were appealing to people who wanted protection from those they considered "undesirable neighbors. . . . Negroes, Japanese, Armenians, or whatever race most jars on the natives."[32] One purpose of zoning was to regulate the type of residence permitted in a given neighborhood—detached houses were regarded as more desirable than apartments or rowhouses, and residents of or aspirants to "better" housing wished to protect their property values by screening out housing of inferior types.

Affluent whites chose the most desirable residential locations in the Baltimore metropolitan area and designed local government land-use and development controls to protect their choices. Property values were safeguarded by government zoning and planning—a form of official race and class segregation that maintained favored neighborhoods by preventing the "wrong element" from moving in. Land-use control, Baltimore's first example of government regulation of the economy, was deployed as a tool of the elite and used to reinforce their privileged positions while creating the illusion that the interest of society as a whole was being served. Planning and land-use control matured in Baltimore into a technique by which the slums—associated not only with blacks but with Russians, Jews, and Poles as well—could be confined to the southeastern part of the city. Mansions for the wealthiest families were developed in the north and northwest. As the city expanded, turf battles developed over the type of housing—and hence the class of people—that would characterize new areas.[33]

By 1922 the city had established a zoning commission whose height and area restrictions effectively confined rowhouses and, by extension, Baltimore's poorer residents, to poor neighborhoods. There was another aspect to zoning. Zoning advocates emphasized how segregating residential, light commercial, commercial, and industrial uses would add to the quality of city life by keeping residential areas free from the noise, pollution, and congestion of commercial and industrial establishments. In practice, however, Baltimore's zoning regulations were very generous to industry, and many existing residential neighborhoods were classified as industrial. As more people left for the suburbs and more land was freed for industry, the remaining low-income population found it had to defend its residential use against more favored industrial uses. Preexisting residential neighborhoods like Fells Point, Locust Point, the Otterbein, Pig Town, and Fairfield, containing approximately eleven thousand dwellings and primarily occupied by blacks and immigrants, were placed in industrial zones.[34]

Zoning in post–World War I Baltimore opened up a "political marketplace."

Brokers and builders used zoning to manipulate real estate transactions. Small businessmen obtained advantageous locations. Large retailers created the "right atmosphere" in the central business district. Heavy industry stifled neighborhood objections to smoke and stench. The rich slowed the rate at which their emptying downtown houses were being converted to flats and boarding houses, and buffered their new neighborhoods from the hurly-burly of the city. The middle class kept their cottage suburbs exclusive of blue-collar rowhouses. The working class fought commercial incursion and the "negro invasion."[35]

Deprived of city services, the poor, predominantly black residents of industrially zoned areas were eventually forced to leave, and their homes were torn down to make way for industrial expansion. They moved west, spilling into recently established black middle-class neighborhoods.

Segregation and the Vernacular Community

The key neighborhoods of Old West Baltimore, Upton, Sandtown-Winchester, and Harlem Park, and the newer neighborhood of Park Heights, were all part of the Western Addition to the city, annexed in 1816. They were not developed, but remained rural until the 1870s, when horse-drawn trolleys converted them into an exclusive enclave for wealthy whites seeking to remove their residences from the congested city center upon which their fortunes relied—much as Harlem developed in New York City during the same period. Baltimore was at the height of its industrialization at that time, and the city center was crowded with the black and eastern European employees of West Baltimore's affluent residents, living as close to their jobs at the shipyards and factories as possible.[36]

When the electric trolley was introduced in 1890, the Western Addition boomed. Black people who lived near their jobs in the center of Baltimore were displaced when financiers and commercial interests created "downtown," a central business district to serve industry, shipping, finance, and retail sales. The blacks, following the lead of their upwardly mobile professional class, moved north and west. (Eastern European workers, displaced by the same process, moved south and east.) Restricted by segregation from moving any further north than North Avenue, or further west than Fulton Street, blacks during and after World War I settled in roughly two-thirds of the area now defined as the West Baltimore planning district. As a result, Upton began to turn black a few years before World War I, though Sandtown and Harlem Park remained predominantly white until World War II. While no black residents were allowed in Harlem Park or Sandtown, prestigious black institutions such as Morgan State College and St. James Episcopal Church were. Morgan State, the city's historically black college, moved into Harlem Park in the late 1800s and then relocated to Northeast Baltimore after World War I. St. Peter Claver Roman Catholic Church was founded in Sandtown-Winchester in 1888. The building now occupied by St. Pius V Catholic Church in Harlem Park was built by a white congregation and sold to a black Catholic congregation in 1931, ten or fifteen years before black people began moving to Harlem Park in significant numbers. These and other such institutions were established before segregation became rigid in Baltimore. They continued to receive their parishioners, who, in one of the many paradoxes of American *apartheid*, walked and worshiped where they could not live, except for the relatively small numbers of resident house servants who lived in alley streets.

Upton was the first area to be occupied by blacks migrating northwestward from the core of the city. At the turn of the century, Upton was a white, almost suburban neighborhood. Its residential structures were built after the Civil War by developers eager to attract the city's affluent white middle class. Upton stood directly in the path of black outmigration from the city's central core. After 1900, blacks from the center of the city and servants who had lived in Upton's back alleys began to move onto the neighborhood's main streets, such as Druid Hill Avenue and Division Street. The Bethel A.M.E., Sharp Street Methodist, Union Baptist, and Sharon Baptist churches all moved into Upton before their parishioners could live there. As more and more blacks arrived in the 1920s, a concentration of politically, spiritually, economically, and artistically developed people produced a smaller-scale version of the Harlem Renaissance of that period.[37] Upton's Pennsylvania Avenue became a bustling, lively thoroughfare for Baltimore's entire black community. The Royal Theater, built in 1927, led a black renaissance that lasted thirty years.[38] The New Albert Auditorium, the Strand Ballroom, dozens of nightspots, and annual Halloween and Easter parades further brightened the street life of Pennsylvania Avenue.[39] A printed guide to Upton recalls the neighborhood's quality of life: "The story is often told by many of the older citizens in Upton that a reveler who happened to celebrate a bit too much could fall asleep in a club or on the sidewalk and upon awakening find not a dime missing from his pocket; the street [Pennsylvania Avenue] was orderly and clean."[40]

By 1910, nearly twenty-five thousand black people lived in West Baltimore, while only seventy-five hundred whites remained.[41] The area had become a magnet for blacks all over the city. By 1930, a large percentage of the city's black middle class lived there, often owning spacious three-story homes on the area's broad avenues and leading W. E. B. DuBois to extol the neighborhoods of West Baltimore as "showpieces" of contemporary black America. By this time many of Baltimore's most prominent black families had established themselves. The Murphys (owners of the *Baltimore Afro-American* newspaper), the Mitchells (Parren Mitchell later became the first black congressman from Maryland since Reconstruction), and the Hughes family (mainly professionals) were among them. A further sampling of prominent family names would include Coleman (publishers), Fitzgerald (politics), Carter (caterers), Smith (importers), and Wilson (insurance). Some of these families had established themselves as early as the 1820s and had been affluent since the Civil War. Much of the black struggle for freedom, dignity, and economic independence was chronicled by the Murphys' family paper.

Arthur Murphy, sitting in the brownstone West Baltimore office of the NAACP (he retired as the local chapter's president in 1992), showed me photographs taken from the 100-year-old newspaper that had made his family's fortune. "My great-grandfather bought a printing press," he said matter-of-factly. "That made all the difference. That's why three-quarters of all the Murphys are college graduates, and a good number of them lawyers. That's why I'm a fourth-generation college graduate. The only thing wrong with that is that there weren't a hundred more like him at the time. The black community has very little experience with power and money and influence that has lasted more than a generation."

Upton, tightly knit and well-networked, as were so many similar segregated communities of the period, suffered under Jim Crow but benefited from the leadership of upwardly mobile, industrious people from Baltimore's prominent black families. An early standout was Dr. Harvey Johnson, pastor of Union Baptist Church and organizer of the Mutual United Brotherhood of Liberty, a predecessor of the NAACP. (Baltimore's chapter of the NAACP is the second-oldest in the country.)[42] "The preachers of the great congregations took the lead in community business," Arthur Murphy's father, William Murphy, Sr., told me. "Sharp Street Methodist, Madison Street Presbyterian, Bethel, Union Baptist. These were great ministers, who provided political and economic leadership. I remember in particular Reverend Bragg of the St. James Episcopal Church and Dr. Harvey Johnson of Union Baptist. Dr. Johnson brought one of the first black lawyers to Baltimore, Everett Waring, a graduate of Howard Law School. He sponsored him while he studied for the bar."

Blacks from all over the east coast began coming to West Baltimore for conventions of the NAACP and black fraternal societies, staying with family and friends in Upton and visiting its churches and entertainment centers. Education was spreading throughout the black community, and as a result of compulsory public school education instituted by Republican Progressives during this period, many blacks learned to read. The *Baltimore Afro-American*, purchased in 1890 by John H. Murphy (Arthur's great-grandfather), grew to nationwide significance, achieving a circulation of 200,000 and annual gross revenues in excess of one million dollars.[43] Based in Upton, the *Afro* was available in New York, Newark, Washington, D.C., Richmond, Raleigh, and Philadelphia as well as Baltimore, and covered the achievements of W. E. B. DuBois, Paul Robeson, Booker T. Washington, Marcus Garvey, and the Harlem Renaissance.

William Murphy, Sr., a dapper, silver-haired man (exactly my father's age, seventy-four, at the time I interviewed him) spoke at great length about the quality of life in Old West Baltimore, but first he questioned me about my background and my family (the kinds of questions my wife, who is from Ghana, tells me to expect in her home country). He placed my family among a group of black middle-class people who lived in Brooklyn, New York, at the turn of the twentieth century. As it turned out, his cousin Elizabeth Murphy and my aunt Norma McDougall had both attended the Atwater summer camp for the children of the black middle class in the 1930s.

Murphy's maternal grandfather was a mulatto house slave who escaped along with a friend from the eastern shore of Maryland. While his comrade continued north to New York City, Murphy's grandfather, like my great-grandfather, went to Baltimore because he had heard there were great opportunities for blacks there. "He worked for white folks, as a waiter, as a valet. He learned the food delivery business, saved his money, and then set up as a caterer. He served only wealthy native whites. He bought a townhouse in an upper-middle-class white neighborhood and left his wife an estate of $157,000 in 1923. You'd be happy to get that much money today, wouldn't you?

"We had accomplished a great deal by that time. Against overwhelming odds. You have to remember that the black man was leveled to ground zero: culture, language, family, religion—all taken away. We didn't have those institutions that other ethnic groups coming to this country have had which have enabled them to stick together. We were constantly reinventing the wheel, and only in rare cases could the successes of one generation be passed on to the next."

Baltimore's black community leaders during the post–Civil War years successfully expanded their influence within local political circles, but later had to devote more and more of that influence simply to retaining the right to vote for blacks in the face of repeated attacks. Possible alternative sources of power—black owned businesses—never emerged as a viable option. While the eyes of many black leaders of the era were focused almost exclusively on the ballot box, there were periodic calls from certain community leaders, in the tradition of Booker T. Washington, to put less emphasis on political advancement and more on developing programs to promote economic self-sufficiency. However, for the most part, their voices went unheeded, and the "rights-based" strategy of black advancement, strongly advocated by W. E. B. DuBois, became the central position of Baltimore's leadership class. Ironically, the very strength of that leadership grew out of the tightly knit vernacular culture that existed in Baltimore's segregated black community.

Blacks in Baltimore followed DuBois more than Washington in their public personas, but applied strong doses of Washingtonianism in their private lives. "Hope for the best, but prepare for the worst," was the watchword then. We can see the synthesis of the two ideologies in the history and contemporary social practice of black Baltimoreans, because it was the black community's vernacular strength that made both the protest and the community-building strategies viable.

═══ Chapter Three ═══
The New Property Versus
the Vernacular Community

When elephants fight, the grass gets trampled.
—African proverb

IN BALTIMORE, as we have seen, black participation in both government and the economy was facilitated by the strength of black vernacular culture. Yet an increased role for government in the lives of all Americans, especially after the New Deal, tended to disrupt vernacular community, partly because government took over functions people had once performed themselves, but also because government was used as a tool to create white and black settlements in which community was attenuated. The more upwardly mobile members of the black community resented their confinement in poor, inner-city communities, and strove to break out.

Segregation and the Black Middle Class

When segregation ordinances were declared unconstitutional, Baltimore whites found other ways to maintain segregation. Baltimore's 1910 land-use control ordinance mapped black and white neighborhoods, designated undeveloped areas to be reserved for blacks or whites, and in some cases converted black neighborhoods to white use. The Louisville, Kentucky ordinance struck down as unconstitutional by the U.S. Supreme Court in *Buchanan v. Warley*[1] was patterned after Baltimore's, which was the first such ordinance in the country. Baltimore's residential segregation ordinance, and similar ordinances in other southern cities, prompted the founding of the NAACP, which was instrumental in the development of the *Buchanan* case. As Garrett Power has put it, the city of Baltimore's history of using land-use control to achieve segregation teaches us to "discount

46

the righteous rhetoric of reform" in the context of many areas of government regulation.[2]

Once the city's "checkerboard" ordinance was declared unconstitutional, Baltimore's mayor sought advice from Dr. A.K. Warner of Chicago on that city's successful efforts to keep blacks out of white neighborhoods without resorting to zoning legislation.[3] Adopting Chicago's tactics, Baltimore public officials and civic leaders sought to maintain housing segregation through official and unofficial pressure on white owners not to rent or sell to blacks, and through slum clearance measures. Local government officials, real estate agents, lending institutions, and private homeowners joined in a conspiracy to keep Baltimore's black population confined to deteriorating central-city neighborhoods.

In the 1920s, when the Baltimore branch of the NAACP was organized, the prosperity enjoyed by much of the city's white community was shared by few of their black fellow citizens. Residential neighborhoods developed during the period of legal segregation remained in a segregated pattern, the state spent on black schoolchildren a third of what it spent on white, and Maryland's chapter of the Ku Klux Klan was one of the largest in the country.[4] Apart from schoolteachers, only 2 percent of Baltimore's municipal employees were black, and 80 percent of the city's black workers were classified as common laborers. Baltimore's Republican party continued to expand its base of support among white voters by repudiating its ties with the black community.

In the mid-1930s, the Baltimore branch of the NAACP was galvanized by a spate of lynchings on Maryland's eastern shore. Lillie May Jackson, a spirited black woman of aristocratic background, led the NAACP and joined forces with Carl Murphy, editor of the *Baltimore Afro-American*, and with progressive black ministers to wring hiring concessions from city businessmen. Thurgood Marshall won a suit to admit Donald Murray, a black graduate of Amherst, to the University of Maryland's law school.[5] Marshall, raised with pride in Upton's tightly knit black middle-class community, had developed a particular enmity for Baltimore segregation.[6]

Racially restrictive covenants, upheld by the Maryland Court of Appeals in 1938 as "private action,"[7] remained legal until 1948, when the U.S. Supreme Court declared all such devices unconstitutional in *Shelley v. Kraemer*.[8] Thus Baltimore's expansion during the years before 1948 was governed by explicit (though private) racial segregation, resulting in historically exclusive racial enclaves for up-wardly mobile immigrants as well as for native whites.[9]

Land-use control in Baltimore influenced New Deal land-use pol-icy. One of the most influential figures in landscape planning during the New Deal was Baltimore's own Frederick Law Olmstead, Jr., who gained much of his experience working for the Municipal Art Society there. As early as the 1940s, the National Urban League (NUL), re-sponding to growing unrest around the country over segregated hous-ing and job discrimination, tried to engage U.S. Attorney General Francis Biddle in a dialogue on ways the federal government could help.[10] Biddle, however, refused to speak with NUL officials, sig-naling to the black community that the Roosevelt administration was content to see discriminatory practices continue.[11]

During the Truman administration, the Federal Housing Adminis-tration (FHA), established by the National Housing Act of 1934, pro-moted and insured long-term, low-interest home mortgages in Bal-timore's lily-white suburbs. The Servicemen's Readjustment Act of 1944 authorized the Veterans Administration to guarantee no-down-payment mortgage loans to veterans. As a result of these New Deal-originated programs, the owner-occupied share of the housing market went from 55 percent to 63 percent in the Baltimore metropolitan area between 1950 and 1960. While this suburban development was tak-ing off, the FHA and VA actually *required* racially restrictive cove-nants—to protect the "property" values of homes they insured. They also refused to insure mortgages in black areas, imitating the early "redlining" practices of private banks.

President Eisenhower's choice to head the Housing and Home Finance Agency (HHFA), Albert M. Cole, was a congressman whose public remarks led black leaders to believe that he would not chal-lenge segregated housing or encourage the federal government to con-front the housing needs of blacks. The NUL quietly signaled their displeasure to Eisenhower, but once again their concerns were ig-nored. At first Cole indicated some willingness to work with black leaders to eliminate discrimination in federally financed housing pro-grams. However, relations quickly soured when Cole, ostensibly be-cause of budgetary constraints, fired Dr. Frank Horne in August 1955. Horne was recognized as the black community's leading expert on housing, and later investigation revealed that the HHFA's budget had increased by approximately $2 million during this time, so that his dismissal could not have been due to financial constraints.[12]

In January 1959 Cole was replaced by Norman Mason, whose civil rights record was only slightly better. Mason was willing to take a stand against housing discrimination, but only in states whose courts had already declared segregated housing illegal.[13] Although Mason did not think federal funds should be used to promote segregated housing, he let it be known that he would not seek the advice of Joseph Ray, Special Assistant to the Administration on Race Relations in the HHFA, who actively pushed for government support of integrated public housing.[14] Mason's approach showed that the Eisenhower government was content to do no more than "moderately prod" local and private authorities to end housing discrimination.[15]

By the time federal practices supporting private housing discrimination were finally eliminated, suburban Baltimore County (which does not include Baltimore City) had established a system of zoning regulations that excluded apartments and set minimum lot and house sizes. Those who wished to escape the taxes and squalor of the city were now limited in their ability to do so by the cost of housing and commuting. Exclusionary zoning, though couched in terms of income rather than race, had the practical effect of reinforcing existing divisions along racial lines simply because fewer blacks could afford the suburban housing made more expensive by such regulations. Further, even though *Shelley v. Kraemer* had held that racial covenants were unenforceable, they were still used extensively, with neighborhood pressure, rather than litigation, as an enforcement technique.

Suburban housing segregation closed off opportunities for Baltimore's poor and working-class residents, many of whom were shunted into public housing if they found adequate shelter at all. Expanded federal taxing and borrowing after World War II and the Korean War subsidized the development and decentralization of industry, and, as the plants moved out of the city, the construction of suburban housing nearby and the roads needed to travel between these newly developed areas and the Port downtown. The federal government thus laid the groundwork for the massive blue-collar suburbanization of the post–World War II period. In the twenty-five years following World War II, industrial plants moved out of northeastern cities and into the suburbs of those cities, drawing with them the housing demand generated by blue-collar workers. This outward migration of housing demand intersected with investment capital's tendency to migrate outward from the central core in search of cheap land. With the aid of federal home mortgage subsidies, the consequent combination of demand and capital inspired a tremendous up-surge of new housing, which a variety of segregation techniques placed beyond the reach of blacks in Baltimore. The displaced blacks lost on both grounds, shut out of the new jobs in the suburbs by inadequate transportation and labor union bias, and prevented from entering suburban homes by housing discrimination and also by their lack of access to jobs and income.

Despite their confinement to the overcrowded city, the wartime economy of the 1940s held many advantages for blacks, as black men joined the defense industry and black women worked as secretaries and clerical helpers. There were strikes and counter-strikes over seg-regated working conditions and disparate pay and promotion scales. When World War II was over, local businessmen and government officials sought to reverse many of the gains won, but the blacks put up a fight. The Interfaith Ministerial Alliance, an association of the city's foremost black preachers formed to reduce interdenominational competition among Baltimore's various black congregations, soon en-tered the struggle for civil rights. Thurgood Marshall won statewide suits equalizing the pay received by black and white teachers, in a campaign conceived by a militant coalition of black lawyers and min-isters.[16] As the civil rights movement picked up steam in Baltimore, predominantly white organizations from the North joined the fray— the American Civil Liberties Union (ACLU), the American Federation of Labor–Congress of Industrial Organizations (AFL–CIO), and the Council of Churches—as well as more militant black organizations such as the Congress of Racial Equality (CORE) and the Student Nonviolent Coordinating Committee (SNCC).[17] Sit-ins and demonstra-tions galvanized black and white students from all over the Baltimore metropolitan area.

Middle-aged, professional black women emerged as a powerful political force in the city. The Organization of Colored Democratic Women, for example, played a pivotal role in Republican Theodore McKeldin's election, first as mayor of Baltimore and then, in 1952, as governor of Maryland. Marshall often planned his strategies at the home of Juanita Jackson Mitchell. Mrs. Mitchell, daughter of Lillie Mae Jackson, was an activist in her own right. Clarence Mitchell, Jr., her husband, was chief Washington lobbyist for the NAACP from 1950 to 1978, and led the struggle to consolidate and strengthen Mar-shall's court victories with federal legislation.[18]

Segregation and the Black Poor

The NAACP did not at first focus on the problems of the poor. Concerned primarily with discrimination, it paid little attention to the U.S. Housing Act of 1937, which was passed for the purpose of clearing slums and blight in cities as well as producing adequate and sanitary housing at a rent low-income families could afford. Other black citizens' groups in Baltimore took notice, however, and in the later 1930s formed the Baltimore Citizens Housing Committee (BCHC), made up of representatives from thirty-two black and white civic, religious, and fraternal groups. The goal of the committee was to "secure the establishment of a racially integrated housing authority and to advise the city on its housing needs."[19] At first Mayor Howard W. Jackson attempted to appease BCHC by agreeing to appoint a committee to study the situation and make recommendations concerning possible uses for federal housing funds. Jackson's committee appointments were heavily weighted in favor of builders and realtors, however, who in general were not sympathetic to calls for federal involvement in local housing issues. Dissatisfied, the BCHC increased its efforts to create a local housing authority under the U.S. Housing Act. Over Jackson's opposition, the City Council of Baltimore declared the need for a public housing program. Eventually Jackson succumbed to the mounting public pressure, and on December 13, 1938, he appointed the first five commissioners to the Baltimore Housing Authority (BHA).

The BCHC turned its attention to securing black membership on the newly created public housing authority, and succeeded in obtaining one black appointment to the five-member board. In 1940 the BCHC disbanded: some participants felt that the committee had accomplished its goal with the creation of the BHA; others had simply grown weary of battling opponents of public housing, who had become more vocal as the city suffered a budget crisis and an accompanying economic slowdown. A number of committee members, however, believing that the BHA needed continued citizen input if it was to be effective, formed the Citizens Housing Council.

Although the CHC's intentions were good, it was principally made up of middle- and upper-middle-class citizens and, unlike its predecessor, had little connection to the neighborhoods that were the targets of the city's urban renewal policies. BHA's job was to study conditions in Baltimore and formulate a plan to clear slums and create low-income housing. In the plan, provision was to be made for the development of one new dwelling unit for every slum dwelling unit destroyed. This provision linked the slum clearance and public housing features of the new law, but, in Baltimore, as in many other cities, the link was broken, and many more low-income units were destroyed than were built.

This pattern was not without precedent. Earlier in the century, black neighborhoods in Baltimore and the alley houses located there were razed to make way for public parks. The traditional policy of excluding blacks from newly developing white areas and containing them in their own neighborhoods had already created crowded and unhealthy conditions in black areas. In Baltimore, the worst slums generally were located near the downtown business sections. These neighborhoods received few city services and did not pay significant property taxes because of the low value of local real estate. They thus became prime targets for removal and replacement by "white housing" or industry.[20] Slum clearance programs provided a way to clear the downtown area of low-income people and spruce it up at the same time. Downtown image, shopping flow, efficient deployment of the labor force, security against crime, and strengthening of the tax base all came together in the minds of city officials.

Plans were formulated and executed that cleared out slums—and the poor and black people who lived in them—but failed to provide the displaced with new units in their old neighborhoods. Slum clearance, in fact, was often regarded as a way simply to get rid of the poor who had begun to accumulate in the city, who burdened the municipal tax base with their need for services, and whose intense social problems drove middle-class taxpayers away. Approximately 90 percent of the citizens displaced by slum clearance were black.[21] The first public housing projects built in Baltimore were specifically designated to house black people uprooted by these early slum clearance initiatives (thus further entrenching the city's segregated residential patterns). Other projects were built "for whites only," one of the most famous being Armistead Gardens on the East Side, which was temporarily converted to wartime housing because of its proximity to Baltimore's industrial sites.[22] One public housing project proposed on vacant land to ease black overcrowding was fiercely opposed because of its proximity to a white neighborhood.[23] CHC worked to achieve racial integration in Baltimore public housing, but with little success.

From 1940 to 1942, thirty-three thousand black people arrived in the city, looking for work in Baltimore's war industry. Their arrival caused an overwhelming increase in residential densities in segregated black areas, and the NAACP began to get involved.[24] Lillie May Jackson of the NAACP, Carl Murphy, editor of the *Afro*, and the Interfaith Ministerial Alliance organized a march on Annapolis in 1942, sending two thousand blacks to protest against conditions in the community before the state legislature. By the end of the war, 6,000 public housing units had been built for blacks, and the membership of the Baltimore NAACP had swelled to 20,000, moving it far beyond its earlier concentration on the "talented tenth."[25] Though more public housing was built, it was still segregated, however. Efforts to integrate public housing were to no avail, and eventually the crusade was abandoned. Today, 91 percent of Baltimore public housing tenants are black.

While CHC could not do much to advance the DuBoisian, "interventionist" cause of integration in public housing, it fared better in its neo-Washingtonian, "parallelist" efforts to organize public housing tenant councils. The councils attempted to create community in the projects and overcome some of the feelings of separation and anxiety engendered in the residents when they were displaced from their original homes and vernacular neighborhood support systems. These councils were especially effective in low-rise units.

Once the tenant councils were formed, however, CHC withdrew and focused its attention on facilitating the work of municipal social service programs. This was unfortunate. In 1953, when the Housing Authority began constructing high-rise public housing projects, the need for community within the new projects was acute, and CHC's organizing expertise would have been useful. The early public housing projects were well designed and constructed. Low-rise units such as McCulloh Homes in the Upton neighborhood and Gilmor Homes in Sandtown-Winchester, at least gave residents some feeling of belonging. Later projects, such as Murphy Homes and Lafayette Courts, however, just outside the Harlem Park neighborhood, were high-rises. These "human filing cabinets" became sources of crime and social alienation, endangering not only their residents, but their surrounding neighborhoods as well. High-rise buildings create a sense of alienation that is especially conducive to the spread of crime. Security is difficult to enforce, and life soon gets out of control. The high-rise projects, all of which were built in black neighborhoods, were characterized by longer periods of tenure, a predominance of broken, large families, and severely antisocial behavior.

Thus, while the federal government was erecting a financial system to facilitate homeownership in the suburbs for white Americans who could not otherwise afford it, low-income blacks were being herded into squalid high-rise public housing projects. The increased residential pressure helped destroy established West Side black neighborhoods like Upton, which, tightly constrained in physical area by official and unofficial segregation, grew even more crowded as a result.[26] "Upton just burst at the seams," William Murphy, Sr., told me. "It used to be a delightful neighborhood, achievers in every area. Good conduct, participation in church life, community uplift, great contacts. Even when times were hard, during the Depression, the people were good. People left their doors open, they reported to parents when kids misbehaved. Every child was everyone's child. These were the things that made Upton what it was."

Later, in the 1950s, urban renewal destroyed many black-owned homes in the southern part of Upton and other West Side neighborhoods (3,100 families were displaced between 1951 and 1964).[27] The encroachment of public housing into the West Side, to shelter blacks uprooted by urban renewal projects all over Baltimore, began to change the neighborhood's population mix. As the city began losing industrial jobs in the 1960s and 1970s, the neighborhood's economic vitality began to ebb as well. Dives and prostitution infested lower Pennsylvania Avenue below Dolphin Street (referred to as "the Bottom"), even as the middle-class strivers of the era attended Sunday services by the hundreds and civil rights rallies by the thousands.[28]

Today, Upton is a deteriorating neighborhood, covering 183 acres on either side of Pennsylvania Avenue. The avenue itself, famous for the night spots that dotted it during the Roaring Twenties, and once the center of shopping and entertainment for Baltimore's black community, is badly decayed. Changes in shopping and entertainment patterns have made poverty the dominant characteristic of the area. Upton's social indicators are now very unattractive. The neighborhood's population dropped 30 percent between 1970 and 1980, from about nine thousand people to just over six thousand. There are fewer children and families now, and single-person households make up a full third of the population. The crime rate is high, especially in the southwest section, across a dividing line created by Pennsylvania Avenue's commercial strip.

Upton is the city's second-largest urban renewal project in terms of physical area, though there were fewer than three thousand dwelling units there in 1980, 20 percent of which were vacant. Thirty percent of the housing stock consists of subsidized dwelling units. Rents are increasing nonetheless—more rapidly than in the city as a whole—and the prices of homes in the neighborhood have doubled in the last ten years. Banks are still reluctant to invest in Upton, but the rapid rise in rents and real estate values indicates that Upton, close to the city core, may be a target for speculators anticipating the movement of gentrification northwest from the center of the city.

Baltimore city government has for some time been looking for ways to salvage Upton, restore the tax base, and prevent the area from becoming any more of a drain on city services and finances. Although a federal program of the early 1970s called for building 1,000 new housing units in the neighborhood, rehabilitation of existing units was to be the primary method of upgrading the housing stock. The Upton project also involved improving services to the area by providing a "comprehensive system of neighborhood, shopping, recreation and health care facilities within walking distance of the residents." Funds for the Upton project were approved by the federal government in 1972, but President Nixon in the same year established a moratorium on all disbursements of federal money for such projects, and the enterprise was stillborn. The city housing agency was left with many deteriorated homes that it had planned to demolish and replace with new construction, using the anticipated funds. Once the center of the city's black culture, host to Baltimore's own black renaissance, Upton today is the most deteriorated of the three neighborhoods that were the center of Old West Baltimore.

The Limits of DuBoisian Strategies

After William Murphy, Sr.'s grandfather died, the family catering business only held its own; it did not grow. The next generation, well educated on the grandfather's money, began, in Murphy's view, to feel that they were too good to prepare food for white people.

"The business just died. Immigrant Jews took over the catering business as the blacks abandoned it. I've never understood that. Blacks in catering were making an excellent living. But the new generation didn't want to put on work clothes. They overlooked the building trades completely. Grocery stores, insurance, even the newspaper business was considered *déclassé*." As blacks abandoned their business foundation, perhaps following the ethos of W. E. B. DuBois ("the talented tenth") to the exclusion of the ethos of Booker T. Washington ("cast down your buckets where you are"), a power elite of ministers, doctors, schoolteachers, social workers, and post office workers emerged.

"There were a few greengrocers. Thurgood Marshall's family in Upton had a good business. Thurgood's cousin Charlie Burns stayed in the business and built a small supermarket chain that prospered into the 1950s, but generally as Thurgood's family became more educated, they lost interest in that business."

While the black middle-class leadership of the NAACP orchestrated its DuBoisian gains, conditions in the black community continued to deteriorate. In 1956, when the BHA and the Baltimore Redevelopment Commission merged to create the Baltimore Urban Renewal and Housing Agency (BURHA), the city still had an inventory of 50,000 substandard dwellings, most of them in African-American communities. Black people were shuffled around Baltimore during the period of urban renewal, just as they were under the rubric of public housing and slum clearance. Between 1951 and 1971, an estimated 25,000 households were displaced, the vast majority of which were black. The residents who were dislodged doubled up in other slums, creating a concentration of low-income, overcrowded, troubled people that no municipality could effectively serve. Blacks, especially, were displaced from the downtown area and piled into the slums of the north and west, touching off a paroxysm of flight from contiguous white, middle-class neighborhoods. Wholesale, low-income blacks were moved into public housing units on the West Side, straining the system with extreme social problems. Urban slum neighborhoods were marked by dilapidation, overcrowding, substandard housing, tension, and violence. Failing buildings and inadequate city services went hand in hand with ineffective schools, alcoholism, traffic in drugs, unwanted pregnancies and a high rate of juvenile delinquency. Even for those individuals who eventually were given or managed to find alternative housing, the experience of relocation was traumatic and undermined the formation of stable family and community ties.

Paul Coates returned to Baltimore from a nineteen-month stint in Viet Nam and encountered Black Power and rising black consciousness. Unconvinced that any of the mainstream black organizations were really making a difference in black people's lives, he was searching, ready to deal with any group that he thought could make an impact on the terrible conditions he observed.

"I was twenty-two, one of those young people who take chances, and sometimes help move things along," he said soberly. "I wanted to throw my energy in with anybody who could do something about the various kinds of shit black people had to deal with. I tried talking to people, but not many were concerned with what was going to happen to black folks, how long were we going to take this stuff. Other people my age were concerned about the world as it was and with how they were going to elevate themselves as individuals within it. I began to be more and more separated from them."

Riots in Cambridge, Maryland, in 1963 and 1967 and in Baltimore in 1968 (along Upton's Pennsylvania Avenue) reflected the anger and frustration of younger, more radical black leaders and the black poor and unemployed whom they recruited into the civil rights movement. Spurred by these civil disturbances, and pressured by the state's business-labor coalition, Maryland passed a public accommodations law, a fair employment act, and an open housing law. Important government bureaucracies were established to implement the social regulation these laws entailed. But the black community was now split between militant separatists and Black Power advocates, on the one hand, and the established middle-class leadership of the NAACP and the Urban League on the other. Neither side had the combination of organizational ability and moral authority they commanded together during the civil rights movement, which wound down after the riots in 1968. White attitudes, particularly in the suburbs, began to harden. Governor Spiro Agnew (1966–1968) became nationally famous as a conservative spokesman who upbraided moderate blacks for not repudiating militant young leaders like Gloria Richardson and H. Rap Brown of SNCC, and Walter Carter and Edward Chance of CORE. Here was a "Great White Hope" who was not afraid to send troops to close down Maryland's black college, Bowie State, in retaliation for a student uprising on campus.[29] Agnew provided the link Nixon needed in his southern strategy, and he left the state to serve as vice-president.

After the riots came the Black Panthers, arriving in Baltimore in 1969, just when disillusionment with the promises of both civil rights and urban renewal was highest in the black community. The Panthers were seen by many as the only black leaders who had not in some way been co-opted by the white establishment, particularly as that establishment acted through government. A 1969 story in the *Afro* reported that the Baltimore Committee for Political Freedom had been formed because of fear that the local police were planning to assassinate Black Panther Party leaders in the city, as Fred Hampton and Mark Clark had been murdered in Chicago. According to the article, the Panthers had access to a church building in West Baltimore (St. Gregory's, in Sandtown) and hoped to expand their free breakfast program from East Baltimore into West Baltimore. They also had a list of forty doctors willing to volunteer their services in a free health clinic the Panthers hoped to open soon. "Baltimoreans will not simply stand by and see the annihilation of a political or racial group," the article quoted members of the committee as saying.

The committee included Dr. Peter Rossi of the Social Relations Department of Johns Hopkins University, William Zinman, an attorney for the Maryland ACLU, and the Reverend Chester Wickwire, a white minister, as well as numerous others. According to Wickwire, the perception of the committee was that Police Commissioner Donald Pommerlau was engaged in a "vendetta" against the Panthers. Pommerlau, police commissioner during much of the latter part of the civil rights era, had been a Marine lieutenant colonel, a combat commander during the Korean War, and an instructor at the Marine Corps School in Quantico, Virginia, before assuming the post of Baltimore police commissioner in 1966.[30] In 1974 it was revealed that he had secretly compiled dossiers on people he considered subversive, regardless of whether they were suspected of criminal activity. (Congressman Parren Mitchell, the Reverend Marion Bascom, and other members of the Interfaith Ministerial Alliance had all been placed under surveillance.) These dossiers were shared with then Mayor William Donald Schaefer, the Federal Bureau of Investigation, and Army Intelligence. Police spying and wiretapping were common during Pommerlau's tenure. The Panther Party was riddled with informants, both from federal agencies, under the FBI's COINTELPRO program, and from the Baltimore police.[31] More than once, members of the Committee for Political Freedom received early-morning calls from Panther headquarters, asking for members to stand vigil outside the building as police with shotguns were cruising around it.

It was about this time that Paul Coates decided to join the Black Panther Party in Baltimore. "I began thinking about the Panthers in early 1969," he said. "I had tried SNCC and the Republic of New

Africa, checking with them at their headquarters in D.C. I used to
see newspapers from the West Coast when I worked at the airport,
and I began seeing all these stories about the Panthers. I met somebody later that year who said he was inside the organization, and he
showed me their Baltimore headquarters. But he turned out to be just
making himself sound important; he really didn't know anybody. So
one day I just went by there myself, knocked on the door, and went
in."

Coates was allowed to enter Panther headquarters but was treated
cautiously. He was, he felt, under suspicion for almost two years, but
later discovered that a police informant had been killed the day before Coates's first visit to Panther headquarters. "The guy had just
walked in and joined a couple of months before. How were they supposed to know whether I wasn't another one?" Coates later found out
that there were three more informers in the Party, none of whom knew
of the existence of any of the others. "Two of them tortured and killed
the third under instructions from the police," Coates said. "The police would meet with them separately right in the alley outside Party
headquarters, and no one—not even the other informers—knew
about it."

Coates started in the Panther Party with small tasks, selling the
Panther newspaper on streetcorners in the black community, working
with the free breakfast program. Little by little he began to identify
with the Party and gradually began to be accepted by other Party
members as one of them. "It didn't happen overnight," he told me. "It
seemed like a big leap when it finally happened. I stayed in until late
seventy-two." Because he had a car, he began to be used more and
more frequently on different kinds of assignments. He worked the
night shift at his job, so he had his days free and was generally
available for Party work. Coates judged that he gained a great deal
from his association with the Panthers.

"I felt that the Party was doing things that would have an impact
on the lives of black people. It seemed like a good vehicle. When I
came in, I had only a limited basis for understanding the world," he
told me. "I just knew it was fucked up. But I had no perspective, no
point of view. No process for sorting out the significance of the things
I was seeing and experiencing, no process for validating my views
against those of other people. In the Party, I began to develop my own
system of political understanding. The Party had a structure in place
to encourage political education. It provided a setting where I could

interact with people who were searching for answers, and with some who thought they knew the answers."

I asked Coates if he was disappointed because the Panthers did not survive as an organization, disappointed at the way things turned out.

"No, not at all. I came away from the Panthers with a sense of the process of social change. The Party had only a limited role in the whole scale of human development. It's like one of those books on the shelf; you pull one out, but there are hundreds left. The Panthers took on a big agenda that they couldn't complete but in the process they accomplished the development of a lot of people. We're always involved in a struggle for the mind, and the Panthers made a big contribution there.

"I miss my comrades, but some of them I still see. We get together because we need to talk about what is, what we're going to do now. Each of us is a product of that experience. I view the world today not as a Panther but as a person who has experienced government repression, my comrades, working with people in the community. It all adds up to the person I am today. A group of us kept the breakfast program going after the Panthers left town, and eventually I opened a publishing operation drawing on things I had learned in the Party. Each of us should do what we do best, and do it for the right reasons."

Interestingly, Coates did not even hold a grudge against Commission Pommerlau (now deceased). "Pommerlau was a soldier, like me," he observed. "We were in a war. The people he represented felt threatened by me and people like me. He had the advantage because he had more men, who were better trained. We were young, didn't have a large arsenal, and didn't have a lot of combat experience. The outcome was predictable. In the Panthers, we understood that going in. And we did it anyway."

The National Black Panther Party, hard hit by the murder trial of Bobby Seale in New Haven and the assassination of Fred Hampton in Chicago, closed down local chapters, including the one in Baltimore. Party members drifted into other kinds of community work. Thus, the young black leadership of the more radical wing of the civil rights movement, often with assistance from both state and national government, self-destructed. "The Panthers were basically a reactive organization," says the Reverend Vernon Dobson, an activist minister. "They were a group of very bright young people who couldn't seem to find a niche in traditional organizations and leadership avenues. Groups like this will crop up from time to time in the history of a struggle, like the breakaway sects in the development of the church. Any attempt like the Panther Party or the Congress of African People cannot survive in the modern context without connecting to an institution that has a history, that can interpret the sweep of events in the black community over a period of fifty, maybe a hundred, years. The only such institution we have is the black church, and it was the breakdown of our communities following the civil rights movement that made black churchmen realize we had to get ourselves together again, and look for new forms of action."

In the meantime, whites were leaving Baltimore in droves. Jews moved out of the communities of the West Side, and blacks moved in. By 1978, two-thirds of the children in city schools were black. Baltimore's *de facto* segregated schools were understaffed, undermaintained, and underfinanced. Baltimore had become two cities—a black inner city and a white outer city and suburban area, the latter growing, the former decaying. While the suburban economy flourished, the inner-city economy was in a depression, and blacks suffered the most.

Turning to government as the key area of the black struggle after 1920, and turning to government as the key area of social support after the New Deal, upset the balance between protest and community-building that black Baltimoreans had hitherto pursued. A certain schizophrenia set in, as the black community struggled against and simultaneously sought benefits from a government that, even when acting in a beneficent manner, remained essentially racist. The social and civic networks and mediating institutions of the black vernacular community showed signs of strain. As an old African proverb puts it, "When elephants fight, the grass gets trampled."

Chapter Four
Picking up the Pieces
at the Grassroots

People in Harlem Park feel the city just doesn't care.
There is a sense of anger, a sense of distrust of the system.
People's morale is very low.
—Jelile Ogundele, director of the St. Pius V Housing Committee

SOME OF the most important features of the vernacular ethnic neighborhoods that remain in urban Baltimore are "community-based" organizations, descendants of self-help efforts pioneered by immigrants and blacks as early as the eighteenth century. These block associations, umbrella organizations, church- and union-based coalitions, and social advocates create a remarkable political and civic landscape. In West Baltimore, as in many similar areas, these church, ethnic, and fraternal organizations, which had been active in the civil rights movement, responded to urban renewal and the costs it imposed on neighborhoods and low-income residents by transforming themselves into aggressive community improvement organizations. Community protests centered on the city's housing and urban renewal programs. They fought planning that was undertaken for business, rather than for people; they called for rent control and for community management of government services and government-subsidized housing. Social activists, including clergy, turned to the creation of parallel institutions at the neighborhood level to try to repair some of the damage that had been done to the vernacular community by overcrowding, state repression, and the loss of middle-class residents. Such voluntary organizations and associations, engaging simultaneously in DuBoisian protest and Washingtonian self-help, surfaced as strict DuBoisian strategies lost momentum.

Black Protest and White Government

As their Republican power base on the City Council disappeared, and with no economic infrastructure capable of lessening the impact of the Depression, many blacks in 1930s Baltimore began to see the federal government (as exemplified by the administration of Franklin Roosevelt) as their savior. Blacks' attention shifted from the Republican to the Democratic party, and from the local government, over which they had once had influence, to the seemingly more humane, but also more remote, federal government. For blacks, as for so many other Americans of the period, the very remoteness of federal politics helped create an illusion of common ground. It was not long, however, before black Baltimoreans began to see flaws in this picture. The various federal programs instituted by the Roosevelt administration to combat unemployment and poverty in the wake of the Depression were often designed to be administered on a segregated basis— as we have seen in the case of public housing and suburban home financing. New Deal legislation encouraged union organizing, but the racism endemic in Baltimore's labor organizations meant that to a large extent black workers remained excluded. The CIO, while not openly hostile to blacks, did not actively seek their participation either. It focused most of its efforts on industries dominated by whites and rarely led a union drive in factories where blacks were in the majority.

Blacks began organizing to press for their rights in New Deal programs, turning to a new politics of intervention that protested against the failure of government (now managing much of social life) to "do its job." Labor was one field, as J. A. Argersinger's history of the New Deal in Baltimore recounts:

> Religious leaders eagerly turned over their neighborhood churches for union meetings and not infrequently used their pulpits to discuss labor issues, keeping their congregations informed of boycotts, strikes, and other CIO activities. At Bethlehem Steel, the Steel Workers Organizing Committee made special efforts to organize blacks and directly linked its activities to the larger black community. Black and white workers cooperated to a degree unexpected in a city so divided by race.[1]

Protest activity increased. The People's Unemployment League (PUL), founded in 1933, not only encouraged racial integration of all its efforts, but also actively recruited blacks to participate in League leadership. Ten of the organization's twenty-five neighborhood boards consisted exclusively of blacks. The City-Wide Young People's Forum, founded in 1931 to help unemployed blacks, grew larger and more sophisticated in response to New Deal programs: "In 1933, the Forum took its cue from the National Recovery Administration, organizing boycotts of businesses that not only failed to display the Blue Eagle, but also refused to hire blacks. This "Buy Where You Can Work" movement resulted in the hiring of blacks at area A & P stores, in five and dime stores and the stalls of Lafayette Market."[2]

Never uncritical proponents of the New Deal, blacks nonetheless called for a more active federal government to reduce the racism and conservatism that locally impeded the programs' effectiveness. The city's four hundred black social clubs and more than two hundred black churches attempted to spread the message of the need for a more enlightened and equitable government: in violation of executive orders, local Works Progress Administration officials in Baltimore discriminated against black workers who sought to participate in various WPA programs.

> Leaders of the CIO and representatives of the PUL routinely blasted the local WPA for racial discrimination. Although [the WPA] regularly tried to discredit [them] . . . citing their alleged ties to the Communist Party, they still grudgingly acceded to minor demands.[3]

In response to the racism they encountered among those administering WPA funds in Baltimore, black community groups sent petitions and letters to local and national WPA offices to demand equal access to WPA jobs. Jobless blacks formed the Baltimore City Colored Unemployed, which called for an end to local discriminatory policies. Black women organized to improve conditions in WPA nursery schools for black children, which were housed in facilities inferior to those made available for white children: "Aggressive citizen action among black residents served to transform one nursery school 'located in one of the worst sectors of the city into a project that won praise not only from local and national WPA officials, but from foreign visitors as well.'"[4]

Throughout World War II and its aftermath, blacks found racism and discrimination in the administration of federal programs in public housing, slum clearance, urban renewal, and suburban housing development, and developed a healthy distrust of the government. This distrust would culminate in the Black Panther Party program of defiance and rebellion. With the Panthers decimated, a "nationalist" alternative promoting independence from government began to fire the imagination of young black men in West Baltimore. Ironically, at the center of the nationalist paradigm lay the dream of reparations: one big shot of government subsidy to transform the damaged black community from a ward of government to an independent, self-sustaining, semiautonomous unit within the society at large. The demand for reparations, as it featured in the dreams of former SNCC chairman James Forman or revolutionary nationalist Omari Obadele of the Republic of New Africa, was a step toward "nationhood" in the political sense. Yet the reparations concept as it worked out in practice was something closer to "Black Capitalism," a pet project of President Nixon for coopting just such energies in the black community. In West Baltimore, the nationalist impulse was translated into this latter form with the development of the Park Heights Development Corporation.

"Black Capitalism"

Park Heights, which lies just above North Avenue, the old segregation line describing West Baltimore's northern boundary, did not have a significant number of black residents until the 1970s. Park Heights had been a Jewish community since the 1930s, with 60 percent of its dwelling units owner-occupied. In 1960, however, blacks began moving into Park Heights in large numbers. By 1970 the neighborhood population was 80 percent nonwhite, and by 1980 it had increased to more than 90 percent. Park Heights today is a neighborhood of some forty-five thousand people, a third below the age of eighteen, and two-thirds between eighteen and sixty-one. The typical resident is a black working-class or lower-middle-class person with a large family (80 percent of households), most of whom moved from West Baltimore seeking a better environment for themselves and their children.

There are approximately fourteen thousand dwelling units in Park Heights, occupied at a vacancy rate of less than 5 percent. Only 20 percent of the housing stock consists of multifamily dwellings, and there is a substantial amount of owner-occupied housing in the neighborhood. Less than 10 percent of the dwelling units in the neighborhood are subsidized (that is, public housing projects, scattered-site public housing, section 8 housing, and section 221(d)(3), 235, or 236 moderate-income housing). Two of the most important public housing projects, Bel-Park (built in 1975 with 274 units) and Greenhill (built in 1980 with 301 units) are for the elderly. Overcrowding in Park Heights has decreased, but rents increased by 50 percent between 1980 and 1990. Homes for sale in the neighborhood have greatly increased in price. A large number of banks have provided mortgage financing for the purchase of homes in Park Heights in the last decade.

Many of the blacks who moved into Park Heights were homeowners from West Baltimore, part of a wave of black middle-class people who began leaving the old community when the barriers of segregation—restrictive covenants, bank redlining, and racial "steering" by real estate agents—fell. Others had their homes bulldozed by "urban renewal" and had no choice but to relocate. The black influx precipitated a large Jewish exodus, but middle-class blacks followed them through Park Heights and into Ashburton, now a prosperous black neighborhood where Mayor Kurt Schmoke lives, and even further, out into the perimeter neighborhoods of Forest Park and Windsor Hills.[5] Blockbusting was common. Park Heights was left with all the disadvantages of an old neighborhood without any of the vernacular social networks that can make living in an old neighborhood bearable. City officials, concerned about the rapid deterioration of the neighborhood's housing stock and the increase in overcrowding, in the late 1960s designated Park Heights as a Neighborhood Development Program Area. Park Heights became the largest urban renewal project in the country. The project—intended to improve housing conditions and the delivery of community services—covered the rapidly changing lower Park Heights area. The Park Heights Development Corporation (PHDC) was formed by local residents during this period.

Morris Iles, the director of the PHDC, was part of these neighborhood changes. A tough-talking, solid man, Iles was an interested newcomer in the 1960s, and in 1969 founded his own block association, which later joined the Lower Park Heights Coordinating Council (LPHCC). LPHCC was a key organization in the transformation of Northwest Baltimore from a predominantly Jewish to a predominantly black community. Forty homeowners who had been displaced from the black community of Franklin-Mulberry (destroyed by the development of Route 40) got compensation and used the money to move into Park Heights. These uprooted lower-middle-class families founded LPHCC to address physical development, human resources, and health care. In 1969 Baltimore passed a "new town" ordinance, which enabled Robert Embry, director of Baltimore's Department of Housing and Community Development (DHCD) and later an official of the Department of Housing and Urban Development under President Carter, to use federal funds to develop a "new town" in the Cold Spring area on the eastern border of Park Heights. Because the legislation required participation from the communities affected, LPHCC was invited to contribute to the planning process. This was the first such opportunity made available to ordinary citizens.

"Community people who got involved were exposed to the actual development process and learned a great deal," said Iles. "They were aware of the signs of deterioration in their community; it wasn't bombed out, but they were already seeing a need for more services and improvements. For starters, they demanded that some revitalization of Park Heights take place along with the Cold Spring new town development."

In response, Embry asked Moshe Safde, a planning consultant for the neighboring Cold Spring New Town, to work with residents of Park Heights as well as with DHCD in creating an overall renewal plan for the area. Many consultants were involved: economic consultants, transportation consultants, health consultants. Park Heights residents began to see a need for an organization to implement this new plan. There was a struggle between LPHCC and the Northwest Baltimore Corporation (a predominantly Jewish organization, rooted in the northern section of Park Heights) over which was to play that role. LPHCC prevailed.

"LPHCC was all young men," Iles told me. "This was unheard of. Community organizing in the black community, like the work of the black church, has always been done by the neighborhood grandmothers and mothers. But we saw the business and economic potential to the plan, and were inspired by it. We were interested in power, not just the delivery of services. Ronald Thomas, who owned the neighborhood McDonald's restaurant franchise, was part of our group. Safde wanted to bulldoze McDonald's, and that's the main reason why Thomas was with us. He was the leader, he had a lot of money."

In 1975 the urban renewal plan was completed and printed, and it projected planning and development in Park Heights for the next ten years. "We still refer to it up here," said Iles. "It covers everything, street improvement, new housing, recreational and social programs. Park Heights is very fortunate as a community to have had that comprehensive plan. It gave us a reference for future implementation."

To implement the plan, the Park Heights Community Corporation was developed in 1976. Its staff grew to nearly fifty, doing basic community organizing, convening groups to plan small area implementation, engaging in land-use planning and rezoning and commercial development in industrial areas. It established a community health center and opened the Park Heights Street Academy, a private school for disadvantaged youths. But the group wanted to move beyond planning and social service. They had their sights set on economic development, a "piece of the pie."

"When PHDC was established, the city only wanted us to do employment, not development," Iles recalls angrily. "Housing was going to go through the city bid process, people from outside the neighborhood doing the work and making the money, not economically empowering or even employing us. PHDC was permitted to do physical development work, as the general contractor, on only one pilot block. We had to subcontract out all the construction work. With the community development block grant [CDBG] money that was available, we renovated forty-eight properties and produced one hundred percent homeownership. It cost us $52,000 to renovate each unit, and we sold them for $10,000. The recipients got a forty-year first mortgage, and paid thirty-seven dollars a month. Five of the people who occupied the homes were on AFDC [Aid to Families with Dependent Children]. These were the kinds of things that were possible when there was a lot of money around."

PHDC's first economic project complied with the city's mandate of job creation. It was a maintenance company. PHDC dreamed up the idea of a preventive home maintenance business: people would pre-pay for maintenance services, while the corporation, by catching maintenance problems early, would minimize the cost of repair. PHDC got a contract with the city to service 125 vacant houses in Park Heights that were boarded up and not maintained because the city crew could not get to them. It then branched out to offer home maintenance services to homeowners in the community, setting up a home maintenance reserve fund for each homeowner that was serviced by a surcharge on mortgage payments. The fund belonged to the homeowner, who received interest on it but could draw on it only for home maintenance and repair.

PHDC then proposed to the city that it service all the city's vacant buildings, three thousand units. A city employee who saw the proposal leaked it to an East Side community organization, the Southeast Community Organization (SECO). According to Iles, SECO copied the PHDC proposal and submitted it as its own. SECO got the city contract and a half-million-dollar implementation grant from the Ford Foundation.

"We raised hell, and the city divided jurisdiction over the vacant houses in half, half for SECO, half for PHDC," Iles said, smiling at the memory. "SECO started with the Ford grant, but PHDC only got $45,000 in CDBG funds to start with. We had no working capital. We used the CDBG money to buy three trucks, but we had no cash flow. We had to work first and get paid later. But SECO had made a mistake. The proposal we originally submitted was only a sketch; we hadn't had time to completely flesh out the actuarial figures for the pre-paid maintenance idea." Without this essential bit of information, SECO by 1979 had spent all the foundation money it received but could not make the business work. PHDC was not inclined to point out SECO's error. "By 1980, PHDC had the maintenance contract for the whole city, and SECO was out of business," reported Iles with satisfaction.

By 1980 PHDC had turned to industrial planning. It was looking at land along the western border of Park Heights, near the old Wabash railroad line, which was all zoned industrial. "When Park Heights was a Jewish neighborhood, there was a foundry, metal plants, auto framing plants, bottling companies, metal fabrication companies, and a lumber yard on this land, near the railroad line," Iles told me. "All these businesses provided jobs for the residents of Park Heights. By the time the neighborhood transformed from Jewish to black, all these firms were gone. PHDC's ideal was to attract business back to this land. We were especially interested in a site at the southern end of the land, which we felt could serve as an industrial park."

PHDC worked with the city economic development agency, BEDCO (Baltimore Economic Development Corporation), on a development plan for this site, forty acres of vacant land just above Park Circle, which had been the site of an amusement park and a drive-in theater in the 1950s. In the 1960s the amusement park was demolished, and a shopping center was constructed on part of the land. The

Metropolitan Transit Authority had plans to use the land for a subway line and thus kept it off the market until 1981, when community opposition forced them to relinquish it to PHDC.

"The city was very excited about developing the site, particularly the small business incubator space," said Iles. (The incubator facility is described below.) The plans for the Park Circle Industrial Park, part of the Neighborhood Development Plan for Park Heights, had been conceived by City Ventures, Inc., a Minneapolis corporation specializing in the development of urban renewal projects and a subsidiary of Control Data, Inc., a corporation engaged in the manufacture of electronic assemblies. City Ventures received a contract from the city of Baltimore to revitalize Park Heights pursuant to the city's comprehensive plan. Their idea was to create an industrial park and have it designated an enterprise zone, so that property tax abatement and investment tax credits for new hiring would be available. But PHDC was not satisfied with the City Ventures proposal.

"We felt that Control Data, the parent corporation, should be involved, and should actually locate an electronic assembly plant in the industrial park and become an anchor tenant," said Iles. Control Data was apparently unwilling to do that, but it assigned City Ventures Incorporated, its planning subsidiary, to develop a technology center and incubator facility, which was built in Elementary School No. 18, across the street from the industrial park. City Ventures renovated the school and also built a 60,000-square-foot addition to it, at a total cost of four million dollars.

In the industrial park itself, PHDC had a 30,000-square-foot building that it hoped to renovate and use to attract the anchor tenant it desperately needed for the industrial park. "There were a lot of fits and starts," Iles recalled. "We tried to start a recycling plant in the big building and got a grant for that purpose, but a truck that had been parked inside the building blew up and destroyed it. The federal Economic Development Administration had agreed to underwrite the recycling plant, but backed out after the fire." Another prospective anchor tenant was undercapitalized, and the business folded.

"We pursued Park's Sausages [the city's largest black-owned company] for a long time, but Park's was not interested," said Iles. "However, things turned around for us when municipal development of the new Baltimore Orioles baseball stadium forced Park's out of their downtown plant. Then they were ready to relocate to Park Heights." In 1987 the industrial park opened, with Park's Sausages as the anchor tenant. City Ventures opened its business and technology center, but it was not long before it folded, leaving behind an outstanding $800,000 industrial development bond. PHDC now owns and runs that center.

In the meantime, PHDC found or developed commercial and industrial tenants for the various buildings that were left. The white-owned Londontown Manufacturers, a large garment-making shop, wanted to move into the industrial park because 60 percent of its workforce came from Park Heights. Most of the concern's workers were female, and wages and benefits were very low. (PHDC agreed to rent to Londontown only if it improved the workers' wages and benefits.) Other large tenants in the industrial park were a plastics firm, a design firm, a computer furniture company, and a group called "Earth Engineering" that constructed its own building. In 1991, PHDC still had four acres left in the industrial park and $1.5 million to develop a 20,000-square-foot building for industrial uses.

The incubator facility has proven to be PHDC's biggest challenge. There are financial constraints involved, because when PHDC took the building over from City Ventures it had to assume $500,000 of the outstanding $800,000 bond. The incubator facility, designed to nurture struggling small businesses, has never been completely filled, and PHDC is still struggling to pay off the bond debt. But an even larger challenge is working with the small businesses themselves and helping them overcome the obstacles they face.

Iles operated a manpower service center for the city until the 1973 recession made it difficult to place people. His approach was to talk to businesspeople, ask them what their plans were, and figure out how he could help them grow, so that when the corporation did expand, he could put his people in. Today, he uses the same approach with the businesses he is trying to support in the incubator facility. The PHDC incubator takes all the risk; all the business tenants have to do is pay $265 a month to rent 400 square feet of space. The large tenants get 7,000 square feet of space, for which they pay three dollars per square foot, utilities included. A telephone, copier, and audio-visual equipment are provided. They get four hours a month of access to a conference room; for more than that, they are billed ten dollars an hour.

"The incubator concept is something that many minority businesses don't relate to," said Iles. "They don't buy into the total concept that underlies the incubator. Instead, each wants all the trappings of business ownership. They won't use the secretaries or the typists, because they want their own. They need business development services, but they don't want to pay. We have had to take a micromanagement approach with these businesses, just to keep them paying the rent." The basic approach is to grow businesses in the incubator until they get bigger, then move them into the industrial buildings. In this way PHDC can keep resources and the potential for job creation in its community.

Iles wants his businesspeople to start thinking bigger. "Businesses have to grow or they die," he says. "If you're making one hundred to three hundred thousand dollars a year in sales, that's not big enough if you're only making 8 or even 10 percent profit. You might as well have a job. I want folks in the incubator to merge. It's very hard. There are four accounting firms in the incubator that won't merge. They won't even form a professional association, they can't even agree on the name that they would call themselves."

Since 1980, PHDC has been using a revolving loan fund to finance commercial revitalization throughout Park Heights. "The businesses we sponsored would grow from three to five years, then they would need expansion capital, they couldn't get it, and the businesses would die," Iles recalled. "PHDC lost $300,000 from the loan fund that way. With the largest businesses that we deal with, we find two and a half millon dollars in sales to be some kind of institutional break point. Internal management skills really have to increase at that point, especially in construction. Minority contractors can't get credit, so they have to be bonded. That means they have to have hard assets, which don't usually show up on a balance sheet. They have to know how to leverage. You need equity of fifty to seventy thousand dollars to get a two-million-dollar bond. The next largest kind of project is suddenly five million dollars. Minority contractors can't get bonds that big. The government could have a ten-million-dollar contract for them, but they couldn't get it because they couldn't get a bond.

"What they need to do is bring their subcontractors into their corporate structure. But again, people are afraid to do this. They're socializing together, going skiing together, doing the full range of things together, but they're scared to give up that ownership interest. They need to start thinking about merging. You get a carpenter, a painter, an electrician, and a person who does HVAC [heating, ventilating, and air conditioning], you get these four trades together and have them merge into one contractor. Most blacks in business in Baltimore are in construction. People need to think about working together and getting bigger together."

Federal Policy Changes and the
Decline in "Black Capitalism"

As U.S. dominance abroad receded after the Viet Nam War, heavily funded domestic development programs such as PHDC became untenable. Under the pressure of increased international competition from Japan and Europe, the reversals of Viet Nam, and the price shocks of the boycott by the oil-producing and exporting countries, U.S. corporate profits began to decline and the post–World War II boom slowed. U.S. business corporations, claiming a need to be more competitive internationally, reduced wages—first for nonunionized service-sector employees, then for unionized industrial workers. Besides targeting labor as the problem, business corporations also mounted a formidable program of lobbying and fundraising for reductions in environmental and civil rights regulation, reductions in social welfare spending, and an expansion of military spending.[6] The redirection in spending priorities was accompanied by an agenda for reducing business costs through cuts in corporate taxes, lowering capital gains tax rates, and increasing the social security taxes paid by individuals. The business position was that the country's economic problems were caused by the various programs of the post–World War II Democratic party's public interest state.

As business was launching this attack, the Democratic party was being buffeted by the aftermath of the domestic upheavals of the 1960s. The civil rights movement in the South brought formerly disenfranchised whites into the political equation as well as blacks. The blacks voted Democratic, but did not register in large numbers. The previously inactive southern whites registered and voted in high percentages, and eventually joined the Republican party under the banner of the Christian Right.[7] On the other hand, the New Politics of the northern, urban Democratic party—peace, environmentalism, and race and gender equality—alienated much of the North's white working class.[8] The inability of the Democratic party to deliver economically to the unionized workers who formed its core constituency—in fact, their abandonment of the unionized working class in the face of the business onslaught—further weakened the party.

Meanwhile, the Republican party was gaining strength. Emerging from its post–New Deal malaise as a coalition of suburbanites, fundamentalist Christians, and southwestern oil men, the party was poorly represented by Goldwater in 1964 but found its voice as Nixon's Silent Majority in 1968. Richard Nixon, the originator of the Republican "southern strategy," was the architect of today's Republican party. He was the first (often through his mouthpiece, Spiro Agnew) to portray Democratic liberals as soft on crime, communism, and racial issues, and the first to make extensive and skillful use of the media for negative campaigning.[9] He turned the tide on the mass movements that undergirded the New Politics of the northern, urban Democratic party. The setback of Watergate removed Nixon, but, ironically, even this debacle achieved a conservative Republican objective—undercutting the legitimacy of the federal government. Moreover, Nixon's program for Republican party revival and the attraction it held for business, suburbanites, and working-class whites, for western money and southern fundamentalists, came through Watergate virtually unscathed. Jimmy Carter's inability to build a coalition of party regulars and New Politics people to support a paradigm for the Democratic party that fitted the new international and domestic context spelled the end of Democratic aspirations to the White House.[10] Ronald Reagan was elected in 1980 with a perceived mandate to destroy the last vestiges of the structures erected by the business–labor–civil rights coalition of the 1960s. He set out at once to implement the business agenda that Nixon had been unable to deliver: cuts in taxes and in social welfare; industrial, environmental, and financial deregulation; a rollback of union and civil rights gains; and increased military spending.[11]

As austerity emerged as national policy, organizations like PHDC became less common. Their economic development functions today tend to be carried on, on a much smaller scale, by state and federal programs that emphasize the training of small business entrepreneurs. Their housing development functions tend to be carried on by voluntary community organizations such as churches, block clubs, and settlement houses, which, in addition to experimenting with nonprofit sponsorship of low- and moderate-income housing, are also engaged in economic development, cultural renovation, school program enrichment, and health care delivery.

"Microenterprise"—Small Small Business

In this less favorable political and economic milieu, microenterprises began generating some interest. The term "microenterprise" (often used interchangeably with "self-employment," "entrepreneurship," "cottage industry," and "home-based business") describes a very small business that may be part of a cooperative or located in a home or on a commercial strip, usually employing fewer than five people. A microenterprise is often started by family members or friends who have the requisite capital and marketable skills. Microenterprises are considered sustainable when they generate twelve to fifteen thousand dollars in net income for the owner per year. Typical successful microenterprises include video production, video rental, florist shops, telecommunications, housecleaning, child or elder care, home repair, restaurants, retail or wholesale bakeries, food catering, janitorial services for commercial sites, bookkeeping, publishing, and dry cleaning.

The Baltimore City Commission for Women took on the development of a microenterprise project in 1988. After a year assessing the economic status of women in Baltimore, the commission invited a number of neighborhood activists, community leaders, and business owners to design a self-employment training project for Baltimore. The Women Entrepreneurs of Baltimore (WEB) developed a microenterprise proposal out of this process, but were preempted by a state and municipally sponsored program, the Maryland Self-Employment Initiative for Development (SEID), which met the Abell Foundation's criterion of involving government. SEID was a four-year demonstration project aimed at assisting low-income women and men to achieve self-sufficiency through business ownership. The initial pilot program is based in the Baltimore metropolitan region and called the Business Owners Start-Up Services (BOSS).

Bonnie Birker, a rosy-cheeked, cherubic, middle-aged woman with a broad, Dutch smile, who makes you think of immigrant women of the early nineteenth century heading to the Midwest in covered wagons, was the first BOSS director. Birker's professional background was in job training, but she began to see that she was training people for jobs that did not exist or were rapidly disappearing because of changes in the organization and direction of the economy. "When you work for someone else, you get locked into a certain salary level. It's easy to get laid off," she concluded. Then she began to specialize in the "self-sufficiency model" of welfare reform, feeling that self-employment was the way to go.

"It's a question of independence," Birker observed. "Self-employment is the best way to get wealthy. But it's also a question of temperament. Some people need the flexibility and room for creativity that goes with self-employment—they need the option to work different hours, to pursue work that develops the skills they're interested in, rather than be programmed for the needs of another person. There are downside risks to self-employment, of course: lousy income, no insurance or medical benefits. But we can limit some of those risks through BOSS by providing group health and life insurance and by lending money to help bridge the income gap when small businesses start up. The present economy is a real scare situation, even for the largest businesses. But the flip side is that, regardless of the economy, there are some opportunities now that didn't exist before—people need lots of services, and these needs can often be filled better by a small, flexible company than by a big business."

Indeed, the large, centralized, and bureaucratic industrial corporations that dominate our economy were designed primarily for mass production and to achieve the economies of scale necessary to saturate markets.[12] With markets saturated, "consumers" became "customers," seeking goods that are not mass-produced but rather are differentiated by the amount and quality of information used in developing the product's design, craft, utility, and durability.[13] Large, cumbersome enterprises designed for the earlier era are having difficulty adjusting to modern economic paradigm shifts from the movement of mass and the accumulation of capital to the accumulation, transfer, and utilization of information.

Customers want goods that are "more useful, longer lasting, easier to repair, lighter, stronger, less energy-consuming," and less damaging to the environment. They want to do business with companies that stand behind their products and continue to serve them after the sale has been completed.[14] Mass markets are being divided into smaller submarkets of customers who want products that are more tailored to their specific needs and desires, both in terms of original design and in terms of on-the-spot adjustments made for a reasonable period after sale. Large companies designed for mass production for passive consumers often find it difficult to make adjustments to suit markets of this size.

In this economic context, increasing numbers of people in poor neighborhoods in the United States are taking risks on alternative and creative types of economic activities such as self-employment. The advantage of self-employment is that there are fewer barriers to entry and people can progress in small steps. Self-employment among welfare recipients occurs frequently enough (18,000 reported cases in 1986) to require AFDC regulations on how to handle self-employment income. Significant rates of self-employment also occur among dislocated workers (especially in construction, manufacturing, finance, and service trades), the disabled, and the elderly.

Bernita Holsey, BOSS's head trainer, believes that the principal obstacle to the small entrepreneur is lack of capital, which in turn is based on lack of collateral and (Catch-22) lack of a credit record. "They can't get their businesses going," she said. "They keep using their profits as a salary, just to survive. They can't recapitalize, can't plow any profits back into the business, and they go under. That's why they need a loan fund."

Microenterprise development programs like BOSS are typically nonprofit revolving loan funds that make very small, short-term loans for working capital to low-income individuals who want to start up or expand a small business. To decrease their risk, microenterprise loan funds often utilize existing community networks to identify persons capable, with help, of starting or expanding microenterprises. Struggling microentrepreneurs face another obstacle: the fear of sharing information and collaborating with other small businesspeople, a problem that Morris Iles has struggled with in his incubator work.

"They're afraid that if they network, ask for help, that someone will take their idea or their business or beat them out of something," Holsey said. BOSS is trying to help recruits develop networks for handling family and social problems and also improve their professional/business contacts, extending them to include credit unions, banks, colleges, businesses, unions, pension funds, schools, community organizations, and public agencies.

BOSS itself went through some dramatic changes. Birker came into conflict with her supervisors because BOSS failed to produce microentrepreneurs at a rate commensurate with the money they spent. Toward the end, Birker seemed overwhelmed by bureaucratic pitfalls. Many of the BOSS graduates did not develop their plans completely, or, when ready, did not receive the money in time. Many spiraled back down into despair. With Birker gone, Holsey has stayed on to train new classes, but BOSS seems to have been recaptured by the social welfare bureaucracy that created it.

Community Self-Help and Advocacy Associations

Problems like those encountered by BOSS persuaded many community organizations to insulate themselves from the social welfare bureaucracy. The high level of technical and political capability that many community organizations have developed facilitates their efforts at self-help. On shoestring budgets, neighborhood organizations have embarked on projects providing all manner of community services—health care, housing, child care, surplus food distribution, small park development, and community clean-up. Some projects succeed; others fail. Community organizations have also battled with downtown interests over highways, pollution, and gentrification. Some organizations have won; others have lost.

The most adaptable of these organizations have survived and continued their work despite decreasing federal support, calling upon a rich history of initiative, creativity, and energy stemming from the struggle for civil rights and for community empowerment in the context of federal antipoverty and Model Cities programs, as well as battles against urban renewal, housing segregation, and environmental pollution. These "second-generation" community development organizations survived program cutbacks and political repression and, phoenix-like, have emerged sophisticated and energetic. They are smaller, leaner, more indigenous, and more in tune with the specific agenda of their local communities than their predecessors, which were more closely tied to City Hall and downtown business interests. There seem to have been paradigm shifts in the arena of community organizing that parallel the shifts in the business world.

In the housing area, many of these smaller organizations have coalesced into a movement to protect the land they are redeveloping from market pressure through the use of community land trusts. CLTs are sponsored by community-based, nonprofit organizations to keep property affordable in changing neighborhoods and reduce the effects of speculation on neighborhood real estate. The CLT purchases or otherwise secures property in areas undergoing or threatened with gentrification, renovates existing structures, and builds new ones. The new or redeveloped housing is sold to buyers who meet income guidelines. The CLT also provides financial assistance to the homebuyer. The CLT retains title to the land upon which the dwelling is constructed, and when the owners decide to move, they are obligated to sell the property back to the CLT for an amount equal to the purchase price plus improvements. The property will then be available for sale to another low- or moderate-income family. CLTs have purchased single-family homes as well as apartment buildings. In a number of cases the CLT has assisted the existing tenants to form a cooperative to purchase their own building.

The CLT model was created by Ralph Borsodi and Robert Swan, who founded the Institute for Community Economics in 1967. The philosophy underlying the CLT is that housing is not a commodity to be bought and sold, but a resource to be shared. Proponents argue that CLTs offer the only opportunity many people will ever have to afford their own homes. Critics have charged that CLTs will just perpetuate ghetto conditions and argue that limiting a homeowner's equity violates fundamental property rights. In a number of states, however, real estate agents and other business groups have lent their support to CLTs. The CLT movement has come to be much more than a collection of isolated, privately supported local initiatives, and is having an increasing and noticeable impact on local and state housing policies.

In their efforts to secure funding for the purchase and rehabilitation of housing, CLTs have drawn on a variety of public and private sources. A number of states, such as Vermont and Connecticut, have appropriated money to finance CLTs. Some CLTs have used money from Community Development Block Grants to pay for rehabilitation, and others have sought donations from private foundations and individuals. In addition, CLTs typically require prospective homeowners to put a certain amount of "sweat equity" into both their own future homes and other CLT property.

CLTs have proven to be good investments. As of 1988, the Institute for Community Economics had lent more than ten million dollars to CLTs and suffered only $2,500 in losses as a result of defaults. CLTs keep their default rates low through the careful screening and education of prospective tenants. CLTs have been formed by churches and a variety of community organizations, as well as by low- and moderate-income people themselves. The typical CLT board of directors is made up of CLT homeowners, representatives of local nonprofit housing groups, and members of the community at large. In the wake of massive cuts in federal aid programs and the rising demand for affordable housing, the CLT model has grown in popularity. The number of CLTs has more than doubled since 1987 and by 1991 stood at more than sixty around the country. Most are located in the New England area, but CLTs can be found in, among other places, Cincinnati, Atlanta, Dallas, Trenton, and Philadelphia.

CLT organizations are typical second-generation community development organizations. Weaned from the need for large federal subsidies, able to depend to a large extent on volunteers, these organizations are free to protect their communities in ways never possible under the antipoverty program, Model Cities, or the early community development corporations (such as PHDC) established by the Economic Development Act of 1964, as amended in 1968. In this respect, second-generation community development organizations bear an important resemblance to the self-help groups and networks previously existing in Baltimore neighborhoods, which were knit together by ethnicity and/or religious belief. This is true, for example, of church-based groups such as the St. Pius V Housing Committee of Harlem Park.

The St. Pius V Housing Committee

St. Pius V Church was established in 1878 in Harlem Park under the guidance of the Josephite priests and brothers and the Oblate Sisters of Providence. It is a leading black Catholic parish in the Baltimore archdiocese. The St. Pius V Housing Committee is a neighborhood development organization sponsored by the church. Jelili Ogundele, the committee's director, is an affable, sharp Nigerian who came to the United States to study financial management for his family's business, but got bitten by the community development bug and took a degree in urban planning from Morgan State University. He volunteered for various neighborhood projects and worked for the Baltimore-based Enterprise Foundation. He had four years of experience as a community organizer prior to coming to St. Pius.

The St. Pius V Housing Committee started as many of the church efforts in West Baltimore have started, with a minister or some other spiritual leader challenging a congregation to do something to upgrade the community surrounding it. Establishing the corporation and getting its tax exemption was a new and arduous process for the people from Harlem Park. They were assisted by the Archdiocese of Baltimore, which at first sheltered them under its 501(C)(3) tax-exempt status, and helped with legal procedures and securing money for start-up costs. St. Pius borrowed from a number of different Catholic institutions (including the Josephites), which they would have to pay back. This was only seed money: they had to look elsewhere for operating funds. Fortunately, community development block grant funds were available.

Harlem Park is characterized by large, gracious mansions (many of which have been cut up into kitchenette apartments) as well as large, single-family, three-story rowhouses that are still quite elegant. (Harlem Park rowhouses contain over two thousand square feet of living space; a typical Baltimore rowhouse has only thirteen hundred square feet.) A person making as little as $25,000 a year can afford to buy one. However, the median income of a Harlem Park resident is between $6,000 and $7,000. Considerable subsidies are thus necessary to make these houses affordable to the local population. The typical prospective buyer for a renovated home is a single female head of household, with two or three children, making $16,000 to $18,000 a year—not enough to qualify for even a subsidized mortgage. Further, with the present gap between what people can afford and what community-based developers can deliver, a number of houses have been vacant for a long time.

Harlem Park was the site of the Baltimore Urban Renewal and Housing Agency's first program of residential renewal in 1959.[15] The principal focus was the demolition and removal of back-alley shanties, reduction of density, and the development of small vest-pocket parks in the alleys, to be called "inner-block parks." People in Harlem Park still feel bitter about their experiences as the guinea pigs of urban renewal in Baltimore. The inner-block park concept worked with the original residents, but things changed after 1959.

The lines of communication between Baltimore city government and Harlem Park residents have been strained ever since. In 1990, the city reviewed and revised the original BURHA plan of 1959, but lack of funds limited implementation. It failed, however, to explain the obstacles, leaving local people angry and alienated. In another instance the city knocked down many of the neighborhood's sizable and attractive houses, without adequately explaining to residents that the homes were too large for economically feasible rehabilitation, given existing zoning and building regulations. Residents today understand only that the Department of Housing and Community Development thought the houses were "too big." They saw many of the mansions go down and others divided into apartments as more people crowded into the neighborhood. As far as Harlem Park residents are concerned, the DHCD has consistently pursued ill-conceived projects that were then dumped on the community with little or no thought as to the impact.

Harlem Park people thus feel "disrespected" by city officials at the most basic level. This perception can proceed from something as elementary as inspectors knocking on doors early in the morning, attempting to verify compliance with urban renewal ordinances but disturbing people's sleep and forcing them to come to their front door in nightclothes. Harlem Park residents question the good faith of government because officials promise things without revealing the limitations of the program or of their own position. Worse, Harlem Park people feel that they are being lied to. Ada Pullen, head of the Harlem Park Neighborhood Council, is perhaps the most vocal resident on such matters.

"Today, community development block grant money is going to private developers and the community is being excluded," she told me. "There's no dialogue; the city people don't tell the Harlem Park people what's going on. What are you going to do in my neighborhood? We want to know. These are young kids downtown making these decisions. Some of us have been at this for thirty years or more. We are not about to let incompetent or indifferent or inexperienced people downtown compromise our community."

"The history of the neighborhood is very sad in that respect," added Ogundele. "The Harlem Park Urban Renewal Plan hasn't been touched or modified in the thirty years since it was first adopted. Neighborhood people feel the city just doesn't care. There is a sense of anger, a sense of distrust of the system. People's morale is very low, there's a lot of apathy. You have sporadic protests, especially to drugs and crime, but they die out quickly."

Today, Harlem Park, a community of nine thousand residents, is rapidly deteriorating. Its homeowners are dying off or selling, and owner-occupied homes are gradually giving way to rentals. The majority of Harlem Park residents are between eighteen and sixty-one. Large families make up a much larger percentage of the population here than in Upton, however—almost 90 percent of the total. Single-person households account for only 9 percent. There were 3,670 dwelling units in Harlem Park in 1980, slightly more than in Upton.

Interestingly, the number of dwelling units in Harlem Park remained stable from 1970 to 1980, and the vacancy rate was 4 percent, lower even than Park Heights' vacancy rate. While overcrowding in Harlem Park has decreased, rents have increased 50 percent. The prices of homes for sale in the neighborhood have skyrocketed, in what appears to be an explosion of speculative activity.

Harlem Park boasts an impressive homeownership rate of 17 percent, primarily due to a small middle-class enclave around Lafayette Square in the northeast corner of the neighborhood. BURHA's successor, DHCD, is renovating the Lafayette Square area, trying to stabilize these few solid blocks as owner-occupied housing. The significance of this enclave of homeownership is underscored by the fact that 54 percent of all dwellings in Harlem Park are multifamily rentals, the highest rate in any of the four neighborhoods surveyed here. Only 12 percent of the dwelling units in the neighborhood are subsidized, compared with 29 percent in Upton.

The social statistics and patterns of Harlem Park overall, however, are bleak. Closer than other West Side neighborhoods to the city core from which blacks originally migrated, Harlem Park is the worst of the four. It is the only one, for example, which showed an increase in the crime rate (robberies, burglaries, and larcenies accounted for most of the increase). Crime seems most severe in a two-square-block area in the southern part of the neighborhood, bounded by Franklin and Calhoun Streets and Edmondson and Carrollton Avenues on the southern edge of the neighborhood, across from the Murphy Homes and Lafayette Courts public housing projects.

Undermaintenance by the Baltimore Public Housing Authority has combined with the lack of community in the projects to further undermine the quality of life. Elevators and plumbing have deteriorated and do not work, and trash is not picked up, leading to accumulations of refuse in hallways, elevators, and stairwells. Facades are eroding dangerously. At Murphy Homes, for example, a twelve-year-old boy was killed by a twenty-pound chunk of concrete that broke away from a twelfth-story apartment balcony. The Housing Authority was aware that balconies were beginning to crack, but did not replace them because of a lack of funds.

Undermaintenance also means lack of security. Idle adults and teenagers lounge in the hallways and common areas of these projects, and crime and violence are common. Projects like Murphy Homes and Lafayette Courts today are havens for drug dealers who terrorize the troubled but generally law-abiding families who live there. Much of the crime in such projects is drug-related. The city police do not have the resources to keep these large, dreary high-rises under adequate surveillance. At present, DHCD has installed a housing police security force, who are not permitted to carry sidearms but do carry spray cans of mace. Their job is to provide surveillance on Housing Authority property and call the city police if a situation warrants it.

Some attempt is being made to deliver social services directly into the projects, but the problems appear intractable, and it is difficult to conceive how the high-rises can be salvaged. Murphy Homes and Lafayette Courts thus remain at the edge of Harlem Park, examples of just how bad public housing can be. When the Murphy Homes project was proposed, neighborhood people cautioned that it would crowd too many people into too small a space. If these units were torn down, one scattered-site unit would have to be made available for every unit destroyed—yet Harlem Park has only 4,000 dwelling units and a vacancy rate of 4 percent. Thirty years after its construction, Murphy Homes is still a problem for Harlem Park. But the city is nowhere to be seen, say community residents.

"Somebody is killed in Murphy Homes every night," said Ada Pullen. "It's fourteen stories high, there are hundreds of families crowded in there. The psychological effect on the children, the effect on their academic performance, is tragic." Children from Murphy Homes and Lafayette Courts cross Franklin Street, the southern border of Harlem Park, to attend Harlem Park neighborhood schools. The schools are forced to handle a level of social disaffection, alienation, and underdevelopment that is quite beyond their resources. Various community groups and parent associations have focused their attention on the neighborhood schools as the primary place where improvement needs to take place. They are presently trying to stabilize the situation, and possibly make some improvements.

To put it mildly, Harlem Park people are bitter and suspicious of the "powers that be." No one wants to be taken advantage of, some do not even want to participate. Jelili Ogundele has to deal with the resentment that results from a long history of community organizations and people being burned by planners and other professionals from City Hall as he works with the community members of the board of directors of the St. Pius V Housing Committee. Ogundele's approach, in this context, is not like the usual community development model, in which the developers decide what they want to do and then negotiate with community organizations for their approval.

"We try to empower people," Ogundele said enthusiastically. "But sometimes we have to tell them you don't make progress without creating relationships with the people you're trying to get to listen to you. Sometimes being really antagonistic is not the way to accomplish what you want. Sometimes people come to the table with the idea that city people can't be trusted and overwhelm them with their distrust. We try to show them how to build networks in the city bureaucracy, how to understand the development approval process. Sometimes they bring lots of complaints to a bureaucrat who has no power to change anything, who doesn't set policy or make decisions. Sometimes you have to go over their heads."

At other times the courts are the appropriate forum. Community-based organizations in Harlem Park recently won a case against some billboard owners. The organizations did not like the messages—promoting alcohol and cigarettes—the billboards were sending out in residential areas to young people. Their protests led to a debate among the mayor, the organizations, and influential groups like the Citizen Planning and Housing Association (CPHA). It was a victory for the community groups. They also won a suit against the landlords of vacant houses for maintaining a nuisance. The houses were awarded to the St. Pius V Housing Committee, and DHCD has promised funding for redevelopment.

As for actual housing development and economic development, that is an uphill battle. "Because of the economy, not much improvement is possible," Ogundele lamented. "There's lots of physical deterioration, lots of vacant houses. We don't expect to see a lot of investment here. And even when we produce houses, we can't necessarily get them to market. What if there's a vacant house next door? It becomes a real problem. And even though we're nonprofit, we still have to pay the bills. There's insurance, taxes, maintenance. Sometimes our insurance policies are canceled for minor infractions and we go into high-risk, more expensive categories. And acquisition costs! You've got to own a building before you can renovate. The Enterprise Foundation has been very helpful in that respect, giving advice on cutting costs and partially funding St. Pius V's first housing project."

The Enterprise Foundation lent them some money, as well as giving them a one-time grant and providing sorely needed technical assistance. "The Enterprise people are very good at teaching; they broke technical issues down into simple terms, but Saint Pius V housing people are still learning," Ogundele told me. Foundation staff members are still frequently called back to give technical advice.

The Harlem Park Community Association, which works closely with the St. Pius V group, is a coalition of several organizations. The Harlem Park Trust was formed to respond to the social problems the city created with the inner-block parks. The Lafayette Square Association was formed to encourage homeownership around Lafayette Square Park, and the Harlem Park Neighborhood Council was founded as a service organization. The Community Association is now trying to organize Harlem Square for homeownership, having since its early days raised money the old-fashioned, vernacular way, with chicken and fish dinners. There were a lot of excellent cooks in the neighborhood and the merchants pitched in as well.

Chairperson Pullen of the Neighborhood Council is a gregarious woman who does not like being confined in an office. She is comfortable in the vernacular, and loves to be out in the street talking with her constituents, finding out how much rent they are paying, and trying to persuade them to use their rent money to buy a house.

"People don't understand how to borrow money—they're not budget wise, they don't have any survival skills, they don't know anything about good nutrition or the quality of life or keeping themselves in houses that are clean. So many of the young people have no training in this area at all. They're listless; they have no desire or ambition. They have to be stimulated and motivated. We have thirty-one-year-olds in our community who are happy to be on welfare. What's going to happen to them? Motivation is the key, you have to have this. If you're a creative person with visions, you can motivate other people.

"This really needs to be happening in the schools. The kids are missing so much, they're so unprepared, and it's so hard for them to catch up. The students have to be empowered to admit that they're just not getting it. The teachers aren't very tolerant of this now. It's really hard to get teachers who are competent and committed. When they don't do their jobs, they just get suspended. They're out of the class but they still get paid. In the Harlem Park middle school there's a group called For and With Parents that's going to lose their funding soon. They were set up to advocate between the school, the parent, and the child. They were developing relationships with the parents, trying to get them to come out to the school. So many of the parents just didn't care, but FWP did canvassing and got them to turn out. The mistake was in just asking for three-year grants. They should have asked for five years.

"We don't understand the city's approach to education," Pullen complained. "Somebody needs to explain it to us. We need money for people who can work hands-on with the parents. The parents feel as uncomfortable at the school as their children do. They don't want to look stupid. It's the same way they felt when they were kids, maybe even in the same school—totally intimidated." People in the community have no faith in the public schools.

All the Harlem Park Council people work as volunteers. They work hard, but they are beginning to burn out. They want paid staff whose only job is to educate the people in the community, help them work on their budgets, help them learn how to control their lives, how to save for a house. This type of money is apparently available from the Baltimore Urban Services Agency for city-funded nonprofit organizations, but the Harlem Park Association is not one of these. Here again, the city's lack of support is a sore point. "At least they could pay for a telephone," Pullen said.

The Need for Public Sector
Involvement and Support: DuBois Revisited

As federal funds for community development tightened during the late 1960s and early 1970s, the Nixon administration consoled big-city mayors with a promise of more direct local control of federal resources. Most urban, housing, and poverty programs were dismantled, and only community development block grant funds were left. Under the new CDBG regime, Mayor William Donald Schaefer of Baltimore built strong ties to neighborhood organizations during the 1980s, but activists in those organizations seldom gained either City Council seats or a position of power based on anything more substantial than the friendship that Schaefer had cultivated with them. Schaefer built a political machine that combined strong relationships with business and professional interests, inner-city ethnic white support on the basis of large-scale citizen participation, and black support based on social welfare. Schaefer put community activists on his payroll, coopting many of the city's once-strident neighborhood workers.[16] Those who refused to play along were shut out. In the process, he was able to divert a significant proportion of the city's CDBG funds away from the neighborhoods and toward the downtown "Renaissance" of Baltimore's Inner Harbor. A small portion was allocated for the cooptation of neighborhood groups.[17]

Even the old and strong church groups were unable to break into city government in a meaningful way. Schaefer had adopted the Richard Daley (Chicago) model of city administration, and kept all power in his own hands while making city leaders feel that they had access to power through him. He was supported by Baltimore business leaders and wealthy families, but also by black voters, despite criticism by black community leaders. The Project Area Committees (PACs) developed to meet the community participation requirements of the urban renewal laws were embarrassed when it became apparent that the new development surge had created housing prices their constituents could not afford, and these constituents, further, were ineligible for city housing loan assistance because of their low incomes. Many of these constituents were forced out of their old neighborhoods, doubling up in other slums as gentrification absorbed their homes.[18]

Much of the formal leadership of West Baltimore's older vernacular neighborhoods disappeared. The few homeowners who remain in places like Sandtown or Harlem Park usually emerge as the leaders of local improvement associations and block clubs. Other formal leaders include the ministers of prosperous churches, whose congregations return each Sunday to worship in their old places, and the owners of local businesses. The primary difference from the previous era is that a much smaller percentage of the formal leadership still lives in the community. Only the grand old churches, still host to the thousands of affluent black exiles who flood them on Sundays, continue to provide some resources and contacts.

As urban programs were dismantled during the Reagan era, programs Schaefer had contracted out to Baltimore's neighborhood organizations were ended, and those programs that remained were transferred to the city's Urban Services Agency, with much less community participation. Coalitions of community groups began to fragment as the battle over urban development in the city became a battle over available city funds. Though city development benefited certain segments of the black community, the black population remained largely untouched by Baltimore's renewal efforts, and community disaffection increased. Mondawmin Mall, a 120-store, black-oriented shopping center in Park Heights, was revitalized in the early 1980s by developer Jim Rouse, head of the Enterprise Foundation. By 1984, only two of the seventy-six stores in the enclosed mall were vacant. A display in the lobby of the mall proclaimed that "center cities across America are reawakening socially, culturally, economically." But underneath someone had written, "This is wrong."

The Park Heights Development Corporation, the St. Pius V Housing Development Committee, and the Harlem Park Community Association are among the very few organizations that managed to keep out of William Donald Schaefer's stable. Yet a "first-generation" community development corporation like PHDC cannot be duplicated in the current era of the U.S. economy. "When you do economic development work, you need two years to get a project from the concept to completion," Morris Iles observed. "These small businesses don't just need money, they need planning and maintenance. Give them enough money to pay an MBA to manage them, or send one with money you lend them. They have to learn how to measure cash flow and negotiate insurance, negotiate long-term buy contracts, and the like. What's needed is to broaden economic strategies to fulfill the need. You have to mix business development with social and human resource development components. And you have to make a way to pay for all this."

PHDC's continued dependence on federal, state, and city contracts and funding complicates its work, especially in times of general fiscal crisis and recession. In 1991, for example, PHDC lost $175,000 of community development block grant money under tightened federal rules. Iles said that the cutbacks would force PHDC to reduce its budget by one-third, lay off staff members, and postpone the planned renovation of low-income housing.[19] "PHDC experiences cash flow problems," said Iles. "We've had to lay off people. Whenever there is a snag on a project, when someone doesn't pay their rent or reneges on a loan, it means we have to let a staff member go. But we'll hang in here as long as we can."

Boss, though much more modest in concept, also foundered on bureacratic constraints and lack of money. Organizations such as the St. Pius V Housing Development Committee and the Harlem Park Community Association, despite their fierce independence, are greatly affected by the actions of city government. A few such small neighborhood organizations are still scattered across West Baltimore, often separated by jealousy and turf battles.

Measuring the costs of their engagement with government, black social activists in the 1970s turned temporarily to "paragovernmental" activity. They maintained their protests and their demands for government relief, support, and protection, but they also began trying to rebuild the mediating institutions of their community. When they made some measure of progress in this respect, they returned to the struggle with government with renewed vigor.

In the 1980s, neighborhood activists in West Baltimore began to get the idea that some citywide strategy was required. "Black capitalism" in isolated pockets of the city was not enough. Dependence on largess from a city government over which they had no control would be a step backward. So they decided to aim for control of that government.

Chapter Five
Black Control of
Baltimore's Government:
A Hollow Prize?

Baltimore remains two cities—one black, one white.
—Michael Fletcher, reporter for the *Baltimore Evening Sun*

BEFORE Kurt Schmoke's election as Baltimore's first black mayor, an editorial in the *Baltimore Afro-American* painted a bright picture of the prospect of black political control of Baltimore. Concluding that control of the "political levers" would have a decisive effect upon the quality of life in the black community, the *Afro* called upon the black community to elect "highly able, qualified, and esteemed blacks" to positions of authority and power. Electing such people, the *Afro* continued, would pay great dividends in "black pride, self-respect, and motivation."[1] But there are limitations to what can be achieved by electoral control of a city.

Segregation: Engine of Black Electoral Power

The demise of the Republican party in Baltimore during the Depression was also the demise of the district-based political machine, the power base that had elected blacks to the City Council since the Civil War. Though black Republicans were elected to the City Council as late as the 1920s, during the Depression the electoral framework in Baltimore changed. A bicameral legislature in which the lower house was elected from small districts, and the upper house from seven larger ones, gave way to a unicameral legislature. The city was still only about 30 percent black, but the small districts of the lower house had permitted blacks to concentrate their votes. These districts were abolished as part of an effort to break the power of the city's vernacular political machines. The seven large districts of the upper house became multimember districts, rendering the whole municipal political system susceptible to middle-class control. The new

91

districts were gerrymandered to cripple black power in the old Fourteenth District of West Baltimore (into the Fourth Ward under the new system). A white, Jewish political machine took over this territory and controlled it by influencing voter turnout and concentrating white voting strength.

It was not until after World War II that the black population of the Fourth Ward reached a number sufficient to challenge the machine, which was headed by Jason Pollack. Pollack was not himself an elected official, but rather a businessman who was one of the most powerful political leaders in the city.[2] In 1954 a group of black Republicans, foremost among them Harry Cole, who later became a justice of Maryland's highest court, challenged the Pollack machine in races for the state legislature. These state races were grounded in districts that were smaller than the councilmanic wards, so that black voting strength could be concentrated. Cole prevailed.

Energized, the black community rose to assert itself. The NAACP, the ministry, and the *Baltimore Afro-American* led a voter registration crusade, increasing the number of black voters in Baltimore from 70,000 to 100,000 between 1955 and 1958.[3] "It was the ministers who motivated people to vote, to get people elected to the City Council," said William Murphy, Sr. In the 1958 elections for state legislature, a black coalition slate of Republican candidates was formed, led by Harry Cole. Verda Welcome, a housewife, civic worker, and former schoolteacher, ran successfully for state senate against the Pollack machine in the Democratic primary. In the general election, Pollack chose J. Alvin Jones, a veteran black politician, to run against Cole in the race for state senate. Cole was defeated in the general election, but Welcome won, becoming the only black politician in the Fourth Ward who was not beholden to Jason Pollack.

"Harry Cole lost to J. Alvin Jones, and the edge was taken off the rebellion against Pollack," the senior Murphy told me. "Jones was from a good family, schoolteachers; he had an engineering degree from the University of Pennsylvania. But he became Jack Pollack's tool. Our historic differences kept us from claiming ownership and exercising power for a long time." Yet the black community kept coming back, despite reversals of this sort. In 1968 Joseph C. Howard was elected as an at-large representative to the City Council. A number of successful campaigns for legal positions followed: William Murphy, Sr., as municipal court judge; Milton Allen as state's attorney; and Paul L. Chester as Clerk of the City Court of Common Pleas. Some of the city's most experienced political professionals—Arthur Murphy, Larry Gibson (who later ran Kurt Schmoke's mayoral campaign), and David Henson (now a real estate developer)—cut their teeth in these races.

By 1970 blacks constituted 46 percent of Baltimore's population. In the late 1960s, black mayors had been elected in Cleveland, Gary, and Newark. In 1971, when Baltimore's incumbent Mayor Thomas J. D'Alesandro III announced that he would not seek a second term, the election of a black mayor in Baltimore seemed to be within reach. Three serious candidates emerged in the Democratic primary: George Russell, Clarence Mitchell III (both black), and William Donald Schaefer. Russell, a former state trial judge and incumbent city solicitor, was a member of the black old guard and sought to build a multiracial coalition for his candidacy. Mitchell, heir to the Mitchell civil rights dynasty and an incumbent state senator, was younger, more militant, and popular with younger voters. Schaefer, a white candidate, was president of the City Council and a power in city politics.[4] Russell took a much larger proportion of the black vote than did Mitchell, but Mitchell's candidacy compromised Russell's performance in black voting precincts. Schaefer, on the other hand, took every white precinct, winning the Democratic primary with 95,000 votes to Russell's 58,000. Schaefer's victory was even more notable given the fact that Russell, who was backed by a blue-ribbon, affluent coalition of Jews and middle-class blacks who were opposed to the Schaefer machine, spent $408,000 to Schaefer's $340,000.[5]

The white political clubs learned to take blacks seriously after that election, however. They ceased bickering among themselves and closed ranks. At the same time that the political clubs stemmed the black tide in citywide elections, incumbents on the all-white City Council moved to insulate themselves from insurgent blacks in their home districts. After the Supreme Court's one-man one-vote decision in *Baker v. Carr*, the Baltimore City Charter was amended to require a redistricting following the results of each census. In 1971, incumbents in four of Baltimore's six councilmanic districts gerrymandered the district lines to dilute the voting power of the city's growing black population.[6] Blacks were consolidated into a 90 percent black Fourth District (covering much of Old West Baltimore), while preserving white majorities in the First, Third, and Sixth Districts (Northeast Baltimore, East Baltimore, and South Baltimore). Slim black majorities in the Second and Fifth Districts were overcome by highly organized white political clubs, which often hand-picked a "token" black to integrate an otherwise all-white ticket.

The cohort of black electoral professionals developed during the campaigns of the 1960s and 1970s licked their wounds and repositioned themselves to bid for power. Then Norman Reeves broke through the power of the Pollack machine in the Fourth Ward councilmanic race. Reeves put together a crack team of political novices who later worked in the watershed campaigns of the 1980s. Notable among them were Billy Murphy, Jr., elected as judge of the Baltimore Circuit Court, and Kurt Schmoke, who became state's attorney. Now they were ready for another try at the mayoralty. Murphy and Schmoke were the logical contenders. The insurgent black electoral team first ran Billy Murphy, who strongly attacked Mayor Schaefer for building a "tourist's" city, underscoring the split between the haves and the have-nots. Though the downtown area was a showplace, serious unemployment, housing, and education problems remained. Murphy asserted that the "restored" city was "filled with children with dashed hopes of a decent education, broken families with unemployable parents, hundreds of functionally illiterate people of all ages, and thousands without low-cost housing."[7]

Incumbent Mayor Schaefer was a formidable opponent. He had an entrenched electoral machine, built over a period of thirty years in the political clubs of the white working-class districts of the city. He was skilled in the use of the media. In addition to coopting much of the city's insurgent community leadership, he had succeeded in revitalizing Baltimore's rotting downtown core. The multimillion-dollar Inner Harbor redevelopment project, a highly acclaimed revitalization of the city's old waterfront, including several striking high-rise commercial buildings, a state-of-the-art aquarium, and Harbor Place, brought international attention to Baltimore and to the mayor. With perfect timing, a city subway was scheduled to open just before the elections took place.[8]

On the other hand, Murphy's flamboyant lifestyle tarnished his appeal to the middle-class female voters who were the core of the insurgent black electoral coalition. Murphy also had some trouble getting the media attention he needed to articulate to the public his assessment of Schaefer's weaknesses and his own strengths. All the Mitchells save Parren (who later served five terms in Congress) supported Schaefer, who also enjoyed the backing of white liberals such as Senator Paul Sarbanes, then-Congresswoman Barbara Mikulksi, and many of the city's most prominent blacks. Despite the fact that three black voters registered to every two white registrations, Murphy lost the 1983 mayoral race, failing even to attain a majority of the black vote (he took 45 percent to Schaefer's 55 percent). Baltimore remained the only major black city without a black mayor.

In 1986 the Morris Goldseker Foundation published "Baltimore 2000," an in-depth study of the city that was intended to provide a framework for public discussions on Baltimore's future. The executive board of Baltimore's Urban League felt that the views of the city's black community were not being adequately represented in this debate, and therefore commissioned a study of their own, entitled "Destiny 2000: The State of Black Baltimore," which was published in 1987. Of particular interest is the section of the report dealing with the black community's seeming inability to translate numbers into real political power.

As early as 1935 the Baltimore Urban League had commissioned similar studies on the status of the city's black community. These early reports focused on the powerlessness of blacks in the political process.

> If ever the Negro Population of Baltimore became aware of its political power, the . . . governmental, economic and racial set-up of the community would undergo a profound change. The political seers have long been aware of the presence of this sleeping giant and have handled him successfully from time to time.[9]

According to the Urban League's 1987 report, written before the election of Mayor Schmoke, little had changed in the intervening decades; the black community continued, for the most part, to be a "sleeping giant." While blacks made up 60 percent of the city's population in 1987, they held just six of the eighteen City Council seats and only three of the city's elected offices: state's attorney, register of wills, and court clerk. "Despite more than a decade of promise, blacks in the past have been unable to win election to the Mayor's office or even wage a serious assault on the position," the report lamented.[10]

The 1987 report was pessimistic about blacks' chances of winning a majority of City Council seats in the 1987 elections, for two reasons: blacks in the city "practice a brand of politics based largely on a concept of concession"; and the city's black voters have "historically proven less inclined than whites to vote the color line." Although blacks and whites registered to vote in nearly the same proportions, blacks were far more willing than whites to vote for candidates of the opposite race.[11] A commentator for the *Baltimore Evening Sun* observed in 1991, "Black candidates for City Council lose by huge margins in white, working-class precincts controlled by old-line political clubs fielding all-white tickets. No black city council member has been elected from a district with a white majority."[12]

The Urban League Report analyzed this issue too:

> To win election to City Council, blacks have had to run in districts with black voting majorities. Of the City's six councilmanic districts, only three—the 2nd, 4th and 5th—fall into this category. However, unlike white voters in districts where whites hold the majority, black majority districts have shown a willingness to elect candidates of the other race. For instance, while blacks make up more than ⅔ of the 2nd District's population, they have regularly elected a white to [at least] one of the [District's] three City Council positions.[13]

The 1987 Urban League report emphasized that even if the black community could achieve the political gains it sought, those gains might not last long: "blacks have a tendency to allow their politicians to drift—to depend on others for financial support. This tendency, to elect and then neglect their representatives, leaves black voters without the access to power that whites in this city have come to value."[14] The report's focus was not so much on criticizing black political leaders, however, as on emphasizing the need for the black community to develop a greater degree of political sophistication.

By the time the results of the 1980 census were made public, it was clear that blacks in Baltimore had overcome the gerrymandering of the past by sheer numbers: Baltimore was now a city with a 60 percent black majority. Yet the redistricting that took place in 1983 merely reaffirmed the lines drawn in 1971,[15] and in 1986 the Baltimore branch of the NAACP threatened to bring a voting rights lawsuit. At the same time a team of electoral activists emerged, having gained in the campaigns of the early 1970s the experience that would enable them to engineer Kurt Schmoke's successful campaign for the mayoralty of the City of Baltimore.

Arthur Murphy is one of this group, a consummate political professional and an expert in the electoral process of representative democracy. He is not concerned about a candidate's party affiliation.

"Party identification is almost irrelevant at the local level," he observed. Rather, Murphy looks for an ideological fit with the perfect Baltimore voter: a black woman, financially independent, probably a homeowner, whose average age is sixty-one, and who is deeply involved in her community.

"You have to hit this voter six times," said Arthur. "By telephone, by mail, on T.V., and on election day by whatever means—four times. The other two times are optional, but they help a lot. The days of door-to-door campaigning are over, because no one is available to volunteer anymore. The successful candidate will need money to hit this ideal voter six times during the campaign." "Do you really want to win?" he asks candidates who come to him for assistance. "Show me the product, and I'll show you how to package it."

In the campaign of 1987, Kurt Schmoke defeated Clarence "Du" Burns, also an African-American, and Baltimore's acting mayor. (As City Council president, Burns had succeeded to the remainder of William Donald Schaefer's mayoral term eight months earlier when Schaefer was elected governor.) Burns's political career spanned forty years. Starting out as a political deal-maker in his native East Baltimore, he built a political machine that earned him the respect of the white political clubs in Baltimore's East Side ethnic neighborhoods. With their support, he won a seat on the City Council.[16] His 1983 election to the position of Council president was engineered by Schaefer and the white political clubs that were the framework of Schaefer's machine. In his quest for the mayoralty, Burns emphasized his ties to Schaefer, who had publicly endorsed his candidacy. By contrast, Schmoke's 1982 victory over conservative white incumbent William A. Swisher for the position of Maryland state's attorney was the product not of traditional Baltimore politics, but rather of a grassroots campaign that was perceived as the first real assertion of the citywide power of black voters. Thus, voters saw Burns as the "machine" candidate, and Schmoke as the candidate of the black community. Schmoke, much more of a "media presence" than Burns, far outdistanced his rival in public opinion polls and fundraising. He led Burns four to one among black voters, and 45 percent to 32 percent among whites.[17] Schmoke was re-elected to a second term in 1991.

Upon his election, Schmoke stressed that he wanted to be seen as the candidate of the city as a whole. "A leader's role is to try to get people to see their commonality rather than their differences," Schmoke said in 1987, identifying Edward Brooke, the former Republican Senator from Massachusetts, as his role model.[18] But in 1991 the seven black members of the City Council broke with the mayor's program of conciliation and, with the help of three white members who saw the handwriting on the wall, staged a palace coup that reversed the gerrymandering of the past. They carved out five majority-black districts, leaving only one district, the Sixth, with an absolute white majority. This coup was engineered over vehement opposition from Mayor Schmoke, who wanted to build white support for his citywide policies and felt that all-black districts would discourage racial coalition politics. The black councilmen, the NAACP, and other activists refused to change their course, pointing to the history of gerrymandering, the domination of the white political clubs, and the historic refusal of whites from the club-controlled, ethnic, blue-collar voting precincts to vote for black candidates.

Segregation: Engine of Community and Regional Decline

The emergence of Baltimore as a predominantly black city had implications other than electoral ones. Baltimore had what amounted to two housing markets until the 1960s, with "respectable" real estate agents operating only in the white housing market. This dual market was officially outlawed in 1968, when the institutionally racist practices of real estate brokers, builders, and lenders were outlawed by the Fair Housing Act. What finally caused the dual housing market to collapse, however, was not a sudden change of heart. Demographics simply overwhelmed the system as blacks became the majority. Between 1930 and 1960, the black population of Baltimore increased from 142,000 to 326,000 as waves of southern blacks were drawn by the industrial opportunities associated with World War II. In 1950 the nonwhite population made up 19 percent of the Baltimore metropolitan area's total population; by 1964 the figure was 23 percent. Meanwhile, the city of Baltimore lost white residents. Between 1950 and 1964, 133,000 nonwhites came to Baltimore, while 145,000 whites left. In the suburbs, the numbers were sharply reversed. Only 16,000 blacks moved to the suburbs between 1950 and 1964, while the white population grew by 440,000.[19]

Block-busting, zoning, and redlining increased racial segregation in the city and encouraged white flight, especially to suburban, prosperous, and predominantly white Baltimore County. "The County" features suburban and rural landscapes, "clean" light industry, and ample land for development. County officials have fiercely resisted the development of public housing in their jurisdiction, and have consistently refused to apply for federal funds that have requirements for low-income housing attached. The amount of money spent per pupil and the quality of education available in Baltimore County represent a prize that suburban residents are particularly eager to protect against encroachment from Baltimore City and its black residents. Baltimore County schools were completely segregated until the 1950s. Three black schools were formally desegregated in 1954, but desegregation did not begin in earnest for another ten years. At that time the black schools were closed, black children were bussed to white schools, and many white parents withdrew their children and put them into private school.

For about ten years after World War II, Baltimore City enjoyed a rate of economic growth similar to that of its suburbs. Manufacturing jobs, the mainstay of the blue-collar working class, peaked during the period from World War II to the Korean War, however, and then declined precipitously, so that manufacturing jobs accounted for only 15 percent of all employment in the city in 1980. As Baltimore's local economy was integrated into the global economy, the city's large manufacturing firms moved their productive operations to Third World cities where labor was cheap and ununionized. The city deteriorated as investment, commercial, and industrial capital fled. The port of Baltimore grew steadily during the war periods of the twentieth century, especially during the Korean War, but by the 1980s the port was declining, suffering from competition from other ports such as Newport News. From a population of just under a million people in the late 1940s, Baltimore lost a quarter of a million people in a single generation. People left the city at rapidly increasing rates: 11,000 withdrew between 1950 and 1960; 30,000 between 1960 and 1970; then nearly ten thousand a year. The result was a population of only 750,000 in 1990.

The suburban region in which Baltimore is located grew according to the selfsame economic indicators that told the tale of Baltimore's decline: retail trade, population, manufacturing jobs, and wealth per capita. Even the municipal pension fund refused to invest in inner-city mortgages, joining instead the rush to the suburbs.[20] While median income for the city in 1980 was $16,000, it was $31,000 for Baltimore County. Nearly 60 percent of the growth of

Baltimore County during the period between 1970 and 1980 was the result of European-Americans relocating from Baltimore City. Federal transfer payments and the city's tax base declined, forcing the city to cut expenditures of $272 per capita while the region as a whole cut only $76. The city's budget was increasingly strained by the needs of a growing underclass. Baltimore, 60 percent nonwhite, has the nation's eighth-highest population of poor families. Slum clearance, urban renewal, and expressway construction demolished many black neighborhoods, displacing 75,000 people between 1951 and 1971, while creating only 15,000 public housing units during this period.[21] (There were 45,000 families on the waiting list for the city's public housing in 1989.) The majority of renter families paid more than half their income for rent; 79,000 housing units in the city are substandard; and 5,000 are abandoned.

Baltimore is an old industrial city plagued by crime, drug abuse, poverty, abandoned housing, high property taxes, and violence in the public schools. Baltimore's favored position as a mercantile center for the Confederate states was disrupted by the Civil War, and its transition to a manufacturing city capable of competing with the more developed industrial cities of the North was never completed.[22] Baltimore did not, like New York and Chicago, aquire the corporate headquarters of aggressive, acquisitive industrial firms. Quite the contrary—many of Baltimore's local firms were taken over by such predatory organizations through mergers and other acquisitions. The city's largest growth has been in the service sector and tourism, both chancy industries at best.

Baltimore City has seven times the rate of welfare dependency of the state of Maryland as a whole.[23] A survey taken of residents of poverty-stricken areas of the city in 1968 reads as an inventory of the problems of the poor and working class then and now. They belong to families in which undereducation is a generational pattern, as members drop out soon after completing elementary school; they feel more oppressed by and suspicious of civilian authorities than helped by them; their neighborhoods are underserved in terms of schools, fire protection, sanitation, and recreation; street crime, poor health, and drugs are endemic problems. They are generally not organized: the adults do not participate in clubs or civic associations, and the youth are not involved in organized sports but rather stay at home or "hang around." The adults suffer from a pattern of unemployment, underemployment, and low wages; for the youth, the pattern is even more pronounced.[24] Blacks make up 23 percent of Maryland's citizens, but 40 percent of those living in poverty.[25]

Baltimore, like many cities, has been forced to deal with the cumulative effects of previously legal practices such as segregation ordinances and restrictive covenants. In a recent University of Chicago study, Douglas Massey and Nancy Denton showed that blacks in large cities (including Baltimore) face a multitude of discriminatory practices in housing markets. They describe this situation as "hypersegregation," defined as:

(1) The degree to which neighborhood percentages of minority-group residents correspond to the citywide minority percentages. A higher degree of neighborhood segregation is considered a sign of hypersegregation.

(2) The amount of potential contact between whites and members of the minority group in areas where minorities live and work.

(3) The extent to which minority neighborhoods are clustered together.

(4) The degree to which minorities are settled in and around the city center.

(5) The amount of space occupied by a minority group.

When 89 percent of Maryland's black population lives in urban areas, and 63 percent of the its white population lives in the suburbs,[26] physical separation makes improbable any significant contact between blacks and whites. Lack of choice in living area has limited access to better schools and therefore to better jobs. If there is no access to the job market or the larger labor force, there is no opportunity to gain personal contacts that would lead to jobs and increased status.

Hypersegregation in the Baltimore metropolitan area can be traced directly to the FHA's post–World War II policy of requiring racially restrictive covenants to protect the "property value" of the developments it insured. Massive federal investments in the suburbs, beginning with the construction of wartime housing, and continuing through the location in suburban Maryland of facilities like the National Aeronautics and Space Administration and the National Institutes of Health, were in fact massive investments in metropolitan segregation. The high postwar demand for suburban housing from whites seeking to escape an increasingly black Baltimore and their use of restrictive covenants and exclusionary zoning to protect their enclaves

combined with the federal government's discriminatory administration
of housing subsidy programs. White suburban families were benefited
at the expense of black inner-city families, and housing production
and suburbanization were skewed into a rigid and continuing pattern
of metropolitan segregation.[27] One important feature of this pattern of
metropolitan segregation is urban sprawl. As land speculators developed outlying districts to facilitate "white flight" to farther and farther
outlying suburbs, the perimeter of the region's developed area was
extended. This urban sprawl, created as middle-income people fled
the problems of the city and set up new housing developments in rural
and suburban areas, has had major and financially costly impacts.

The environmental impact of urban sprawl on the Chesapeake
Bay watershed, a tremendous natural resource for Maryland and its
immediate region, has been striking.[28] The Chesapeake Bay provides
food, recreation, commerce, and industry to 13 million people, and
has made Baltimore one of the five major U.S. ports on the North
Atlantic, and one of the top three commercial fishing centers on the
east coast.[29] The Bay also depends on a complex and delicate environmental balance of fresh water and sea water, mixed in a shallow basin
surrounded by thousands of miles of grassy shoreline. Soil is eroded
during construction of new suburban subdivisions (up to six truck-
loads per year from each acre of land being developed), and this
sediment, introduced into the watershed, damages the wetlands that
are the shallow-water habitats of ducks and geese and deprives fish
and other aquatic life of oxygen. Sediment also causes a decline in
the submerged aquatic vegetation that provides food and shelter for
waterfowl, fish, and shellfish. Submerged aquatic vegetation declined
more than 30 percent between 1984 and 1987.

These injuries to the environment are exacerbated by air pollution
due to automobile exhaust. The air pollution is harmful to humans
and plant and animal life in its own right, but in addition air pollution
finds its way to the Bay indirectly, through acid rainfall. Trees and
grass, which filter out pollution from storm runoff, are replaced with
slick pavement. Residential runoff pollution—not only sediment from
erosion taking place during construction, but also oil, lawn fertilizers,
and other toxic materials disposed of by the typical suburban household—has an immense environmental impact. Toxins, sediment, and
trash now cloud the once-clear waters of the Chesapeake Bay. During
the period from 1950 to 1970, wetlands were lost at the rate of 2,800
acres per year, for a total of 56,000 acres. And still, 2.5 million

people are expected to move to the Chesapeake watershed area by the year 2020.

Protection of the Bay requires that limits be placed on suburban sprawl, with fewer large home sites, more compact developments, and restrictions on the conversion of farmland for residential subdivisions. In 1980 the Virginia and Maryland legislatures established the Chesapeake Bay Commission to coordinate interstate efforts to reverse the decline in the Bay's quality and productivity. Subsequently, Pennsylvania and the District of Columbia, as well as the Environmental Protection Agency, joined in the effort to preserve the Bay and its watershed. In 1987, all four jurisdictions, the Commission, and the EPA signed the Chesapeake Bay Agreement, which established a framework for addressing the Bay's problems. The agreement recognized the importance of planned, regulated development in preserving the Bay and required the establishment of a panel of experts to report, by December 1988, on the "anticipated population growth and land development patterns in the Bay region through the year 2020, the infrastructure requirements necessary to serve growth and development, environmental programs needed to improve Bay resources while accommodating growth, alternative mechanisms for financing governmental services and environmental controls."

The panel, called the "2020 Panel" consisted of three members each from Virginia, Maryland, and Pennsylvania and one each from the District of Columbia, the EPA, and the Chesapeake Bay Commission. Their major conclusion was that unplanned, scattered development has not only threatened the survival of the Bay, putting Maryland's environmental and resource base at risk, but is also undermining the state's economic viability. The roads, schools, and sewer systems required by the sprawling development have so strained Maryland's fiscal capacity that it is scarcely able to pay for anything else. Thus, the exodus of white, middle-class residents from Baltimore to the outer suburbs is not only causing an environmental problem but has also ironically (or, perhaps, tragically) undermined the state's ability to provide Baltimore with the support it needs as it loses more and more of its middle-class tax base.

Baltimore's tax base is further compromised by the urban disinvestment strategy known as "redlining"—that is, discrimination by banks and thrift institutions against loan applications from poor and minority neighborhoods, once outlined in red on a map kept in the lender's office. Redlining today has become more subtle and sophisticated, part of the corporate and institutional culture. Loans for improvement, renovation, or repairs are barred, inner-city homes underappraised, and exorbitant down-payments demanded to discourage borrowers. Lending discrimination of this type can occur at a number of points in the lending process. At the preapplication or origination stage, when applicants are merely seeking information about what loans are available and what loans they might qualify for, undesirable applicants, or applicants from undesirable areas, can simply be discouraged. Buyers eager to close on a sale contract will simply move, as quickly as possible, to another bank. At the loan processing stage, foot-dragging and other delays may lead an applicant under time constraints to apply elsewhere. A lender may also discriminate in the credit check phase by letting desirable customers explain away slight or even important irregularities in their credit records, while using these as an occasion to deny credit to undesirables.

When the collateral is property located in an undesirable neighborhood, real estate appraisers often illegally consider the neighborhood's racial characteristics. Weighing such characteristics was once an explicit part of appraisers' training, and the practice continues on an unofficial basis. The terms offered and conditions imposed in an underwriting may also differ according to an applicant's race. Credit may be available only in a form an applicant cannot use, or at interest rates an applicant cannot afford, for example. Finally, private mortgage insurance (PMI) may provide another opportunity for discrimination in lending. Most buyers cannot afford to put down the required 20 percent or more when they buy a home. To get a loan with a smaller down payment requires PMI. Using techniques similar to those used to steer blacks away from mortgage credit, lenders can deny them access to PMI.

Despite laws against discrimination in lending, enforcement and monitoring remain a problem. In 1989 a survey found that Baltimore had one of the nation's highest loan-rejection rates for black applicants. A study done in 1988 by Ann Shlay of the Institute for Policy Studies at Johns Hopkins University found that the majority of home mortgage loans in the inner city were going to neighborhoods in the process of gentrification and that comparatively little credit was being extended to neighborhoods where the majority of residents were black. The banks' unwillingness to invest in such neighborhoods, combined with their readiness to invest in the suburbs, exacerbates urban decline, white flight, and urban sprawl.

The irony of redlining is that banks engaging in the practice frequently maintain branches in the same decaying neighborhoods in which they refuse to invest, collecting depositors' savings but failing to recycle the funds within the community in the form of mortgages and home improvement loans. As a result of such practices, members of minority groups and the poor trapped in the city by segregation, exclusionary zoning, and high commuting costs increasingly face an environment in which lack of maintenance is the norm and even basic building systems such as boilers, plumbing, wiring, and roofs are affected. As residential and other options disappear for these inner-city dwellers, the rates of murder, suicide, and drug abuse dramatically increase.[30]

Policies to reduce metropolitan segregation and foster open housing are some of the most hotly contested issues in Maryland politics. Parren Mitchell, Maryland's first African-American Congressman (representing the Seventh District of Baltimore City, now represented by Kwesi Mfume), witnessed extremes of racial hatred in the late 1960s when activists and religious leaders speaking in favor of fair housing laws had to be physically protected from hostile crowds. When Maryland's fair housing laws were finally passed, they failed to give the state Human Relations Commission power to remedy the widespread use of racially restrictive covenants and "steering." In response, communities mobilized to initiate their own legal complaints, and a new phase of the civil rights movement in Maryland began. Baltimore Neighborhoods, Inc. (BNI), a nonprofit citizen's organization created in 1959 to help create an open housing market in the Baltimore metropolitan area and maintain viable interracial neighborhoods, brought twenty-six housing discrimination lawsuits in the 1980s alone. BNI actions have included civil suits and complaints to the Federal Department of Housing and Urban Development and the Justice Department, the Maryland Real Estate Commission, and the Maryland Commission on Human Relations, as well as conciliation and mediation. Resistance to integration continues, however, and in some neighborhoods it continues almost unabated.

The prospects for a frontal assault on exclusionary zoning—a more subtle tactic against integration because income rather than race is the putative basis for discrimination—do not appear bright in Maryland. The U.S. Supreme Court has set high entry barriers to federal litigation on exclusionary zoning matters, so that litigants have little choice but to bring their claims to state courts and to base their arguments on state constitutional rights. Some notable successes have been registered in state courts, but the typical state court response to an exclusionary zoning challenge is that courts are not set up to function as a "super zoning board" and that complex social problems are better dealt with by an elected body. The New Jersey Supreme Court's 1975 *Mount Laurel* decision and its progeny brought the exclusionary zoning problem before the public in that state.[31] Elected officials using zoning ordinances to exclude people were held accountable because of the prolonged attention that court battles focused on the problem. Low- and moderate-income groups were made aware of zoning decisions that escalated housing costs in the suburbs. This exposure, along with the strong legal remedies fashioned by the Court, compelled the state legislature to act. The Maryland high court has taken no such bold step, however, despite the presence of Harry Cole, the court's first black justice, appointed in 1978.

As a consequence, the Maryland state legislature has been able to sidestep the issue of exclusionary zoning. Legislators want to avoid a conflict with municipal officials, who may bear considerable responsibility for state legislators' electoral success. Legislators also must reckon with voters who favor exclusionary zoning for its putative fiscal advantages and environmental benefits, and who see it as a useful device for maintaining social and racial homogeneity. Exclusionary zoning thus remains a popular mechanism. The right to construct housing in an exclusive, homogeneous, suburban municipal unit is of great financial value to builders and developers, who in turn will provide funds and other support to local officials to protect the privilege. Suburban officials who rely heavily on such patronage will seek to protect their power base, regardless of whether they themselves are racist or have a phobia against lower-income persons.

Racial Division and Political Opportunism

The division of Baltimore and its metropolitan area into a prosperous white and a declining black community has exacerbated racial tension—whether the reason for the division has been race or class (and it has probably been both). In 1989 two white men were indicted by a federal grand jury on charges of housing discrimination, conspiracy, and illegal use of explosive devices. The two had firebombed the house of an African-American woman in the Baltimore suburb of Dundalk. One of the conspirators lived two blocks away from the family. The family escaped the house unharmed, but later moved away.

In November 1990 highly publicized racial incidents took place in Highlandtown and Remington, two ethnic white neighborhoods of Baltimore. In one case a black man was chased into the path of an oncoming pickup truck and killed. Mayor Schmoke, at the behest of the NAACP and the Ministerial Alliance, organized a citywide summit on race relations. Held at the City Convention Center, it was the first meeting of its type not only in Baltimore but in the entire country, according to John Ferron, director of the Baltimore Human Relations Commission.[32] The great majority of the two thousand-odd people who attended were black, however. A small number of white professionals (usually connected to an agency or organization relating to racial issues) were there, but there was virtually no participation by the city's major businesses or business groups. The meeting was picketed by skinheads and a small group of working-class white ethnics carrying Confederate flags.

There were no panels of experts or lectures at the summit. After the mayor's greeting, the meeting was totally interactional, the participants breaking into smaller groups to discuss topics such as race in education, cultural diversity, and the relationships among blacks, Koreans, and Jews. The most diverse of these smaller groups was the workshop on religion, including Muslims, Jews, Roman Catholics, Baptists, African Methodist Episcopalians, Korean Presbyterians, Mennonites, and others.[33] The groups reported back to the plenary meeting, and these reports were forwarded to the Community Relations Commission for recommendations. Issues emerging from a preliminary reading of the reports included:

> lack of understanding of cultural differences between different ethnic groups; deteriorating race relations; how has corporate America impacted our lives; the responsibility of the media in helping to improve race and intergroup relations, i.e., to be active, rather than reflective; the important role education must play in preventing and addressing prejudice and bigotry in children; economics and its impact on racism; the need for government to make a firmer commitment to human and civil rights; the plight of minorities relating to employment."[34]

The reports also indicated that those in attendance felt that the summit had not attracted the people who most needed to hear its message, and suggested that the summit be continued in Baltimore's neighborhoods, and perhaps even elevated to the regional level so that white suburbanites would be included. The whites who did attend seemed unwilling to challenge the prevailing impression in the workshops that the lack of black advancement in employment and education was due to white racism alone. In contrast, speaking for the many whites who did not attend, Bryan Moorhouse, editor of the *Enterprise and Inner Harbor News* of Baltimore wrote:

> The average white citizen who lived his life socially and peacefully among his friends was usually unaware of Black Americans other than what he occasionally read in the papers. Suddenly, with the rise of civil rights, riots and disobedience he became painfully conscious that radical changes in his mode of living was [*sic*] disturbing his equilibrium.
>
> Legislative pressure laws, rules and regulations were enacted to create a semblance of equality. This looked fine on the surface. Underneath, however, there was a constant bubbling of discontent from the majority who felt their individual constitutional freedoms were being imposed upon to support a minority who snarled and bubbled with "we shall overcome" for it wasn't enough to satisfy.
>
> Money to underwrite social programs, most of which did little to improve things, was wasted by the millions. This resulted in the horrendous tax problems that now confront us. A subculture of nonproducing citizens grew into its third generation. Major cities in our country are subsidizing in one form or another better than 50% of their population. This burdens the working taxpayer to a point where he moves away for relief complicating things much more. . . . Something has to be done![35]

This is precisely the image that Lee Atwater, and before him Richard Nixon, strove to create in the minds of white ethnic working-class voters in order to pry them away from the Democratic party on the national level. Racial demagogues have been aided—consciously or unconsciously—by a host of others: by the media, by the business executives who abandoned the New Deal coalition in search of lower governmental costs, by the real, deteriorating conditions in the black community, and by middle-class black leaders who seem more concerned about their rights vis-à-vis whites than their responsibilities to the less affluent majority of the black community.

Something does have to be done, not only about the real conditions in the black community that reinforce the stereotypes that too many whites hold, but about racist manipulation of the media and of political debate, about isolation of the races from one another except in the most unfavorable of circumstances (criminal acts and competition for jobs and education), and about the lack of leadership and involvement being provided by successful black people who should know better. Many of the middle-class black participants in the summit, for example, felt that the answer to improving racial relations was for a leader "at the top" to simply say, "Do it."[36]

What is the mayor of Baltimore going to do about this problem in the long run? What is the Ministerial Alliance going to do? Initial recommendations included measures to insure greater fairness in the courts, race relations classes in public school (pointless unless conducted on a regional basis, as 80 percent of the children in Baltimore's public school are black),[37] civilian participation in police review boards, and pairing black and white church congregations, as Baltimore Clergy and Laity Concerned have been doing since late 1989.[38] George Buntin, executive director of the Baltimore chapter of the NAACP, urged participants to carry the message to their communities, churches, and synagogues, and begin dialogues there. Human Relations Commissioner John Ferron predicted that the groups convened at the summit would continue meeting, particularly the workshops on business and religion.

The true frontier, said Wiley Hall, columnist for the *Baltimore Evening Sun*, "exists in the workplace, in the classroom and in the courts where justice is done."

> Every day, the races clash—silently, but with ninja-like ferocity—in the political arena where priorities are set, values are defined, and leaders are determined . . .
>
> "Who gets promoted on the job, and why?"
>
> "Where do people choose to live or shop?"
>
> "Into which programs are public funds allocated and what are the goals?"
>
> This is the frontier, where the races clash, where resentments and misunderstandings fester. This is the racial no-man's land and it has existed for so long and it can get so ugly in there that between bouts most of us have trained ourselves not to think about it, not to see it.
>
> So let me say this quickly, before my own memory fades: For all of its flaws, the city's summit on race relations . . . ventured, albeit timidly, into areas where most of us fear to tread. . . . Through all

the predictable rhetoric and sermonizing, occasional moments of honesty and understanding peeped through. I left there thinking: We can do it. The races are not that far apart. All we need to do is talk. The problem is, we rarely do.[39]

Baltimore remains two cities: one black, one white (64 percent of Baltimore's voting-age population lives in voting precincts that are either 90 percent white or 90 percent black).[40] The city boasts a refurbished downtown, with vibrant and renewed upwardly mobile neighborhoods filled with people returning to enjoy an urban renaissance, but it is also hobbled by a deteriorating and troubled area just outside downtown, marked by high levels of unemployment, segregation, and school dropouts. Mayor Schaefer's popularity and reputation as father of the city's downtown renaissance were based on the redevelopment of the Baltimore harbor area, which was possible only because of high levels of federal aid to the city. Between 1980 and 1990, the federal government's share of the Baltimore city budget was cut in half.[41] This decline in federal support, making large-scale economic projects less and less possible, throws into sharp relief the reality that the "other" Baltimore is more and more a city of a black underclass who need services but who cannot generate the tax dollars to pay for them.

Further, Baltimore's predicament is complicated by its relationship to the state of Maryland. Given the decline in federal support for cities like Baltimore, issues of municipal finance, racial integration, economic development, and many others will be increasingly determined by what happens in the state capitol at Annapolis. As early as 1980, Maryland was experiencing the problems faced by most states as the national economy weakened, as business interests sought to reverse social welfare and labor gains, and as the country absorbed the shock of dramatic shifts in the balance of international trade. The rate of growth of per capita income in Maryland first slowed, then declined.[42] The discouragement of Watergate, the failure of nuclear power, an apparent environmental crisis, and growing distaste for the "rights" movements of the Democratic New Politics among the majority of Maryland's white citizens combined with a realization that families were weakening, schools eroding, cities deteriorating, and crime and drug use increasing.[43]

Marylanders, like citizens of the country at large, have been convinced by conservative propaganda and media repetition that liberal government spending is the problem. They are not interested in progressive taxation, local school tax base equalization, and consumer, civil rights, or environmental legislation.[44] They have imposed ceilings on state and county taxes.[45] The Democratic New Politics in Maryland collapsed as business withdrew, labor became a conservative special interest group, and college students switched from social activism to corporate careerism.[46] Today, Maryland is relatively prosperous, fiscally conservative, postindustrial, and suburban. While blacks make up 25 percent of the state's population, they hold only 16 percent of the seats in the state legislature.[47]

The city of Baltimore, once the seat of power in the state, is now the state's greatest liability, spending more than it earns to poorly educate and manage a socially volatile, declining, majority-black population. As the city has lost population, redistricting robs it of more and more representatives in the Maryland state legislature. At the same time, representation from Baltimore's more politically conservative suburbs is increasing.[48] Of the six political subdivisions that make up the Baltimore Regional Council of Governments (Baltimore City and five suburban counties), a local journalist notes, "only Baltimore City remains majority black, overwhelmingly Democratic, almost totally impoverished, and completely dependent. Instead of bitterness and hatred pulling the races further apart as they have in the past, the catalyst this trip is economics. Money is making blacks blacker and whites whiter, and the division is sending thousands into leafy isolation in the rims around Baltimore, turning the city into an abandoned welfare colony."[49]

Various efforts are being pursued to revamp the state tax structure, impose a commuter tax, and otherwise divert more public money into Baltimore. Tax Equity for All Marylanders (TEAM), a coalition of public interest groups, has lobbied hard in Annapolis to restructure state taxes so that all localities can provide essential services. (Baltimore presently attracts poor people from other jurisdictions because it provides services and housing.) The results have generally been disappointing. It is the challenge of city government and the local community-based, civic, religious, and nonprofit sector to find ways to collaborate in initiating processes that can improve the neglected areas of Baltimore despite the lack of support from the federal and state governments, and encourage suburbanites to help support the city's cultural facilities, which they use. Otherwise, the Baltimore to which Kurt Schmoke succeeded as political leader will be nothing more than a $2 billion bankrupt corporation.

Great expectations were raised as the black community's electoral majority began to add up to political control of the city. But, like the civil rights activists before them, black electoral activists tended to focus on the power of government, and underestimated the potential of their own community. The vernacular community of black Baltimore, left behind once more, weakened further. Antisocial and self-destructive behavior increased just as the black middle class entered the corridors of power. Whites in opposition sensationalized such behavior, using it to excuse delays in black progress and promote "white backlash." The problem remains unsolved. Black Baltimore and its white suburbs remain two cities—one black, one white.

John H. Murphy, Sr. (center) sits outside the offices of the Baltimore Afro-American with his staff, many of them relatives. (Copyright 1990 Afro-American Newspapers Archives and Research Center, Inc. Reprinted with permission.)

Baltimore's vernacular black culture brought these boys together at the YMCA in 1912. (Copyright 1990 Afro-American Newspapers Archives and Research Center, Inc. Reprinted with permission.)

Vernacular culture brought out the parishioners of Sharp Street Methodist Church in 1944 to hear Eleanor Roosevelt (center), here accompanied by Juanita Jackson Mitchell (left). (Copyright 1990 Afro-American Newspapers Archives and Research Center, Inc. Reprinted with permission.)

This same culture produced leaders like Thurgood Marshall (seated second from right), here conferring in 1952 with the Brown v. Board of Education litigation team. Constance Baker Motley, now a U.S. Circuit Court judge, sits to his right. (Copyright 1990 Afro-American Newspapers Archives and Research Center, Inc. Reprinted with permission.)

Carl Murphy, crusading editor of the Afro. (Copyright 1990 Afro-American Newspapers Archives and Research Center, Inc. Reprinted with permission.)

The desegregation of Gwynn Oak Park, Baltimore, 1963. (Copyright 1990 Afro-American Newspapers Archives and Research Center, Inc. Reprinted with permission.)

Pickets march against segregation in downtown Baltimore, 1961. (Copyright 1990 Afro-American Newspapers Archives and Research Center, Inc. Reprinted with permission.)

A voter registration drive down Pennsylvania Avenue, between Upton and Sandtown, 1966. (Copyright 1990 Afro-American Newspapers Archives and Research Center, Inc. Reprinted with permission.)

Some of Baltimore's 1971 "new wave" of black political activists, filing for various city and state offices. From left: David Allen and his father, Milton Allen; William H. Murphy, Jr. and William H. Murphy, Sr.; and Leroy H. Carroll. (Copyright 1990 Afro-American Newspapers Archives and Research Center, Inc. Reprinted with permission.)

Parren Mitchell, the first African-American elected to Congress from Maryland since Reconstruction. (Copyright 1990 Afro-American Newspapers Archives and Research Center, Inc. Reprinted with permission.)

Blacks in Baltimore have also been active in the labor movement. (Copyright 1990 Afro-American Newspapers Archives and Research Center, Inc. Reprinted with permission.)

W. E. B. DuBois, branded a communist, settled in Ghana, where he is seen at 95 years of age entertaining President Kwame Nkrumah in his home, 1963. (Copyright 1990 Afro-American Newspapers Archives and Research Center, Inc. Reprinted with permission.)

The Black Panther Party had its greatest success among low-income and working-class Baltimore blacks, who were bypassed or alienated by the civil rights movement, the labor movement, and most black politicians. (Copyright 1990 Afro-American Newspapers Archives and Research Center, Inc. Reprinted with permission.)

Today on Pennsylvania Avenue, at the border of Upton and Sandtown, the great leaders of the past have faded, and little activity seems to be taking place.

But parishioners flock to churches like Bethel A.M.E., on Druid Hill Avenue in Upton.

Muslims attend services at Masjid Al-Haqq, also in Upton.

In Sandtown, members of the New Song Urban Ministry renovate rowhouses from the ground up.

Ella Johnson, chair of the Sandtown-Winchester Improvement Association, spends long hours behind her desk.

Imam William Shahid (left) of Masjid Al-Haqq offers advice while having lunch in the Masjid's cafeteria.

Darnell Ridgely always has a positive attitude.

So does Athena Young, who has pledged, for her children's sake, to fight for her community of Sandtown.

Chapter Six
Church, State, and Neighborhood: Forums for Citizen Action

The city lacks the spirit, the essence of struggle. Maybe the
political system can't give birth to what we need.

—Reverend Vernon Dobson, member of
Baltimoreans United in Leadership Development (BUILD)

BLACKS IN Baltimore remember segregation as a cruel symbol of in-
equality, but they also remember it as a context for stable black vernacular neighborhoods, with a strong work ethic and closely networked local economies.[1] While well-meaning middle-class black
people mobilized, lobbied, and politicked, often, but not always, on
behalf of the entire black community, they sometimes lost contact
with low-income black people, and so lost sight of their needs and
aspirations. The limited results of black electoral achievements demonstrate that formal political empowerment alone is unlikely to galva-
nize the black community's informal leaders to root progress and development deep into the underclass. The support networks that once
were the greatest resource of vernacular West Baltimore must be re-
created. A leadership approach that relies more on networking within
the community, and less (or at least not exclusively) on "big bang"
political and economic strategies, is needed to create a more lasting
improvement in the black community, and to include all of its members in the work of change as well as in the rewards of change.

Economic Limits to Black Electoral Success

If black control of the city is not to be a hollow prize, Baltimoreans
must find a way to reeducate and train their poor and unskilled (most
of whom are black) and thus create a better-educated and more productive workforce. Baltimore must change its image of urban crime,
congestion, and decay, not only to hold on to its present middle class,

113

but also to attract more middle-class people to relocate within the city. Maryland's Regional Planning Council recommends the formation of a technology development fund, which would use the region's universities to recruit technologically based firms and encourage entrepreneurship. This proposed fund would also underwrite incubator facilities, brokerage for venture capital, a technology exchange and transfer program, and grants to match corporate giving. The Greater Baltimore Committee (a progressive business group) seconded this vision in 1991, calling for a turn to biotechnology and other life sciences—"industries of the mind"—to jump-start the city's economy.[2]

This type of "big bang" economic development was first employed during Mayor Schaefer's administration in the development of Baltimore's Inner Harbor. The Inner Harbor Project created a minor economic "miracle," which, unfortunately, looked a good deal better from the distance of national coverage than it did from the close-up perspective of Baltimore's relatively unchanged inner-city neighborhoods. The objective of the Inner Harbor Project was to attract suburban shoppers into the city, thus generating employment opportunities for Baltimore's residents. Programs were designed to increase retail development, alleviate traffic congestion, increase employment, and thereby increase city revenue through property taxes. The focus was on the waterfront, downtown, and transportation systems, and not on where people lived.

Despite an investment of over one billion dollars, Baltimore continued to lose middle-class citizens, industrial employment, and tax revenue, simultaneously experiencing a growth in its low-income population. While tourists were flocking to the redeveloped Inner Harbor, Baltimore's young people were quietly flunking out of school. The black and poor people who occupied the downtown area before renewal were left worse off as their homes and communities were destroyed to make way for large transportation and infrastructure systems that were eventually underutilized by the businesses for which they were designed. Baltimore, the nation's eleventh-largest city, despite a resurgence in downtown economic activity, remains "one of the nation's poorest cities, with declining blue-collar employment, a faltering education system, among the highest teen-age pregnancy and infant mortality rates in the country, a deficient health care system for the poor, and a crisis in housing."[3]

"Big bang" projects alone cannot solve Baltimore's fiscal and political problems. Even if they could, the bailouts of our troubled financial sector, the costs of the Persian Gulf War, and the inability of the federal government to stem our trade and budget deficits do not bode well for any creation or even expansion of federal urban aid. The 1992 riots in Los Angeles did not change this basic economic equation. Combined federal, state, and local spending on social programs during Reagan's presidency dipped to less than 21 percent of the gross national product (GNP), lower than any other major industrialized country. (France, Germany, Italy, and Sweden, for example, each devote 30 percent of their GNP to social investment.)[4] Poverty and unemployment increased almost immediately, but the trade balance, despite business's claim that its agenda would make U.S. firms more competitive, continued to decline. The United States became a debtor nation, its $150 billion merchandise trade deficit exacerbated by its extensive borrowing from the foreign nationals attracted by our high interest rates.[5] More and more, foreign capital (especially British, Japanese, and Arab) came to bridge the gap between our national income and our national expenditures.[6] Still, the public deficit climbed—not because of wasteful social welfare programs, as business propaganda argued, but because of Reagan's program of raising defense spending while cutting taxes on corporations and the wealthy.[7] By 1991, highly leveraged U.S. firms were paying half their earnings in interest on outstanding debt, keeping financial markets very unstable and bringing accumulated national debt to $3 trillion.[8] Corporate bankruptcies, the falling value of residential and commercial real estate, and dampened consumer spending touched off a decline in bank lending and business borrowing. Businesses scaled back spending and output, resulting in lost jobs and lower wages.[9]

The national recession, compounded by a Maryland recession, does not establish an atmosphere attractive to large-scale new business investments in Baltimore. Further, in those cities that have made a transition from industrial to service-sector employment (a change projected for Baltimore by the Greater Baltimore Committee), middle-class whites have reaped the benefits, while unemployment among blacks and the working poor has sometimes actually increased. Milwaukee's service-sector, technology-based economic recovery, for example, crushed the city's poor black neighborhoods. Blacks in Milwaukee now have one of the highest unemployment rates in the country.[10]

Election or Participation—Which
Way to Political Power?

In West Baltimore, the city's Fourth Councilmanic District, drug shootings, unemployment, inadequate housing, and the city's highest rate of teenage pregnancies continue to obscure the neighborhood's rich history.[11] As in other black communities in Baltimore, a sense of apathy has crept over the Fourth District, which is "represented" by officeholders with black skin. When Baltimore's councilmanic districts were redrawn in 1991, Councilwoman Sheila Dixon (D-4th), waving her shoe, said that whites in the city would now find that the "shoe was on the other foot," and that black voting majorities in all councilmanic districts save the First would change the complexion of the Council. But despite voter registration drives by churches, fraternities, sororities, and community groups, voter turnout remains low in the Fourth. Residents feel that the politicians simply ignore them.[12] A plethora of black candidates so divided the black vote in the redrawn Third District that two white incumbents and a white independent candidate easily coasted to victory in 1991.[13] A more serious attempt was made at organizing black voters in the redrawn Sixth District when new boundaries brought in Harlem Park and deleted a high-turnout white neighborhood. In the first elections under the new system, a black candidate, Melvin Stukes, bested a white incumbent from the legendary Stonewall Democratic Club. Still, Stonewall's other two candidates squeaked by.

Ironically, just as blacks succeeded to citywide and district-level power in Baltimore's electoral arena, efforts to register black voters began to drop off. Only 35 percent of the city's eligible voters turned out for Kurt Schmoke's second mayoral campaign.[14] When asked to comment, David S. Bositis, a senior research associate for the Joint Center for Political Studies, a Washington-based black think tank, observed that this should come as no surprise: "The purpose of political activity is to win elections, it's not to get people to participate." Lower-income blacks are the traditional targets of voter registration drives because they are less likely to register on their own. Bositis observed that with the increasing class stratification within the black community, voter registration might actually be harmful to a black candidate like Kurt Schmoke, whose strength lies with black middle-class voters.[15]

Because of the city's financial straits, inherited from its predecessor, the Schmoke administration cannot deliver patronage jobs to hoist lower-status blacks out of poverty. In addition, HUD, in an unusually critical report, questioned the city's ability to administer community development funds and required it to return over $5 million after determining that city housing officials had inadequately monitored expenditures.[16] A hiring freeze and other budget-tightening strategies stabilized the city's bond rating but simultaneously undercut any hope that Schmoke would be an employment Messiah for the city's black working class, as Marion Barry had been in Washington, D.C. Schmoke reduced the city payroll during his first term and began his second term by announcing a turn to austerity.[17] These conditions are not likely to endear Schmoke to less affluent blacks over the long term.

The middle-class black women who form the core of Baltimore's insurgent electoral coalition still love Kurt Schmoke, however—"the earnestness in his manner, the self-deprecating wit, the boy-next-door wholesomeness" described by a local journalist.[18] Baltimore's black middle class is large and more successful than ever before. But the problems of the black poor and working class have gotten worse.[19] In the housing arena, Baltimore contains between five and twelve thousand vacant housing units. During Schmoke's first administration, about a thousand units were being rehabilitated annually, and action was being taken to transfer abandoned units to community groups, but nearly a thousand more units were being abandoned at the same time. Street violence continued unabated.

Kurt Schmoke began his first term as mayor speaking about neighborhood and community participation in housing and community development. He planned to focus as much on "building human infrastructure" as on high-visibility physical development projects.[20] Schmoke's first administration undertook some very important—indeed, unique—policy initiatives. He lent his support to job training and "community-oriented" approaches to police protection of neighborhoods. In keeping with his campaign themes of making Baltimore the "City That Reads," Schmoke's administration established learning centers for the city's 200,000 functional illiterates. Spurred by the Maryland Alliance for Responsible Investment, a statewide public interest organization, Schmoke translated his campaign promise of a community development bank into a functioning agency, the Community Development Finance Corporation (CFDC), a $40 million community development bank that made $20 million worth of loans to renovate 600 homes. The Nehemiah Project to erect 283 new homes in Sandtown-Winchester shows the influence of community-based groups such as Baltimoreans United in Leadership Development (BUILD).[21] Community activists like Schmoke's people-oriented agenda, a welcome change from the downtown-focused development policies of William Donald Schaefer.

But Schmoke's style and his agenda do not match. His public persona, one with which whites are comfortable, reflects his training at Harvard and Yale, but not the vernacular of his black roots. His middle-class, low-profile, squeaky-clean image, which his handlers feel helps him in doing his job, getting himself reelected, and keeping himself from becoming a target, has created a problem in another sector. "Kurt doesn't inspire the people," observes the Reverend Vernon Dobson. "When I used to walk the streets with Parren Mitchell after his election, it was like a party. People filled the streets, trying to speak to him, trying to touch him. Kurt doesn't have that from the people. They don't know him."

Before his first term was over, Schmoke had already begun to be characterized as a "laid-back technocrat with a 5,000-kilowatt smile" and little substance.[22] He attempted to improve communications at the grassroots level through such techniques as holding Mayor's Forums in neighborhood community centers and broadcasting half-hour shows on television channel 54, but he could not and preferred not to become a "media animal" like his predecessor, who had put his name on everything that was built in the city. "I'm not the kind of mayor who's going to waste the city's money painting my name all over town when Baltimore has so many other important things to spend money on," he said in 1988.[23]

"He does have a thrust that makes sense, and I think if he articulated it, it would make governance better," said Schmoke supporter Arnie Graf, an organizer for BUILD, the citywide religious and civic coalition that enjoys access to a mayor whom many see as inaccessible. "People often don't see where we're going. . . . Even if they see something happening in their neighborhood, if it's not connected to a larger vision, you set people adrift, without a sense of hope."[24] Arthur Murphy agreed. "Kurt has had trouble establishing meta-values for Baltimore. Schaeffer renovated downtown, and everyone in Baltimore felt proud. 'The City That Reads' was a good start, but Kurt didn't know how to market it. He's got to keep pushing it, referring to it in every public appearance. His handlers are already focusing on the problem, urging him to refine the slogan to 'The City That Reads to Its Kids,' a metaphor for the need to save the youth through education."

Schmoke's detractors complained that "he has not worked hard enough to build the coalitions necessary to implement his programs and that he is aloof and lacks the common touch."[25] Throughout the city, Schmoke was being criticized for being ineffective and insulated at the same time that he continued to gain national recognition and prominence. Part of this discontent stemmed from the inability of his staff and close advisers to keep him abreast of developments in the neighborhoods, but concern continued to grow in the black community regarding his ability and willingness to address a "black agenda." There is a feeling that Schmoke has set his sights on higher office—Senator, perhaps—and does not want to wrap himself in black issues and a black style that might make him unelectable. "Jesse Jackson in 1984 and 1988 made himself clearly a black candidate with a black agenda," said Reverend Dobson. "He'll never be elected to national office. But he's done great things for the black community right from the position he's in."

It is at the level of appointments that Mayor Schmoke's visionary policies have most clearly broken down, and considerable controversy has been generated by his personnel decisions. Schmoke's first-term appointments in some key positions were either controversial or lackluster. Richard Hunter as school superintendent and Barbara Bostick as warden of the city jail both left their positions under cloudy circumstances.[26] Bostick was passed over by state authorities as warden for the jail when Schmoke negotiated its transfer from city to state control, and charges of mismanagement had been rife during her tenure there.[27] Yet she was later appointed to an important community empowerment role (see Chapter 7). "Kurt doesn't know how to wield power," said one community elder who asked not to be quoted by name. "Maynard Jackson [Atlanta], Ernest Morial [New Orleans], Harold Washington [Chicago]—they knew how to wield power. They used the city government power to let contracts and created a lot of business and work for black people. The white business community was hopping mad, but these guys just told them that blacks had the power now, and it was their turn." (To be fair, other community activists point out that mayors today, especially black mayors, operate with less federal money and more scrutiny than the stalwarts of the early days, men like Morial and Jackson.)

These problems suggest that Schmoke is the representative of Baltimore's black community, but not its leader. A leader knows his or her people and, while prepared to speak in clipped middle-class tones, is also comfortable in the streets, in the vernacular. Schmoke is not part of the large, interlocking pattern of networks that characterizes Baltimore's vernacular black community, and, as a consequence, he cannot keep his finger on the pulse of what is going on. This concerned Arthur Murphy, because, without such connections, he did not see how the mayor can exercise the leadership that the black community of Baltimore needs. "Who's talking to him, helping him make policy?" Murphy said. "I have no idea—I don't know if he has any backup, any advisers who understand the needs of the black community from a deep, historical perspective, who understand how to build institutions in the black community. He's not talking to anyone from the political and leadership circles of black Baltimore, so far as I know."

Something was missing: a sense of community that would urge middle-class, successful "New Wave" black politicians like Kurt Schmoke to develop—outside their own inner circle of trusted advisors—the coalitions that are needed to implement their visionary policies for the black poor and working class. Something was needed that would permit Baltimoreans of different classes as well as different races to cooperate in building a new sort of community, one based not on "representation," but on participation; not on alienation, but on collaboration and sharing. Skimming along the top as the people's "representative" will not do the job. Political, social, and economic development must be rooted deep into communities, using techniques that involve those who would benefit, calling upon them to participate and create new social forms. To Kurt Schmoke's credit, he has called for just this type of initiative. This cannot simply be wished into existence, however. It does not come out of the pages of a blue-ribbon report any more than from the smoke of a backroom political deal. Luckily, there are people in the city who can help him to build the kind of coalitions and informal, grassroots networks that will be necessary to accomplish his objectives.

Reverend Dobson has reflected on Schmoke's difficulty in implementing the same visionary, community-oriented policies that distinguish him from most other mayors in the country. He described the mayor as honest, sensitive, and intelligent, but with a limited conception of what is needed to rebuild the black community. "The city lacks the spirit, the essence of struggle," Dobson said. "Maybe the political system can't give birth to what we need. The mayor needs to connect to the institutions of the black community, especially the church. One person can't do the job alone, no matter how much power he has."

Participatory Democracy and the Black Church

When most African-Americans think of community as a series of networks among people trying to live useful lives and treat one another with respect, we think first of the black church. The ideology of community found in the Old Testament Book of Genesis was developed by the Jews in an attempt to create a new community out of a people brought closer together by oppression, and this literature has struck deep, resonant chords in black people's history since the time of slavery. Distinguishing characteristics of this community include a commitment to equality of rights and responsibilities for those within the community, compassion toward the vulnerable and dispossessed, and a conviction that the spiritual maturation of the human race points toward the removal of oppressive structures and their replacement with "forms conducive to the well-being of all creatures."[28] The history of the Judaeo-Christian ethic is one of struggle to keep the divine spark in human community alive in the face of pressures inducing hierarchy and institutionalization. This charismatic tradition as it appears in Christianity is associated with the breaking down of invidious differentiations between people, with the custom of sharing goods in common, and with an end to self-centeredness and greed.[29] Networks binding Christians (and, more recently, Muslims) in the African-American community's charismatic tradition have emerged from and reflect their pursuit of righteousness, compassion, and justice.[30]

Cornel West points to black theologians' lack of a social theory that relates black oppression to "the overall makeup of America's system of production, foreign policy, political arrangements, and cultural practices."[31] This failure made it appear that as black theologians spoke to their congregations and to the public at large about the "liberation" of the black community, they meant nothing more than racial equality and middle-class status within the context of the public interest/regulatory state. Thus, their demands began and ended with "equality before the law, equal opportunities in employment, education, and business, and economic parity with whites in median income."[32] In other words, black "liberation theology" has too often been little more than a reflection of the middle-class goals of the established civil rights movement. West feels that black theologians have made an important contribution by emphasizing the ways in which culture and religion strengthened the black struggle,[33] but they still have important contributions to make in demonstrating the ways in which popular culture can produce "sets of habits, sensibilities, and world views that cannot possibly be realized within the perimeters of the established [oppressive] order."[34] In order to round their analysis out to a true theology of liberation, West insists, black theologians need exposure to progressive concepts of participatory democracy in the economic and political spheres.[35]

The synthesis of cultural and religious energy with participatory democracy in the economic and political spheres of which West first spoke in 1982 is a model that has even more relevance now. The public interest/regulatory state that many black theologians took as their primary reference point is in decline. The pretensions to power of black elected officials have too often degenerated into petty squabbling or, worse, remoteness from the communities they were elected to serve. The black church is an important locus for building an alternative because it is "financially, culturally, and politically free of corporate influence."[36] In an interview, Father Robert Kearns of St. Peter Claver Church in Baltimore envisioned for the church the special role of contributing to the religious awareness of parishioners and "spreading God's special love for people who are victims" as espoused in the Scriptures, people who are poor and oppressed. This mission is to be carried out in a way that empowers individuals and their community, helping them to "analyze social situations, make decisions for themselves based on that analysis, and work in a collaborative relationship with one another to carry out their decisions."

"The community has seen the importance of organization and collaboration. The American value system based on individualism can be a trap. If your own self-interest is your only motivation, you don't make as much progress as when you collaborate with others," said Kearns. "Community revitalization is also important because the youth have become less and less tied to community institutions. The media now provides their role models; they are trying to live out what they see. The community must provide a different set of images—rootedness, pride in the accomplishments of members of the community, and feelings of loyalty, connectedness, and proprietorship in the neighborhood."

Bethel A.M.E.: Spiritual Uplift
and Community Development

As mentioned in Chapter 1, Bethel A.M.E. Church was founded in 1817 (though the congregation dates to 1785). By 1970 Bethel had become a middle-class church with very few members, and its glory days seemed over. Most of the congregation lived outside the city and commuted to the church. In the 1970s, however, when Cecilia and John Bryant became the pastors, Bethel started to attract people again. From 1975 to 1988, the Bryants, who were social as well as spiritual activists, created programs that attracted similarly motivated people and kept them involved in the church. John Bryant had been in the Peace Corps in Liberia and there developed a whole new conception of the spirit world. He saw the Holy Spirit in Afrocentric terms. This was something many groups in the black community found attractive—from cultural nationalists to pentecostal worshippers.

Reverend Bryant told his new congregation that it was fine to raise your hands and shout during the services. This was very far from the standards laid down by Daniel Paine, one of the church's first ministers, who was very much against the deeply spiritual expressions of African people and decried spiritual songs as "cornfield ditties." Reverend Bryant, on the contrary, led his congregation back to their vernacular roots. Even people who had been successful and moved to "the County" did not have to feel guilty: they could give money to Haiti and Africa. People quit their jobs and went to Africa to do evangelical and support work. There was an opportunity and encouragement to serve. They developed a credit union and a food coop for the secular types. Leronia Josey, a successful lawyer whose office walls are covered with autographed pictures of well-known politicians, spoke of the Bryant years at Bethel, her face glowing.

"There were lots of flags to rally around, a sense of possibilities. You were part of a larger enterprise. This is how the Bryants tapped into the Holy Spirit. Other pastors just seemed to want to keep building new sanctuaries and new buildings. But Bethel was about service. You'd come into services at eight o'clock on Sunday morning and

Reverend Bryant would have something planned for you. Some committees would meet all night, but they would find a way to involve you that complied with your schedule. They took away all your excuses." In 1979, the Bryants set up the Gethsemane Counseling Center because there were many doctors and psychologists in the church who wished to provide this service to the community. Soon, Bethel expanded into a full range of social services.

The new pastor, Frank M. Reid III, is a fifth-generation minister; his father was Bishop Reid, and there have been two bishops in his family. His style is completely different from John Bryant's. Yet Bethel continues to grow. "John was an activist," Josey observes. "Reid is an administrative type, a CEO, he follows up on things and demands accountability. John would say, 'Go do it and I'll pray for you.' Frank doesn't micromanage, but he wants you to run everything by him. He says that if you're a two-million-dollar concern, you can't operate with horse and buggy techniques. Some of the super-spiritual people were upset, but it's a classic sequence to go from activism to management.

"Some of the ministers who were running programs had to be removed. They'd get up and leave in the middle of a program to go to a religious meeting in some other state. If you criticized them about it, they'd say you weren't saved, that you were a heathen. You don't close down all centers every time there's a religious meeting. The ministers also had to learn that when they were running outreach centers in the community, they were there to meet people's temporal needs. You can't ask people, 'Have you given your life to Christ?' as soon as they come in the door. That's disrespectful if you don't know people. Bethel continues to walk the line between the spiritual and the temporal. It's very difficult, very exciting, very challenging. We're trying to build people's self-esteem. People ought to have options, regardless of what they do with them.

"We're building a nation; we have to help the kids," Josey mused. "Frank is working on the new generation. He says we can't let them go. He's trying to mentor young ministers. He has a junior trustee board and a group of junior stewards for the church. We have to grow leadership, give young people an opportunity to give reports, to speak. We have to prepare them, show them respect. The church is 40 percent male now—this is great. The kids have to see strong black men. Bethel is introducing martial arts, and 'take back the streets' programs. The police came out one night because they saw all these black men 'taking back' the streets. The congregation had to explain to the police what was going on."

In 1990 Bethel dedicated its William Smith Memorial Family Outreach Center. Bethel is at the edge of Upton, near Druid Heights, a neighborhood once described by W. E. B. DuBois as the showpiece of middle-class black America. The Reverend Quismat Alim, a luminous minister who has a parish in Cambridge, Maryland, is the director of the Center. She told me that the Center was the result of a challenge to the Bethel congregation from Reverend Bryant, who recognized that the congregation, prosperous and living in the suburbs, were oblivious to, if not actually contemptuous of, the people who lived in Upton. People complained to the minister, "Your congregation members park their Mercedes on our lawns, but they don't speak." The importance of greeting those one meets, even strangers, is a vernacular tradition that stretches back to Africa itself.

The Outreach Center, named after a prominent, deceased member of the Bethel congregation who was once an assistant director of the City Planning Commission, has a $100,000 annual budget. Speakers at the dedication, including Representative Kwesi Mfume, Mayor Schmoke, and State Senator Larry Young, observed that Bethel was doing more with a hundred thousand dollars than the city government could do with nine times that amount. They applauded this example of what middle-class people can do, particularly in the communities from which they sprang.

"The harvest is great, but the laborers are few," observed Frank Reid, who is Mayor Schmoke's half-brother. Though Reid is also a Yale graduate, he is nonetheless comfortable in the vernacular, and used vernacular styles of speech to call upon the assembled gathering to follow Bethel's example, come back to the community, and get involved. "There are fifty thousand families on welfare in Baltimore. There are thirty-five thousand working families who live below the poverty line. The city is not in good shape; there's hardship and homeless people. Bethel chose to act because it's time to turn things around, time to take a step. The Center began as a vision in the minds of Bethel's congregation many years ago. Great things begin from small things; a great tree grows from the smallest mustard seed. This building, this Center, is the beginning of a great work, which must extend beyond Bethel. We must share our vision. Vision adds to our eternal life. Where there is no vision, the people perish."

With dynamic preaching and leadership as well as sound administration, Frank Reid has constructed a mega-church based on black activism, neo-Pentecostalism, and traditional family values. Yet Reverend Reid stands aloof from other churchmen in the city, including those involved in the Interfaith Ministerial Alliance (which, along with the Baptist Ministers Conference, accounts for three hundred members of Baltimore's black clergy) and those involved in BUILD. He feels that Bethel is so large and its service program so comprehensive that he does not need to work with anyone else; he reaches out to the entire Baltimore black community on television and cable broadcasts of his sermons.[37] But the civic revival Baltimore needs requires more than individual churches, no matter how large they are; coalitions must be built among many people who are doing good work. BUILD is such a coalition.

Baltimoreans United in Leadership Development—
Power, Spirit, and Community

BUILD is based on an organizing model developed by Saul Alinsky, who taught that ordinary people possess the ability to solve their own problems. It seeks to effect change on a citywide level while retaining a focus on developing the leadership capabilities of its individual members. Harry Boyte has described BUILD as one of several organizations that are harbingers of a "third way" of civic engagement, "neither intimate nor innocent, not countercultural but not settling for welfare either."[38] BUILD is a coalition of forty-five affiliated churches, the resident leaders of public housing projects, and three local unions—the teachers', the school principals', and the hospital workers'. These constituent organizations, sometimes referred to as "mediating institutions," are the typical building blocks of an Alinsky-style organization.[39] BUILD charges each adult member dues of five dollars apiece. For large churches, that can amount to more than five thousand dollars a year. BUILD accepts no government money and takes foundation grants only for individual projects not essential to the group's survival. The organization is biracial and has about thirty-five thousand families as its base. It bridges the gap between the establishment and Baltimoreans who lack political and economic clout.

BUILD's goal is to become a strong, interfaith, multiracial citizen-power organization by: (1) empowering poor, working-class, and middle-class communities; (2) negotiating on behalf of such communities with corporate and elected political power; (3) developing leaders trained in the public skills of citizenship; and (4) renovating mediating institutions such as churches and unions into places where values are formed and families nurtured and protected. They work for economic and community development that raises the real and effective incomes of low- and moderate-income people, not only by providing jobs, but also by providing assistance in public school curricula and instruction. Several of BUILD's member churches have taken this program a step farther, providing low-cost, subsidized services such as day care, transportation, and health care.

BUILD grows out of Baltimore's Interfaith Ministerial Alliance, a coalition of church leaders that began in the black community in the 1940s as a means of overcoming interdenominational competition and bickering. In the mid-1950s, the Alliance became involved in the civil rights movement, which sensitized many preachers to the needs of people outside their own congregations. By 1958, the Reverend Marion Bascom, the president of the Alliance, was able to sponsor a march on City Hall and a rally drawing fifteen hundred people to demand jobs, desegregation of public accommodations, and decent housing. Senator Jacob Javits of New York and Jackie Robinson (the first black in major league baseball) addressed the crowd, creating tremendous enthusiasm in the black community and establishing the Alliance as an important organization existing outside the traditional forums of the NAACP and the Urban League. In the 1960s and 1970s, under the leadership of the Reverend Vernon Dobson and the Reverend Wendell Philips, the Alliance pulled in support from the NAACP, the Urban League, and CORE, as well as the Mitchell family (Parren Mitchell had recently been elected to Congress as the first black Democrat from Maryland in U.S. history). Because of their connection as Morehouse College alumni, Martin Luther King and a core group of approximately twenty activist ministers in the Alliance shared strategy and financial support. King raised more money for SCLC in Baltimore than in any other city besides Atlanta, his home base. His Poor People's Campaign, which set up a tent city in Washington, was staged from Baltimore.

Beginning in the late 1960s, the Alliance began to talk about ways to move the black community in Baltimore beyond civil rights and into an economic and political position of substantial equity. The Alliance supported the upstart political campaigns of Parren Mitchell and others in the early 1970s. Kurt Schmoke's campaign for state's attorney in 1980 was supported by Reverend Bascom's church, of which Mayor Schmoke is still a member. But the Alliance wanted to move in the areas of housing and economic development as well as political access. It was at that time that BUILD was conceived.

Some of the credit for BUILD's success is owed to the Industrial Areas Foundation, an umbrella organization based in New York that provides the full-time staff for BUILD and similar organizations centered in New York, Texas, and California. After a rocky beginning, the IAF was able to work with BUILD to develop the organizational skills it needed to succeed in a political environment and to become politically enfranchised through numbers. The objective was to capture some of the political power enjoyed by businessmen, politicians, and bureaucrats and use it to advance the goals of the community at large. BUILD credits its success and longevity to the organizational discipline IAF provided. The initial contact with the IAF was made through the cooperative efforts of Reverend Dobson and Monsignor Clare O'Dwyer, who had worked together against blockbusting. They networked into the Ministerial Alliance, the Catholic hierarchy, and the white Protestant denominations to develop support for an interracial community development organization. They contacted IAF, which brought interested clergy from all three networks together to create BUILD. Monsignor O'Dwyer engineered BUILD's first grant ($70,000) from the Catholic Campaign for Human Development.

According to Arnie Graf of the IAF, BUILD's principal organizer in the early 1980s, if one wants to effect long-term institutional change, "something has to happen to people. We can dream up all the programs we want, but we can't dream up people." Graf said that people who become active in BUILD become different people, gaining confidence that they have the power to solve their problems. BUILD's goal is not to teach dominant power, he observed, but "relational power," the power of mass participation. BUILD, however, has not always had a reputation as a coalition-builder: its perspective from its inception was that power was the name of the game. As Reverend Dobson told me, BUILD embarked on a five-year plan to develop the capacity to represent the poor in the "corridors of power." While many community-based organizations form around a particular issue and dissolve once the issue is resolved, BUILD was able to thrust itself into the forefront of all of Baltimore's urban issues. Its voice was heard, even sought after, in developing Baltimore's plans to promote more jobs, housing, and industry. They refused to accept a token role. BUILD's aggressive tactics offended some of the groups that are now its closest allies.

Those tactics were also very effective. For example, in the early 1980s the state of Maryland created a fund to guarantee home mortgages to low-income residents, but the program foundered in black areas of Baltimore because the city's banks refused to participate. Unsuccessful in their attempts to meet with the president of one bank in which BUILD members had over $2 million in deposits, BUILD leaders decided to take more direct action. One day hundreds of BUILD members went to one branch of the bank and tied up the teller lines requesting change. Outraged, the bank manager called the police. When they arrived, a security guard demanded that they arrest the BUILD members on the charge of "making change." The police laughed and returned to headquarters. BUILD had made its point, and ultimately an agreement signed with that bank and three others enabled more than five hundred inner-city residents to buy their own homes. This action was part of a series of public confrontations and private bargaining sessions designed to achieve BUILD's two major goals: to get Baltimore's business community to help the poor and to get them to take BUILD seriously.

One of BUILD's greatest challenges on the local front came in 1983 when it successfully fought Baltimore Gas & Electric's attempt to form a holding company that would have led to increased rates for city residents if BG&E's diversified businesses lost money. Thanks to BUILD's efforts, the Public Service Commission granted BG&E only half of the sought-after rate increase. BG&E's hiring of a consultant to deal with and counter community organizations during its battle with BUILD is illustrative of the respect enjoyed by the organization throughout the business and political community. BUILD established itself as a political watchdog for Baltimoreans on statewide issues as well when it fought the insurance industry's attempt to charge higher rates to drivers within the city than to suburbanites.

BUILD prides itself on being nonpartisan. Remaining neutral in electoral politics keeps BUILD's options open and gives candidates a greater interest in hearing its agenda. However, BUILD leaders recognize the value of being able to turn out large numbers of supporters and the message it sends to politicians. During the 1987 mayoral election year, BUILD conducted a citywide petition drive with the goal of signing up 75,000 registered voters who supported its "municipal agenda." BUILD then used the approximately seventy thousand signatures it obtained as leverage with candidates, publicly requesting that they either adopt BUILD's agenda or state what portions they disagreed with, along with the reasons for their dissent. BUILD thus ensured that whoever was elected as mayor would be forced to consider their concerns.

As a consequence, BUILD's relationship with City Hall has improved. Mayor Schaefer was not particularly supportive of BUILD, and, in fact, he and the group clashed on several occasions. In contrast, Mayor Schmoke actively sought the support of the BUILD churches during his first mayoral campaign, and he has endorsed many of its programs. During Schmoke's first term, BUILD was regularly briefed on city policy by the mayor or by his top advisers.

BUILD became important because it saw the "big picture" and had the resources to bring together the data to show how housing, education, and health care interrelate. In its role as advocate, it could take political positions more readily than a neighborhood group, which might have a vested interest in maintaining good relations with their elected representatives. BUILD's capacity to bring together a diverse group of people enabled it to bring a substantial amount of pressure to bear on the state capital as well as on City Hall. It started out by attacking the system from the outside, but its increasingly sophisticated use of partnerships with city officials and the business community has brought it into the mainstream of city development efforts.

Unlike a neighborhood organization or even a citywide coalition that focuses on a single issue, BUILD has the capacity to concentrate on a broad range of issues that affect the city as a whole, and the resources to build a constituency that transcends a particular geographic location. Once seen as a confrontational antagonist, BUILD has become the mainstream voice of thousands of previously voiceless Baltimoreans.

In 1987 nearly three thousand people attended BUILD's annual convention. It proclaimed a new municipal agenda, which was endorsed by the city, state, and federal elected officials in attendance as a vision for Baltimore. This agenda for citywide transformation proposed changes in education, employment training, neighborhood development, health care, and city finance to overcome a milieu of "disconnected souls, defeated schools, abandoned houses, violent, drug-infested streets, and overflowing jails." In the area of education, BUILD has called for school-based management to create neighborhood school autonomy. In employmènt training, it advocates "enrichment centers" to retrain unemployed workers for the skills required in a service economy. In housing and neighborhood development, BUILD advocates tenant management of public housing and community-oriented (rather than incident-oriented) policing. In the area of municipal finance, it recommended looking at a commuter tax and statewide tax reform geared toward improving the financing of Baltimore municipal services, and particularly the operation of public schools. BUILD worked with the Greater Baltimore Committee to start the Commonwealth Program, which provides jobs or college scholarships to Baltimore high school students. BUILD helped put together a $30 million package for the renovation of the West Side neighborhood of Sandtown-Winchester, and it was in a position, by June 1991, to summon Baltimore's entire Maryland state legislative delegation and upbraid the politicians for their lackluster support of statewide tax reform.[40]

As BUILD's influence has grown, however, the city as a whole has had to reassess its priorities in the face of serious budget constraints. As of March 1990, Baltimore did not have the funds to maintain basic services, much less start new projects. Baltimore is now more dependent than ever on its nonprofit sector, and in particular on groups like BUILD, which are skilled in bringing together private and public sector partnerships designed to improve the quality of life for all of Baltimore's residents. BUILD thus stands at the intersection of church, state, and neighborhood.

At this juncture, BUILD must be cognizant of the functions of government, which it must monitor and, in some cases, assume as an adjunct to elected officials. The first of these functions is *electoral*: "(1) demand aggregation, articulation and transmission; (2) leadership recruitment, selection, and promotion to public office; and (3) citizen education, mobilization, and participation in the political process."[41] This electoral phase involves reaching out to the public and persuading them to support a candidate. The role of a community-based organization in this phase is easy to comprehend, especially in terms of demand aggregation and citizen mobilization, and BUILD has acquitted itself well in this area. Identification of leaders to seek public office is more difficult, because the party and the media have a great deal to say about who will run.

It is in the second phase of these paragovernmental functions, *governance*, that an organization moves from protest and electoral mobilization to the delivery of public goods. This phase involves the ability to affect the implementation of policy by elected and appointed officials. Here, BUILD is much weaker. To strengthen its position, BUILD needs to be able to influence "(4) policy formulation and decisionmaking; (5) conflict adjudication over policy decisions and administration; and (6) service delivery and resource allocation to [its loyal members]."[42] This governing phase involves crafting compromises among those members of the public who make their presence felt in the governance process. There is a danger here, however. It must be very tempting for BUILD to simply cast itself as a special interest and make deals behind closed doors, especially as its clout in corporate boardrooms and political backrooms increases. Most Alinsky-style organizations, in fact, walk a fine line between denouncing the powerful and accepting their largess.

At the very least BUILD needs to perform a kind of "shadow government" role in this second stage, exposing, monitoring, and criticizing the political and economic establishment of Baltimore as well as using its political clout to gain rewards from that establishment on behalf of BUILD constituents. While this critique need not be ideologically driven (Alinsky hated ideology), the rank and file members must be actively involved in the process of critique and empowered to carry it on without constant tutoring. The IAF has struck a balance in many of its organizing efforts by developing a "practical theory of action" through which rank and file members are exposed to the dynamic equilibrium of citizen politics, the interplay of "power, mediating institutions, public life, the meaning and management of time, judgment, imagination, and self-interest."[43] More recently, they have begun to expand their theory to identify distinctions between behavior and expectations appropriate in intimate personal relationships and those appropriate in the confrontational world of public action.[44] In this context, too, BUILD faces related but contradictory perils. Constituents may feel that they have been "sold out," or they may come to perceive the establishment as their provider, making it less necessary for them to support BUILD. Either way, the organization would become alienated from its constituency, and the cause of community empowerment disserved. Ironically, both these constituent reactions can occur simultaneously, and this is especially likely to happen when communication between the leadership and the rank and file becomes one-way and filtered through layers of bureaucracy, and when rank and file members have no continuing role in the political discourse of the organization.

The first problem is well illustrated by Robert Fisher's statement (probably influenced by Max Weber) that "all formal organizations tend toward bureaucratic control, toward organizational maintenance objectives superseding other goals, and toward defusing citizen participation by giving the impression that since an organization already exists to carry on the struggle, personal sacrifice for the cause is no longer necessary."[45] The second issue is not as obvious. On the one hand, an ideologically driven political discourse within the organization and between the organization and other political actors can degenerate into histrionics and posturing, while political activity degenerates into one-way mobilizations, usually led by charismatic males.[46] A politics of empowerment rather than of ideology lends itself more to the kind of interaction and discourse that roots civic capacity deeper into the community, often bringing forth female leadership that is focused more on community-building than on macho power conflicts. On the other, unless the organization goes beyond reacting to power relations and empowers its members with a structural analysis of such relations, the willingness to engage in the confrontational politics that is sometimes needed can fade away. And with that, the very "people power" upon which Alinsky-style organizations rely can vanish, leaving only memories of past rallies as the political capital upon which the organization trades. BUILD's credibility and effectiveness greatly depend upon its ability and willingness to nurture its roots in the communities it purports to serve. As an umbrella group, it must also be sure that each of its constituent organizations maintains the grassroots linkages that permit it to speak as an authentic voice for its community.

The IAF has adopted the position that the church is the primary mediating institution in the black community. Unions, schools, and ethnic clubs, all of which surfaced in black communities like Old West Baltimore, are now on the decline. The church is the last link with the vernacular community, but even in the black church there are strong counter-pressures. A process of divestment is going on, Reverend Dobson observed. "First the white congregations divested and moved to the suburbs, leaving behind some very fine buildings that black congregations took over. But now the black congregations want to move to the suburbs, too. The ministers are trying to invest in the community, to make it difficult for the congregation to leave. They believe that spiritual growth takes place in the 'community of need,' with all its pain and danger, rather than in a withdrawn, pristine, monastic sort of spiritual experience way out in the suburbs."

Ironically, many of the white churches from the suburbs are now trying to sponsor projects in the inner city because they miss the challenge of a community of need. For Reverend Dobson, a key point that people too often do not understand is that spiritual growth is not monastic: it does not involve a pulling away from people. It comes from struggle, from interaction with others. "Our witness depends on this," he told me. "The mega-churches are leading us to anonymity. Five thousand parishioners, all strangers, sitting in an auditorium or watching T.V., waiting for some mesmerizing experience that they then have to take home and connect to their own lives. It's an illusion. The reality of life can only be worked out in struggle and in concert with others."

BUILD tries to impress a twofold message upon the ministers it recruits into the organization: not only will people grow and develop as they address the citywide issues that are on the larger organization's agenda, but leadership must also be trained to deal with the issues of concern to the congregation and the local community. At present, however, the churches with significant resources are middle-class, and many have little contact with marginal people. Their parishioners travel from the suburbs to worship in inner-city churches. A positive sign is that these churches tend to remain located in the black community; while they are not "of" the community, at least they are "in" it, and can sometimes be prevailed upon to reach out to the marginalized community that surrounds the church itself.

Boyte has drawn attention to BUILD's symbol, which depicts the organization as a tree. The roots signify the "private foundations of public life" and the trunk and branches, "symbols of the visible public world, are expressions of maturity, although they continue to draw sustenance and support from their roots."[47] BUILD must pay a great deal more attention to these private roots. In its "social movement" origins, IAF staffer Arnie Graf felt that BUILD focused far too much attention on mobilization rather than deeply rooted organizing.[48] IAF staffer Gerald Taylor recognized the potential for deeper roots in Baltimore when BUILD was being started. He remarked upon the "density of community ties," the "overlaps and friendship networks" that existed in the city's black neighborhoods.[49]

To what extent can this more deeply rooted process take place? To what extent do the churches go beyond providing services to become an engine of community empowerment? To what extent do they, as Reverend Dobson suggested, engage the poor in the "liberating force" of the gospel? "The church is supposed to renew that experience over and over; that is its mission," he said. "Let's take the church at its best; and link that up with active and awakened people, and with schools and families. I hope the church can do this." A joint renovation effort of the Mayor's Office, the Enterprise Foundation, a local community organization, and BUILD in the neighborhood of Sandtown-Winchester, discussed in Chapter 7, has furnished a proving ground for Reverend Dobson's hopes.

Ironically, the black middle class can progress only by embracing the very community that they have been trying to escape. Civil rights and electoral victories are hollow when they are not powered by, and shared with, the entire black community. Those members of the community to whom such benefits have not yet "trickled down" must be provided with the resources, training, opportunity, and respect necessary for them to chart a path for their own development, just as the middle classes before them have done. A key part of this strategy is the revitalization of the vernacular community support networks and mediating institutions that launched the success of the talented tenth.

═══════ Chapter Seven ═══════
Community Building in
Partnership

The only way the process of empowerment can continue
is if new leadership continues to surface, not always to stand out in
front, but also to fill in the gaps, to maintain communications and
dialogue among all the people in the community.
—Darnell Ridgley

BALTIMORE'S nonprofit housing providers have expended a tremendous
amount of time, energy, and creativity in the effort to give Baltimore's
low-income population access to decent housing, and an extensive
system of networks is attempting to remedy the lack of low-income
housing caused by racial and economic discrimination. The emphasis
has been on bricks and mortar, however, and the development of the
city's human resources has lagged behind. Thus, a number of houses
in a particular neighborhood may be rehabilitated, but other factors
that also affect the neighborhood's stability—crime, drugs, lack of
employment, and a poor education system—remain unaddressed.
Concern over such issues led to a drive by the mayor, BUILD, and the
Enterprise Foundation to attempt a broad-based, comprehensive renovation of an entire neighborhood. Sandtown-Winchester was selected.

As the urban experts Neil Pierce and Curtis Johnson have observed, it is too early to celebrate the breakthroughs resulting from
this "Community Building in Partnership" effort. What might be accomplished is really inspiring: "Local schools managed by the principals, teachers, and parents—not a central school bureaucracy. Tenant management teams to run public housing projects and develop
citizenship centers. Enrichment centers to provide job training that
might lead to middle-class futures." Community-oriented policing,
"police officers placed on permanent neighborhood assignment to prevent crimes, not just search for criminals and pick up bodies," is also

a possibility. And it all could be done with no more money than is funneled into Sandtown today for various forms of government largess—welfare, Medicaid, food stamps, and the like.[1]

A pivotal feature of the process remains the involvement of community residents, however, not just in the planning process, but also in the implementation. Too often planners completely disregard the question of how plans are to be put into practice, or who is to put them into practice. Too often implementation means getting the community's token support for a process that planners have initiated and will continue to control. Sandtown residents will, of course, benefit from the physical changes that are going on in their community, but they must be empowered in a much deeper way. Broad-based community involvement and comprehensive participation will be necessary to insure the accountability of the process in Sandtown, which businessmen, politicians, community leaders, social service bureaucrats, and private foundation staff are all struggling to control.[2]

Sandtown as a Setting

Sandtown (as residents call the neighborhood of Sandtown-Winchester), is a community of approximately twelve thousand people plagued with vacant, boarded-up properties and vacant lots dating back to the early days of urban renewal during the 1950s. Unemployment is high, and there are a significant number of female-headed households living at or below the poverty line. Sandtown is virtually all black; 40 percent of its residents are below the age of eighteen; 45 percent are between eighteen and sixty-one; and 13 percent are over sixty-one years of age. There are more large families in Sandtown than in Upton, but there are also many single-person households on the verge of homelessness. The population decreased by one-third between 1970 and 1980, and the pattern of serious crimes has been uneven. Murder and burglary decreased, though rape stayed the same. Robbery, aggravated assault, larceny, and auto theft have increased dramatically. The overall crime rate in Sandtown is still higher than anywhere else on the West Side. Crime seems to concentrate in the northern section of the neighborhood, near the light commercial strip of North Avenue.

Sandtown is characterized by absentee landlords, housing abandonment, and arson. There is a great deal of dilapidated alley housing of the type inhabited by blacks in Baltimore for generations. Of the approximately forty-six hundred dwelling units in Sandtown, about 30 percent are multifamily dwellings, and just under 20 percent of the single-family homes are owner-occupied. Sixteen percent of the dwelling units in the neighborhood are subsidized. Overcrowding in Sandtown has decreased, the vacancy rate now standing at about 5 percent. Rents have increased by half during the last ten years. Homes for sale in the neighborhood have increased in price from roughly a tenth of the citywide mean to a quarter of it. The houses increased in value 117 percent in this period, compared with 158 per cent in Park Heights and 183 per cent for Baltimore as a whole. Unlike Park Heights, which is experiencing a great deal of new private mortgage capital investment, banks have not yet begun investing in Sandtown to any appreciable extent.

Because of its large number of multifamily units, abandoned buildings, and vacant lots, Sandtown is ripe for extensive development despite the reluctance of the private sector. The city Department of Housing and Community Development (DHCD) quietly acquired and cleared properties as part of a comprehensive strategy that made Sandtown a prime candidate for the Baltimore Nehemiah Project (described below) and brought in the massive infusion of capital needed. When Sandtown residents appealed to Mayor Schmoke for aid in reclaiming their neighborhood from drugs, crime, unemployment, and inadequate housing, he was ready.

Community resident Athena Young carried on a street survey of Sandtown, with my assistance, in the summer of 1991. Her impression was that her community was filled with a great many people trying to make it on their own—lots of beauty parlors, carryout restaurants, and auto repair shops being run out of yards and small buildings. In some cases, she observed, people would do better to move a block away, but because they have not done any market research, they are unaware of the competition until they actually set up shop. The diversity that we observed in our first assessment was amazing. Sometimes there were three churches in a block, from storefronts to the massive St. Peter Claver and the New Song Urban Ministry, newly moved into a renovated building across the street from Gilmor Homes. We passed evidence of Muslim and black nationalist activity: a Muslim carryout on Carey Street, the Nation Builders (2) bookstore on North Avenue, and the home of a Rastafarian, with a Haile Selassie emblem and handwritten, apocalyptic messages posted in his windows. On "black business row" on North Avenue across from the Nation Builders (2) bookstore, black street vendors who live in the area come out around lunchtime and stay until dusk. Arabbers (black vendors who sell fruit, vegetables, and fish from horse-drawn wagons in West Baltimore) gather on Winchester Street, at the stable of Sandtown's senior Arabber, whose street name is Fatback. There they collect their produce and merchandise to sell on the streets of Sandtown. Fatback's stable was later bulldozed to make way for the Nehemiah Project.

We passed a small house that appeared to be a Veterans of Foreign Wars post. We passed a fire station, a police station, a gas station, and several larger business sites, including a stationery manufacturer, a heating oil company, and a paving concern. We took note of three doctors, two lawyers, a dentist, a realtor, a tailor, a shoemaker, and two barber shops. There were a number of funeral homes, one dry cleaner, one hardware store, and two laundromats. There are three elementary schools, Gilmor, Kelson, and Pinderhughes (another elementary school and a high school in Sandtown have been closed and converted into apartments). The Lafayette Square Multipurpose Center, the Lillian Jones Recreational Center, the Urban Services Agency on Gilmor Street, the Carroll Health facility for the elderly (then under construction), and the Baltimore Project (prenatal counseling and referral) all are located in Sandtown. Evidence of the Nehemiah Project was clearly apparent, as well as some earlier renovations and rehabilitations. And, of course, there is Gilmor Homes, a low-rise public housing project occupying several square blocks and situated directly across from Gilmor Elementary School. This was our preliminary inventory of the resources of Sandtown. About two weeks later, at Young's practical suggestion, we checked our street observations with the telephone book. The white pages and the yellow pages corroborated most of our observations although the storefront churches generally could not be found in the telephone book. The Arabbers, of course, were not listed.

The Nehemiah Project

The federal Nehemiah Housing Opportunity Program, enacted by Congress in 1988 at a cost of $20 million, authorizes HUD to make grants to nonprofit organizations to enable them to provide loans to low-income families for the purchase of newly constructed or substantially rehabilitated houses. The Nehemiah program, named for the Hebrew leader who organized the rebuilding of Jerusalem, was conceived to permit massive intervention in inner-city neighborhoods, and was made available only to cities proposing a project with a scale large enough to make a significant impact. The program is designed to assist organizations like the East Brooklyn Congregations, a network of Brooklyn black ministers who conceived the first Nehemiah Project, which enabled 700 low-income families to purchase their own homes. That group of ministers, like BUILD, was organized by the IAF and BUILD considers it a sister organization.

In 1988 over eight hundred BUILD delegates, Mayor Schmoke, Governor Schaeffer, Senators Mikulksi and Sarbanes, Representative Mfume, and scores of religious and lay leaders gathered at St. Peter Claver Church in Sandtown to announce a collaboration among BUILD, the city, state, and federal governments, and the Enterprise Foundation. Mayor Schmoke committed $11 million in land, site clearance, and municipal services; Governor Schaefer promised $11 million in low-interest mortgage financing. The principal BUILD denominations and the city's Catholic, Episcopal, Methodist, Lutheran, and Jewish organizations have together contributed $2.2 million in interest-free construction loan funds, to be made available for a term of seven years. In early 1989, the federal government pledged $4.2 million in Nehemiah Opportunity Grants to provide interest-free secondary mortgages of up to $15,000 each, to help reduce the size of the first mortgages homebuyers will need to purchase. Loan repayment will be deferred until the new owner leases, sells, or otherwise transfers the house.

The Enterprise Nehemiah Development Corporation (a subsidiary of the Enterprise Foundation) serves as project developer and is the recipient of BUILD construction loan funds. Its board of directors consists of three Enterprise Foundation representatives and three BUILD representatives. No action can be taken, no check can be signed, without the agreement of both groups. The $28 million Nehemiah Project will build 225 new, modular homes for low-income families in Sandtown, as well as rehabilitating 17 rowhouses. Seventy-five new modular homes are scheduled for Penn North, a community located just north of Sandtown. The overall plan calls for the elimination of seventy vacant dwellings and commercial and industrial units, and for the expansion of the commercial development of North Avenue (the northern border of the project area). In addition to the Nehemiah Project proper, the city has undertaken a major sanitation project, and the Gilmor Homes public housing project is being modernized with funds from the HUD Comprehensive Improvement Assistance Program (CIAP).

The Nehemiah Project in Sandtown is not limited to physical re-development, however. It includes a planning, service, and community action component, called "Community Building in Partnership" (CBIP). The CBIP concept is to approach community development holistically, involving community residents and seeking to evoke from them a commitment to a real change in their neighborhood.

The Concept of Community-Building in Partnership

Mayor Kurt Schmoke began developing the idea of community-building in partnership after he visited a model community in Israel. Schmoke was impressed with the idea of a self-sufficient, self-maintaining community and made individual responsibility and community volunteerism major themes for his second term in office. In January 1990 Schmoke established the Sandtown-Winchester Task Force to guide the CBIP planning process, with representatives from a local community group, the Sandtown-Winchester Improvement Association (SWIA), as well as the city, the Baltimore Urban League, BUILD, and Enterprise. BUILD committed itself to develop social infrastructure and community support, particularly working through its member churches in the project area to organize new homebuyers into a mutual support organization. It was to draw upon its relationships with public schools and the corporate community to further the success of the project.

The task force formally began the process in May 1990 with a public meeting in Sandtown, attended by some four hundred residents—every kind of community person. There was a free meal for all participants; no one was turned away. The participants, broken down into small groups, were urged to "think and dream about what you want." Darnell Ridgely, a big, fair-skinned black community advocate with fire-red hair and outrageous fingernails, was transferred by Mayor Schmoke from her job supervising the city's Community Development Block Grant program to staff the CBIP project. Ridgley, Francis Green (a consultant), and members of the CBIP Task Force facilitated meetings to be sure that the process remained open and community-driven. At first, the community people did not believe them. They were waiting for the city staff, the Enterprise staff, the experts, to take care of things. The staff refused, and forced the people to deal with the issues.

"If you don't have a sense of what people really want, any physical or institutional changes made in a community will simply revert," Ridgley observed. Eight work groups along the lines of community concerns were formed, consisting of community members and staff from the city and the Enterprise Foundation. BUILD's small staff made it impossible for it to match the activity of the city and Enterprise in this regard.

The Physical Dimension

Allan Tibbels, director of Sandtown Habitat for Humanity, was selected by SWIA to chair the project's physical development committee, which was charged with developing a housing plan for Sandtown-Winchester. (Habitat for Humanity International is a nongovernmental organization promoting the development of affordable housing all over the world; see Chapter 8.) The summary statement of the first round of meetings of the SWIA project proposed as a first step the creation of a neighborhood-based housing development entity and a nonprofit real estate company. These entities were to buy, hold, and dispose of property in Sandtown to complement physical development plans, and to insure that profits from publicly funded projects are directed back to the community for further development activity. The primary objectives were the creation of affordable housing for everyone in the community (i.e., housing for which residents pay no more than 30 percent of their incomes, with special attention to households earning less than $10,000 a year), and the raising of Sandtown's homeownership level from one-fifth of neighborhood residents to one-half by the year 2000. Members also wished to develop resident councils in all public and assisted housing projects in the community to screen prospective tenants and demand a higher level of maintenance and management of their buildings. The committee was also concerned about the amount of vacant land and the many vacant housing units in Sandtown. (The committee's concern with junkyard and other unsightly land uses conflicts with an economic development plan that deals with people who are doing auto repair in their yards or in vacant lots.)

Although Habitat International's philosophy is to encourage the development of owner-occupied, single-family housing, the CBIP task force recommended that homeownership also be promoted through co-operatives and mutual housing. "Cohousing," pioneered in Denmark, is the latest word in such cooperative living and construction arrangements. In a cohousing venture, each family (or individual) owns or rents its own dwelling unit within the community. The units are similarly designed, low-rise homes arranged in rows or clusters. Each unit has less living space than a conventional private home to reduce expense and encourage the use of larger structures that include a kitchen and dining area, where common meals are regularly served, as well as children's play areas, laundry facilities, and so on. The community is also surrounded by common outdoor areas, such as green spaces, courtyards, soccer fields, and gardens. Though parking is available, it is not adjacent to the units but rather kept just within walking distance, making the settlement safer and encouraging interaction.

The cohousing community is managed only by residents, who all participate in committees or work groups. Though most of the existing communities arose from groups of friends who simply decided to change the way they lived, many of the residents have found cooperative decision making very difficult. Some people whose ideals diverge from those of the group leave. Yet most of the people who choose to join in this effort bring with them a vision of community that enables them eventually to accept the validity and utility of group decision making. These people find themselves uplifted through the process of democratic participation. Once residents of cohousing communities have endured the difficult process of interaction and affiliation, they usually move in and stay. The key problem in developing cohousing in Baltimore would be integrating the cohousing units into the larger neighborhood. In Sandtown, the condominiums developed by the Housing Assistance Corporation and SWIA on Fulton Avenue were very insular. The homeowners' association that developed inside the condominiums was too detached from the community outside, and caused a good deal of resentment. The organizers of the Sandtown project want to avoid such results.

The Economic Dimension

The residential phase of the project will be complemented by employment opportunities generated by development schemes planned for the area just across North Avenue in Penn North. As part of the scheme, Penn North has been designated an enterprise zone and will receive some of the Nehemiah money for economic development, particularly along the Pennsylvania Avenue corridor, where property is already being acquired. Sandtown's stretch of Pennsylvania Avenue once boasted extensive wholesale produce concerns. Some of the wholesalers have left, but the few warehouses that remain employ a considerable number of people. Present plans call for the remaining warehouses to be physically rehabilitated, while the deteriorating warehouses will be demolished to make room for other types of businesses. Unlike the businesses Schaefer recruited to the Inner Harbor Project, the new businesses slated to be developed in Penn North (such as light manufacturing and assembly facilities) will make extensive use of unskilled and semiskilled labor and will be able to employ large numbers of neighborhood people. The employment planning group for the Sandtown-Winchester Task Force, referring specifically to its desire to involve agencies like BOSS in Sandtown's economic and employment development, also expressed an intention to encourage the development of small business, microenterprises, and community jobs and skills. This is an important step, because these more basic devices can root the process of development into the community, creating informal economic networks through which the impact of development capital can be multiplied.

Thus, CBIP shifts the focus of economic development away from "big bang," large-scale, remotely located projects, like the Inner Harbor, which may broaden the tax base and create jobs, but which do not generate benefits that can "trickle down" to working people and the poor. Without an economic network connecting the lower economic levels with the upper ones at which "big bang" development intervention occurs, "trickle down" cannot take place. A greater emphasis on networking and mentoring, and a determined attempt to engage voluntary associations such as churches and community-based organizations in operational activities, will strengthen the impact of these projects.

Building on the utility and accessibility of small businesses, microenterprise loan funds and community-based organizations will not only develop viable self-employment options for the disadvantaged, but also begin to revitalize the municipal economy. In a restructuring economy, expanding self-employment opportunities is as important to economic vitality and competitiveness as it is to the goal of greater economic opportunity for all our citizens. Microenterprises can reno-vate a municipal economy at the most basic level, providing self-employment for the economically marginal and revitalizing urban markets by creating as well as meeting demand. The potential impact of self-employment includes the generation of additional businesses and jobs induced by the new role models, revitalized communities, new attitudes, and changed institutions. And, not insignificantly, eco-nomic networks created at the lower levels of an economy can help funnel down the benefits of "big bang" interventions that take place closer to the top.

Athena Young of Sandtown was one of the stronger students in the first BOSS microenterprise class. Before coming to BOSS, she had al-ready developed plans for a business, but kept getting turned down by the banks. Figuring that if she had a house for collateral, they might lend her money, she started looking into city programs for low-income homeownership. To her disappointment, she found that "low-income" was something of a misnomer: in fact, no low-income person could afford the houses the city was offering. But her quest for a house induced her to network, and she learned these new skills rapidly. In the end, it may well be that the search for a house was more impor-tant to Young than getting the house. She learned how to call people and follow through and nail things down.

"The government agencies like the Urban Services Agency, that's where you start," she said. "But they can't solve your problem. The churches, they're mainly concerned about your soul, you know. They want you to pray before they'll give you anything. And the community organizations are so scattered. I'd like to see all these different sources come together so people wouldn't get so worn out going from place to place. The way it is now, it's really discouraging. So many people live with problems all their lives. Others go to social services for one thing, then to the churches for another. Once the problem is solved, though, they become complacent again."

Networking among business, financial, social service, women's, community development, and neighborhood groups can provide in-valuable contacts for the microentrepreneur. Networking, which is fa-cilitated in the black community by a command of the vernacular, can directly link an individual's capacity to produce with available re-sources and with consumer demand. Such relationships can reduce unprofitable competition, increase program efficiency, create more ef-fective program targeting, enhance credibility, and, therefore, produce better results. Community-based organizations provide not only clients, a local economy, physical space, and fiscal and social supports, but also political support for microenterprise development, building coalitions around economic issues and advocating supportive policies from City Hall. A good training/mentor program can help link these community business and social networks together.

Bernita Holsey of BOSS argued that microenterprises, once begun, can better withstand pressures due to economic reversals than the giant multinational behemoths can.

"With big business, it's the line they're in or nothing. That's the reason for all those suicides during the Depression. That's why they have to get bigger—to diversify, to hedge their bets. But that makes them bureaucratic and unmanageable. And then they're right back where they started. But small business people are very resourceful," she said, with a wry smile. "Especially blacks. They may be limited in terms of sales, but they can still make quick shifts, moving easily from selling food to computer programming to elder and day care, for example."

Small businesses can "think faster, change more quickly, establish better internal communication, and tailor their products and services to smaller markets."[3] Home-grown businesses, cottage industries, service companies, small stores, design firms, and contract manufacturers "fly under the commercial radar of the big corporations, free to create their market niche."[4] Microenterprise development is a community strategy that enhances and utilizes existing human and capital resources, and it proceeds best when microentrepreneurs are networked together. Thus, an alternative paradigm for economic development is presented—a people-centered, do-it-yourself endeavor that proceeds in incremental steps.

BOSS trainees are quick to shift gears if an initial idea does not seem feasible. Athena Young's first business idea was a candystore, for example, but when it proved infeasible, she switched to preparing herself to do desktop publishing for community organizations. It was her focus on community service that remained constant. She wanted to stay in Sandtown and give something back. She wanted to be a local role model, and prove that someone from the neighborhood could accomplish something. She first thought of the candystore because she remembered the black owners of the corner store on the block where she grew up. They got up every day and went to work.

These are the kind of upwardly mobile working-class and lower-middle-class people who do not live in the community any more. "They're extinct, a dying breed," said Young."There's nothing for kids to relate to. Kids don't really want to learn negative behavior; there's just no other examples available. But we're re-learning. If you sweep out in front of your door, pretty soon other people start doing it, too. It makes an impression. We've got to do more of that."

Young often talks about her community and how it could be pushed in a positive direction. "Don't drive people away from your stoop if they're sitting there. Talk to them." Of all the BOSS students, she was probably the most excited about the prospect of pursuing her business goals in the context of her own neighborhood. She is not one of the elderly civic ladies, the "grandmother types" that Morris Iles referred to as running the churches and the neighborhoods, and that Arthur Murphy described as the backbone of the city's black electoral strength. She is not retired. She is raising children and trying to make a living, yet she still finds the time to be involved in her community.

Though the CBIP Economic Development Task Force states as one of its objectives the promotion of entrepreneurship among community residents and the development of a merchants' association, members are still focusing more on the kind of high-profile, "big bang" projects that can be carried forward only with significant government assistance. Microenterprise approaches should also be stressed, however, because they can be duplicated in communities without the tremendous influx of public funds that Sandtown has recently experienced. Young, for example, felt a need to find the entrepreneurs who are working out of their homes and have not reached the level of setting up shop in a separate building. The first step is probably to contact the street vendors who come out to North Avenue, one of Sandtown's two main commercial thoroughfares. Another possibility is to use community bulletin boards, such as those set up in supermarkets. Observing that several young men in the neighborhood cut hair in their homes, Young wondered whether the barbers and beauty parlor owners of the community might be willing to teach some of their skills at the Resource Center conceived as part of the Nehemiah Project.

This led us to a discussion of the concept of a skills bank, described by the Community Information Exchange in Washington, D.C. A key technique for economic networking, a skills bank or skills exchange is a registry of people signed up to sell, rent, or barter their products, services, tools, machinery, or working space, specifying in advance what they have to offer, the time it will be available, and any other conditions they have set for the exchange. By setting up a skills bank, a community-based organization can match residents' skills with residents' needs, facilitate work on community projects, develop a referral file for employment outside the community, and generally raise the level of mutuality in the neighborhood. Registrants can also be solicited from outside the community—from service agencies, area colleges and universities, businesses and corporations. Or the system can be designed to encourage bartering among community residents alone. A barter system works best when it is not limited to an exchange between person A and person B, but rather sets up a banking system in which A's service to B earns him or her a credit that can be used to "purchase" services from any participant in the skills bank. The credits are based on a dollar figure for the work done. Operating the skills bank is a fairly low-cost endeavor, requiring perhaps a half-time staff person and some minimal printing, mailing, and telephone costs. Part of the Sandtown project involves re-creating public schools as part of the support network for the entire community, and a public school might be a good place for a skills bank to be housed. The skills bank concept can also be expanded to include a learning exchange, in which people share their skills or teach "perspective" courses on religion or philosophy, environmental concerns, creative writing, and the like.

The Civic Dimension

In the Spring of 1990, when the CBIP planning process was announced, Athena Young was one of the four hundred Sandtown residents who attended the community meeting. She was attracted to the idea of the public school as a community resource center, the use of task forces to implement the visions expressed in the meeting, and the "Afrocentric, holistic approach." The critical challenge for the CBIP project at the outset was to retain such community interest and involvement. Too much city and Enterprise staff intervention, and the residents would feel the job was going to be done for them. Not enough, and the residents would feel abandoned and apathetic.

"It's very important to find and cultivate the informal leadership of the community," Darnell Ridgley observed. "The formal leaders are the homeowners, the stable folk—the people who are articulate, the people who have something. They're very important—they are the

traditional leadership of the black community, and we're lucky to
have them. Too many of them leave the community, abandoning the
struggle. But the only way the process of empowerment can continue
is if new leadership continues to surface, not always to stand out in
front, but also to fill in the gaps, to maintain communications and
dialogue among all the people in the community."

Ridgley summed up her task in the spring of 1991 as follows:
"Empowerment means teaching people how to take care of themselves. People are ready to work hard and want to be recognized for
what they do, but they also want limits. You have to know how to
move from the conceptual to the concrete; otherwise you lose people.
Few people want to sit and plan for four, five hours. People have to go
to their jobs and work, you have to understand this. We've been
working people to death [in the CBIP planning process] since October
of 1990. It's important not to waste people's time; you can't get them
all stirred up with last-minute proposals. A facilitator needs skills to
deal with community people in this kind of process to keep them
involved over a long period of time."

The key to successful social action is to insure that the process
remains community-driven. Ridgley advised starting with the formal
leadership and beginning a process that enables one to discover the
informal leadership, and recruit them as well. Personal contact is
very important, and the contact must be maintained. An additional
component, obviously beyond what government can supply, is the
spiritual direction needed for lifestyle changes that can reduce sus-
ceptibility to drugs and crime, and increase motivation for school
achievement. From the outset of CBIP, Ridgley was convinced that
city and Enterprise staff should not be at the center of this process.
She felt that mediating institutions such as churches, social clubs,
and community centers were vital partners.

By the Summer of 1991, Darnell Ridgley was no longer project
manager for CBIP. She had earlier proved very useful to the mayor in
managing the Community Development Block Grant program, and she
was reassigned to that program when problems surfaced between
HUD and the city administration. At the same time, Barbara Bostick,
the former warden of the city jail, was assigned essentially to take
Ridgley's place at CBIP. Arnie Graf of BUILD mentioned that the sym-
bolism of making a former prison official the head of citizen empowerment was, at best, unfortunate. Some community leaders, formal and
informal, complained that Bostick seemed removed from the process

and from the people, and apparently more comfortable with the technocrats and professionals Enterprise had brought in to the project.

CBIP's overall objective was to build a "viable, working community in which neighborhood residents are empowered to direct and sustain the physical, social, and economic development of their community." All public and private support systems were to be focused on this objective, creating a community "fulfilling to existing residents, which provides for community economic self-determination, while also being attractive to potential new residents." The CBIP work groups established in October 1990 were followed by a meeting in May 1991 to mobilize community residents once again and involve them in an intensive "charrette," or planning process, to review the results of the work groups and chart Sandtown's future development. Attendance at this meeting was disappointing, however, down to 150 people, despite organizing efforts by SWIA and BUILD during the summer of 1990. The staff and leadership of the various task forces met, discussing issues with those community residents and others who were present. Although attendance was disappointing, community representatives and city and Enterprise staff forged on, formulating plans in all key areas.

After this second CBIP community meeting, Athena Young became very concerned. The poor turnout seemed to have undercut the meeting's usefulness as a means of ascertaining community wishes. It had not been sufficiently advertised, more flyers should have gone out, more doors been knocked on, she insisted. Apparently many others who attended that day felt so as well. Thus, despite the energy of "informal" leaders like Young, the CBIP concept began losing ground. Without continuous and extensive community participation, physical redevelopment started getting ahead of economic development, and civic development lagged even further behind. Housing was being built, but the "social infrastructure" that was supposed to be the showpiece of the project was at a standstill. BUILD was only peripherally involved. The project was being carried forward mainly by Enterprise and the city, and Enterprise was taking the lead.

Angela Murray (a pseudonym) is an executive of one of the foundations Enterprise has solicited for funds for its "social infrastructure" project in Sandtown. She was troubled by Enterprise's ever-expanding role there and led me to believe that others in the foundation circle felt the same. "Enterprise shouldn't be growing," she said. "They've got holding companies to handle all the money they receive, they're becoming big conglomerates. They're developing relationships with banks, not with people. They're not about empowerment, or if they are, they don't know how to go about it. They should be creating capacity in communities. Instead, they're developing capacity in themselves, and the communities that they go into have to keep asking them to come back to do the work. My impression of Enterprise in Sandtown is that they're being very heavy-handed. The community people that they trot out look like window dressing. It seems as if Schmoke's people are hardly involved at all. Enterprise is running the whole show."

"Jim Rouse is really getting on in years, and he's not really the CEO of Enterprise any more," a Baltimore community organizer, who asked to remain anonymous, told me. "He wants Enterprise to focus on social and community development, not just physical development, and he's picked one man, Pat Costigan, to make that happen. The only place they're doing it is in Baltimore, so they have a lot on the line. Costigan's approach has been to try to get lots of financial support for the project, bringing in lots of other foundations and philanthropic groups." (A mark of Enterprise's power, and its approach, seems to be its ability to create critics who wish to remain anonymous.)

Athena Young, speaking as a community representative at a briefing held by Enterprise for perhaps two dozen foundation executives, warned that focusing on physical development alone was like building a shiny new car for the Sandtown community without providing the means to maintain it. "Without oil, that car won't run, it will break down quickly. The oil is the soul and spirit of the community, brought to the project by active, continuous participation," she said. But Enterprise and the city continued to fall short on bringing in the community. Roslyn Branson, former head of Family START, a federal and state-funded social service coordination project on the edges of Sandtown, was engaged by the city as a part-time consultant to work on improving relationships with the community. Yet Branson herself had left Family START amid allegations that she could not effectively reach out to community people. Young told me in February 1992 that as far as the community was concerned, the ball had simply been dropped.

"Things were really jumping in the beginning. Now we don't hear anything from anybody. They are just not letting people in the community know what is going on. They respond to my calls now, because I guess they think I'm a troublemaker. But other people just get ignored. Harold, you've got to feed people every day," she said. "They need attention and recognition. You can't just throw them a scrap every couple of months and expect them to believe that things are changing. They have to feel it as part of their lives. Coming in every couple of months and spending a lot of money to rally people just won't do it."

Darnell Ridgley, before her departure, recognized that support for community organizing and development is essential. Support systems have to be rebuilt in black communities, devastated by the loss of middle-class leadership and institutional leverage. "All black children are affected by what is happening in low-income black communities today," Ridgley maintained. "Sandtown is a good place to start. It is a real community, with all the problems, all the history, and a tradition of solidarity, of dealing with problems within the borders of the community." Until she left the Sandtown Project, Ridgley expected eventually to expand the formal leadership of Sandtown with a permanent management structure that would represent an ongoing commitment on the part of the city (ideally, the Mayor or a representative was to be a member): a large pool of community people trained in reading budgets and balance sheets, meeting procedures, and the like. She hoped for a sortition process (rotating leadership) so that a large number of these trained community people would actually participate in the process of CBIP governance.

"Community involvement must go beyond block parties and health fairs," Ridgley said. "People must have something to do, must feel needed. Many of their differences will be resolved in the context of collaborative work." She wanted the community contingent in the management structure formally divided into a board, which would meet with outside funding sources and policymakers, and a much larger community advisory group, from which board members would be selected and to which the board would remain responsible, perhaps through a periodic vote of confidence. The advisory board would be strengthened by rotating leadership and continual leadership training. Advisory board members would have to keep records so that those who took their places would not lose the history of what had happened on the board to date. Ridgley wanted the community to invest itself in the project and keep reinvesting. The community advisory board would provide the board of directors with its mandate to speak for the community on external matters. The management structure as a whole was to have responsibility for determining which aspects of the community plan would be acted upon first. As plans were implemented, the management group would have to keep track of programs as they evolved and changed, trying wherever possible to latch on to and build upon what already existed in the community.

In the spring of 1992, with Ridgley gone, Barbara Bostick representing the city, and Enterprise running the show, this projected governance structure based on a compact between the "parties" (the community, the city, the Enterprise Foundation, SWIA, BUILD, and the Urban League) seemed far off indeed. The stakes had gone up for all players because Sandtown (along with Washington, D.C.) had been named as the site for the 1992 Jimmy Carter Community Work Project, in collaboration with Habitat for Humanity International, with which former First Lady Rosalyn Carter is affiliated. Jimmy and Rosalyn Carter were scheduled to work with Sandtown Habitat during a "blitz" construction of ten homes in June 1992, the first phase of a 100-house joint venture between Sandtown Habitat and the Enterprise Foundation. Their preliminary site visit in March of 1992, with the press, the city staff, and the neighborhood organizations and churches all agog, exposed the fault lines in the "partnership" that had been constructed in Sandtown.

While Enterprise and the city told everyone that BUILD was handling the community-organizing aspect of the project, Reverend Dobson and Gary Rodwell, BUILD's lead organizer, insisted to me that BUILD was not consulted, not involved, and had been marginalized in the process. "That just sets us up," Dobson remarked. "I've got to talk to Jim Rouse and tell him that we're pulling out unless we are involved, and permitted to do the kind of job that we're really capable of."

Ella Johnson, the chair of SWIA, is a large black woman with graying hair, a determined, almost professorial manner, and a delightfully sweet voice. It took many telephone calls to find a time when Johnson was not rushing off to one meeting or another. As she moved wearily into the conference room where our interview was to take place, slowly sat down, and began to speak about the prospects for Sandtown-Winchester under CBIP, she seemed physically burdened by the weight of many disappointments.

"There are twelve thousand people in Sandtown. The people in Sandtown who have been involved in the CBIP process are the most well-off," she said. "The people who own their own homes, or have a job. Even the people who get helped by Habitat, Allan Tibbels' group, are folks who have a job, or who have a history of employment. The working poor in our neighborhood come out and sweep the streets, but even they are a far cry from the most damaged people. All the folks who are converging on our community in the CBIP process have a very limited idea of what community involvement really means. We've got to reach way down deep, get those people who have almost given up, to really make a difference here. Otherwise you're always skimming the cream off the top, and people get the idea that something's happening in the community, but it's not happening for them. It's nice that the mayor is around a lot, [presidential candidate Bill] Clinton came to Sandtown, that's more attention than the community has had for a long time. But there's been no money to dig deep into Sandtown, to reach the really poor, since Reagan was elected.

"Nehemiah, big as it is, is still only 273 new housing units. Over the last seven or eight years, 580 units have been added to the community. These units have helped the people who got them, but they haven't had an effect outside the block where they've been built." She rested her head against her hands, folded in front of her, as if she was offering a prayer. "Sandtown is really poor. There are lots of problems, high unemployment, female-headed households. People don't realize how serious it is. Folks have been on social services for a long time. You don't turn that around overnight. It will take five or six years before you see any difference at all. CBIP will address lots of these problems together, holistically, and that's very exciting. But it's going to take a long time, and continuous work, before you see any results you can measure."

Earlier that morning, I had met Barbara Bostick and Pat Costigan. The meeting was held in Costigan's office, and he ran the meeting. A red-haired, intense Irish-American with metal-rimmed spectacles and the breezy manner of an executive, he was all business. "We need to get this project evaluated," he said. "We've got to show our funders and supporters a base line, where we began, and a successive track record of what we've achieved, how far we've come."

Bostick, on the other hand, was hesitant, almost demure throughout the meeting. Slightly built and fastidiously dressed, with a soft voice, she spoke for another constituency in CBIP—the Mayor's Office. Her primary concern was that the expectations of Sandtown people not be raised to unrealistic levels, that all the major players in CBIP stay in the game, that no one leave the table or take offense.

Put the four major players together at one table—the city, Enterprise, SWIA, and BUILD—and you have four very different approaches to the community's problems, four different, strongly held mindsets about what the problem is and how it should be approached. Perhaps the starkest contrast was between Ella Johnson and Pat Costigan. Johnson, with the weight of experience, starts and stops, many failures and that minimal number of successes necessary to keep her and her group going, was sure that the renovation of Sandtown's social and civic infrastructure, its sense of community, and its quality of life, was going to take a long time and would be hard to measure. Costigan, in a hurry, pressured by his supervisors and funders to show quick results to justify the money being spent and to qualify for more, was talking about evaluating a process that, in Johnson's view, had barely begun.

BUILD, for its part, is unwilling even to stay at the table as long as organizing is not going on. Ella Johnson told me that SWIA had begun an effort in February 1991, during Darnell Ridgley's tenure at CBIP, to organize Sandtown block by block, to counter the disappointing results of organizing attempts under CBIP during the summer of 1990. "We were looking at four- and five-square block areas," she said. "The people were starting to see the problems of the whole community by starting with the problems on their own block. We had people working on cleaning up their streets, we had citizen building inspectors starting up, people had something to do, they were getting involved. Then we were going to link them up to look at things that affected everybody—crime, vacant houses, things like that."

It was in May of 1991 that the disappointing second charrette was held, and, soon after, Enterprise staff and city staff proceeded ahead, apparently assuming the community had lost interest. Ironically, it was this development and others like it which followed that left community people feeling shut out and apathetic, in a sort of self-fulfilling prophecy. Then the foundations came in to observe, and they wanted to know, 'Where was the community?' So Enterprise and city staff had to go back to the drawing board on community involvement.

"There are powerful players here," said Johnson. "Smaller groups like SWIA are getting shoved around, elbowed out of the process. Even the city doesn't have the leverage it used to. Under Model

Cities, federal money used to go right to the mayor. Now, it goes to a joint venture that Enterprise is part of, and the city doesn't have the final say as to how the money gets spent or how the project proceeds. And groups like Enterprise are still making developers' profits and drawing all the talent that used to go to city administrations."

Johnson echoed my own thoughts. Earlier in the day, Costigan and Bostick had wanted to know what I thought of the CBIP process, from what I had seen so far. "There's an old African proverb," I told them. "When elephants fight, the grass gets trampled. What I see is a set of four really powerful players—Enterprise, the city, SWIA, and BUILD—struggling to make CBIP come out right from their own institutional perspectives. They create a pretty strong wind at the top. If the process isn't rooted really deeply into the community, it will be blown right over. I think you have some catching up to do on the ground. I don't think that you should feel particularly disappointed that more progress hasn't been made in organizing the community in that way, because very few people know how to do that."

"Yeah," said Costigan ruefully. "Every time we turn around, some graduate student pops up who's just done his Ph.D. thesis on community organizing and thinks he knows how it's done. That's why we've tried to keep this quiet, why we haven't marketed it yet. Lots of people want to jump on board the train as soon as they see it's rolling. There's a great deal of organizing capacity in Sandtown—the churches, the service agencies with outreach functions, formal and informal leadership. There's lots of history, lots of agendas. We want the whole thing to come together, create unity out of diversity. That's why we wanted to hold off on the organizing until the community came up with a vision. Then we could fill in the details."

It was, of course, the decision to have large meetings, develop a vision out of such meetings, and then narrow participation to small planning groups that created the perception in the community that nothing was going on, that they had been hoodwinked, again.

"We're struggling to keep the top-down stuff from taking over," Bostick said. "We know it can't be a quick fix. But we had to do some programmatic things right away, so people could see some results. Things are happening. We're advertising jobs in the community newsletter, and the Urban League tells us that there's a pride in people's voices now, when they call in for jobs that must be filled by Sandtown residents. 'I'm from Sandtown,' they say.

"We tended to work with the vocal and articulate people to make things happen, to get the newsletter out, get the word out," she continued. "Now we've got to make it clear that we haven't anointed those people as community leaders. We know the process hasn't served the whole community yet. We wanted to go door-to-door with that newsletter; we had five thousand copies printed. But we just didn't have the personnel. We're hoping it will get circulated and recirculated throughout the community. There are so many people beyond the most vocal, people we don't even know about. We're trying to find a comfort level here. Like Pat says, there are so many experts, so many people wanting to get involved, we don't know when to say, "Enough." Someone is always showing up, like you, who has something we need to hear. There is a wealth of knowledge, a lot of networking going on, people giving us their cards, telling us to call them if we need anything. When do we reach closure? We don't want this to be another letdown for community people, like the old urban renewal efforts in Harlem Park. What happens after Kurt Schmoke isn't mayor any more? Sandtown will still be there."

Costigan shared with me a newspaper article that Jim Rouse, founder of Enterprise, wrote for the *Miami Herald* on transforming the lives of the poor. (Enterprise has a project in Miami as well.) The letter emphasized the approach Rouse and Enterprise know best: bringing public and private resources to bear on changing the physical and social service dimension of the community. Thus, the conditions in which community pride and involvement can grow are created. The agenda for the physical and service transformation comes out of a planning process in which community leaders and volunteers work with experienced professionals. Yet the Rouse/Enterprise method, as it has developed in Sandtown, has too much of what Harry Boyte describes as the "therapeutic" approach, and not enough of the "empowerment" approach. In the therapeutic approach, experts define and diagnose the problem, generate the language and labels for talking about it, propose the therapeutic or remedial techniques for problem-solving, and evaluate whether the problem has been solved. In such approaches, community involvement is placed in the framework of representative rather than participatory democracy. Even in the middle-class milieu of everyday politics, people are demanding more accountability from and contact with their leadership. In a community in which the civic and social fabric has deteriorated as much as it has in Sandtown, even more contact and involvement is required.

As of the spring of 1992, Enterprise's priorities for community involvement and organizing were plain in its draft report on CBIP, which Costigan showed me so that I would have complete information from all sides. The report revealed only a relatively small amount of money ($80,000) allocated for community organizing, and there were indications that community organizing would be relegated to the later stages of the CBIP process.[5] The report referred to community organizing as "subjective" (and presumably less important).[6] Clearly, it was these subjective elements of CBIP for which it was most difficult to secure funding, because business, government, and foundation personnel want to be able to measure results in quantitative terms. In this way the money that was available for CBIP probably drove the process. Enterprise directed its funding pitch, apparently, to where staff thought patrons wanted their money to go—for physical development and social services. Less funding was requested for community organizing than for any other item save community surveyors, sanitation training and education, and the community newsletter. The impression one gets on reading the CBIP draft report is of a top-down process with a therapeutic spin to it—service, but not empowerment.

In a community of twelve thousand people, a great many more than two hundred have to be continuously involved to make the process work. Jim Rouse's *Miami Herald* piece brimmed with enthusiasm and energy about CBIP because he was directly involved, making decisions, meeting people, networking, getting feedback, being challenged. Rouse and others like him who engage, admirably, in tackling the problems of poor people need to understand the need to share with community people the prestige of being identified as a person with something to contribute, of being presented with a problem and trying to solve it. Many people in the community must have access to such experience. Street fairs, charrettes, and mass meetings will not accomplish this. It was time for the city and Enterprise to resume block-by-block organizing. If that was not done, it would not matter how much money was funneled into the project—a great many people were going to be very disappointed in the results. At a later meeting with Costigan, Bostick, and Lenny Jackson, a canny, sharp SWIA organizer who has been hired for CBIP by the Mayor's Office, I was informed that CBIP's budget for community organizing had been tripled.

In Sandtown, an attempt is being made to rebuild the social as well as the physical infrastructure of one of Old West Baltimore's most famous neighborhoods. Government officials, church leaders, community organizers, and nonprofit foundation executives have come together in an uneasy alliance to accomplish this objective. It is clear that there are many obstacles and that all the players have a lot to learn about the Sandtown community as well as about each other. Many wrong turns will be taken before the right path is found. The stakes are high, and the results, whether success or failure, will be far-reaching. The key factor is the involvement of the community, its existing institutions, and its remaining vernacular strength.

Chapter Eight
Base Communities:
Citizen Action
at the Grassroots

The power does not reside simply in the culture but in
the forms of organization that our ancestors have handed over to us.
If we exist today [as a people], it is because there is something
in our traditions that has helped us continue living.

—Juanita Vazquez, liberation theologian

ALTHOUGH organizations like BUILD are necessary to create new frameworks for citizen action in the public sphere, particularly in setting public agendas and formulating public policy, something smaller, more indigenous, more flexible, and more intimate is required for policy to be implemented on a daily basis, to be rooted deep into a community. When the large rallies and meetings are over, when the organizers have gone home for the night or have taken off for the weekend, there must *still* be a reason for people to continue to participate. Otherwise the same special interests that tend to subvert the formulation of public policy in the therapeutic state will surely subvert the implementation of policy as well. Without support and reinforcement from a peer group, even "informal leaders" like Athena Young are reluctant to get involved: there is too much intrigue, too much hassle, too much energy wasted. Politics, Young told me, is populated with people who do it just as a job, "wimps" who want good things but cannot get them done, and "devil's advocates," who are evil and try to make things as difficult as possible. The residents of Sandtown will need a stronger sense of their own power if they are to take charge of the CBIP process and rebuild their community's social and civic life. If more is to occur in Sandtown than renovation of its physical plant and economic environment, community residents will first need access to the kinds of empowerment techniques BUILD organizers are skilled at teaching. But they will also need something more: participation in small, intimate "base communities," peer groups of a dozen or two dozen people, in which they can evaluate the day's struggles, commiserate with one another's failures, celebrate success, and plan for the next day's fight. This kind of personal, intimate contact with trusted others is a necessary building block for Harry Boyte's "third way" of citizen engagement. Citizens involved in public debate must also have a safe harbor in which they can try out their opinions and receive succor and support for the bruising public combat Boyte describes. Families are not large or diverse enough to perform such a function. Churches are too large. The contact must take place in a new, smaller form of association in some ways similar to the social units liberation theologians in Latin America have called *comunidades eclesiales de base*, which translates as "ecclesiastical base communities," or simply "Christian base communities."

Base Communities: Origins and Utility

Base communities started from a variety of experiments with small-group Bible study in Europe and Latin America, primarily among Catholics. After the Second Vatican Council, priests and nuns organizing in small communities in Latin America during the 1960s began using the Bible to guide small groups in reflecting on the spiritual dimension of community organizing. In other cases, social action grew out of Bible study itself.[1] Carlos Mesters, a Latin American liberation theologian, pointed out in "The Use of the Bible in Christian Communities of the Common People" that the "text" (the Bible) had to be discussed in the "con-text" of the community, bearing in mind the "pre-text," that is, the physical conditions in which the community existed. He concluded:

> When the [base] community takes shape on the basis of the real-life problems of the people, then the discovery of the Bible is an enormous reinforcement.
>
> When the community take shape only around the reading of the Bible, then it faces a crisis as soon as it must move on to social and political issues. . . .
>
> It doesn't matter much where you start. You can start with the Bible, or with the given community, or with the real-life situation of the people and their problems. The important thing is to do all you can to include all three factors.[2]

Under these conditions, Mesters stated, "the word of God becomes a reinforcement, a stimulus for hope and courage. Bit by bit it helps people to overcome their fears."[3]

The base communities of Latin America were truly revolutionary instrumentalities. Working with passages from the Bible, rural and parish priests and nuns first gave the poor and downtrodden a sense of self-worth, a sense that God loved them, not just the rich for whom the established Church seemed designed. Once that point was made, it was only a matter of time before the people began to see that individual human beings who have self-worth should not be subjected to dehumanizing conditions: grinding poverty, disease, violence, and lack of economic opportunity. This was not Christian treatment. In El Salvador, the base community response to such treatment was nonviolent; it involved preaching the message of self-worth to more and more people. When the military government responded by trying to stop the movement, in some cases assassinating priests and members of the base communities, the communities pressed on, just as civil rights workers pressed on in the United States in the past, just as Eastern Europeans and Russians pressed on in the face of government repression before the disintegration of the USSR.[4]

The importance of base communities does not lie in the radical, quasi-Marxist class analysis with which they are associated in many people's minds. This type of analysis may very well have been appropriate for the conditions faced by the Latin American poor, but no analysis of their condition would have made sense to them unless they first felt worthy of a better life. It was the joint interpretation and celebration of the hopeful messages of the Bible that empowered these people, giving them a sense of direction and purpose as well as a sense of self-worth. As Pablo Galdamez put it in 1983, "Our communities started with people. People looking for salvation. Salvation that went by the name of happiness, friendship, love, justice and peace. A great number of people in El Salvador were looking for this, because they didn't have it."[5]

Practical considerations determine the size of a base community. It should be small enough that its members can learn from one another and share a common vision or goal, yet large enough to realize, or at least approach, the goal. The optimal size allows a level of participation that gives individuals a sense of identity and self-realization, and an area of control separated from opposing values that may detract from their goals. This situation should not be secured simply by excluding "undesirables," however. A principled basis for exclusion from and inclusion in the group itself is as important as the standards of conduct observed by each member.

Members of a base community come together in friendship and cooperative activity, their livelihoods and sense of being, of personhood, somehow defined, refined, reinforced, by the group. Such people might be found today in a microentrepreneurs' peer-lending circle, in a Bible study group, among Afrocentric cultural activists cooperating in a foodstore, or in a group of environmental activists. A base community might spring up in a small firm of civil rights lawyers, in a core group of activist ministers, in a collective of low-income housing activists, or among parents of sixth-graders in an elementary school. They might be discovered among the alumni of a law school clinical education program, members of a family reunion group, residents of a cohousing settlement, or a team of lobbyists from different public interest organizations. Nursing mothers' support groups or nonprofit social service organizations might be another location. Wherever people are coming together to engage positively with their own living conditions and the conditions of those around them, peer groups of informal leaders are emerging and networking among themselves, often across what appear to be very diverse issue areas. In such a fashion, base communities are formed.

Nurturing intimate bonds within a neighborhood (or, by extension, a church or a unit of government), essential to the development of base communities, may seem at first antithetical to the development of political clout in representative democratic structures.[6] It is, after all, to a society of strangers that Locke's message was addressed.[7] And it is a society of diverse strangers who have learned how to deal with one another (albeit at arm's length) that, for Matthew Crenson and Harry Boyte, constitutes the source of political strength and vitality. Indeed, diversity and friction may make government work more vigorously than social uniformity and friendship. Representative government seems to function best when society itself proceeds in representative fashion—when a relatively small number of highly developed individuals come forward to manage social life, while the large majority of lesser folk acquiesce.

Lateral political relationships, with a social character, actually impede representative government. Perhaps "unresolvable" disagreements with neighbors encourage us to lose ourselves in the anonymity of representative society.[8] Laterally integrated neighborhoods, churches, and even governmental units, characterized by a great deal of informal political discourse among equals may well prove impotent in a representative government context.[9] Clout in a representative democratic system seems to flow to neighborhoods and churches which are dominated by upper-status people and in which little lateral political discourse is permitted to detract from the vertical political integration necessary to function effectively and efficiently in a representative government milieu.[10] The more powerful a neighborhood or church is, the more "vertically integrated" it is—that is, people identify with, and follow, their leadership.

But clout in the representative democratic milieu is not the sole objective of people who form base communities. Rather, it is *community* in the sense of lateral integration, making constant resort to the hierarchical structures of representative government (and the market) less compelling. Shorn of its Marxist trappings, and contextualized for urban North America, the base community model idea is cousin to the "free spaces" described by Sara Evans and Harry Boyte: physical and social locations in which people can develop the strength and capacity and definition necessary to challenge the dominant hierarchical matrix of the public and private bureaucracies with which they must contend. The importance of vernacular culture is particularly relevant as we look at the creation of base communities. As Boyte puts it, one of the strongest themes of democratic, participatory social movements has been the "repair and revitalization of memories, communal ties, and voluntary associations weakened by modern corporate and bureaucratic institutions," especially the "buried insurgent elements" in such traditions.[11] Base communities are cells that root deeper into human life the vitality Boyte sees in the "third way" of citizen engagement in public affairs.

Baltimore, like any other city, is too large to be a base community. Contrary to the observations of Gerald Frug, the shared interests that allow people to overcome feelings of alienation are overwhelmed by a city's diversity.[12] Most people are incapable of forming an emotional and intellectual bond on such a large scale. Further, Matthew Crenson demonstrates that even neighborhoods, while more conducive to participatory democracy than the city, are still too large and impersonal to be base communities. In fact, Crenson's book on neighborhood politics suggests that neighborhoods are polities, not communities, in which a kind of "social compact" emerges among residents who mutually recognize a common public and ethical space as "their" neighborhood.[13] Neighborhood is a "framework in which residents may begin to construct personal agendas of local problems and issues."[14] It is like a nation, a corporate, "ideological community" deliberately advocated, advanced, and constructed.[15] Baltimore is justly proud of its reputation as a city of neighborhoods, each with its own unique characteristics. Neighborhood organizations have been important catalysts for change throughout the years of the city's development. However, the type of intimacy and solidarity furnished by base communities has very little to do with neighborhood identity. The neighborhood is "turf" in the way that a nation is. Even the neighborhood, it seems, is too large and variegated to be held together by communitarianism.[16] Finally, most community organizations, though smaller than neighborhoods, are too acclimated to government and business hierarchies to form base communities. If our goal is participation, we will be disappointed if we rely solely on community-based organizations that use representative techniques to politically integrate their neighborhoods, and whose leaders minimize participatory activity, merely mobilizing their neighbors when a show of force is needed downtown.[17] This can be a problem as well with "megachurches," which can become insulated from outsiders by their own success.

Baltimore's Emerging Base Communities

On the West Side of Baltimore, peer groups that display some of the characteristics of base communities have already begun to develop. People involved in the various civic, community, and economic development activities of these Baltimore neighborhoods have gone a step further, and reached out in fraternity and sorority to their peers, beginning the process. Baltimore's base communities exist in many different forms and stages of development. They are not all religious, but all seem to be spiritual at one level or another. And, most importantly, they tap into the kind of networking that has traditionally been a great source of strength for the vernacular black community.

The BOSS Microentrepreneurs

I discovered that base communities were forming in Baltimore when I interviewed members of the founding group of students who participated in the BOSS microenterprise program. The interviews conveyed that the BOSS students were, above all, survivors and networkers.

Many of them also were civic-minded in the sense that they wished to give something back to the community. When they encounter a problem, they network. They go and talk to somebody, usually at some government agency, sometimes simply a friend, and they are referred to people who can help them.

"Just read the blue pages of the telephone book until you find some agency that's supposed to help," said Athena Young. "Maybe you make ten calls, but you'll get connected. Someone will help you." I remarked to Ameen Bahar, from Upton, that this advice reminded me of the fairy tales that have children meeting cruel and dangerous people but also fairy godmothers and helpful elves. "Sure," he said. "Fairy tales are all about education."

Bahar, natty and wiry, with a direct gaze and diffident manner, was wearing a three-piece suit when I interviewed him. He had been a room service operator for hotels—lots of hotels, here and there. "I was sick of working for other people," he said. A friend had told him, "Ameen, you're broke and you're working. Does that make sense?" So he decided to quit his job and go on welfare until he figured out what he was going to do. He had just gotten custody of his three-year-old son and wanted a new start. A neighbor got a letter from a social service agency telling her about the BOSS program, and she told Bahar about it.

"I've always been a supervisor or a manager," Bahar said. "I knew I was going to be my own boss one day." He wants to start a restaurant. He wants positive, successful people to come, who will be attentive to the entertainment and discussions that will go on there. He wants the restaurant to have a spiritual ambience, where people can focus on what needs to be done in his community, on the youth, and on other pressing issues. It will serve "Hilal" food, prepared in the Muslim style. "Not just physical food but food for the spirit and for the mind." (Immediately a name for the restaurant came into my mind—"Food For Thought.")

Jackie Turner, from Harlem Park, had her first networking experience about ten years ago when her mother's social security check was about to be cut drastically just as she had to go into the hospital. Turner went to the social service office and struggled to prevent the cut. She found out about options like the "home visit," and was referred from one person to another, finding several fairy godmothers and godfathers along the way. She did a complete follow-through on the job she had to do, not missing a detail. After that, she felt confident that she was a person who could get things done.

The students from the first class of the BOSS program are pioneers. They have a strong sense of mission. They consider themselves very fortunate; they want to succeed and to make it possible for more people to get the opportunities they have received; and they want to give something back to their communities. "We're capitalists," said one. "But we're concerned about the community, we want to show people that there's something better. And that doesn't mean getting on T.V. like Spike Lee and advertising sneakers that cost a hundred and fifty dollars. How are black kids going to get those shoes without stealing or selling drugs?"

The BOSS students are also very supportive of one another. "Being in this class is affecting the way I deal with my daughter," said one student, Joanne, from Park Heights. "I'm learning a lot. This is a social and cultural network, people are very close. Ameen is going to do a program to celebrate our graduation, a skit in December. We don't want anyone to fail. We'll never get another opportunity like this one."

The students had different views about whether everyone in the program would succeed or whether only some would. Bahar felt that it was very important that the students not become dependent on the program. "It was because we were trying to become independent that they were interested in us in the first place. We get free training here. It's up to us to put it to work. And we can't stop doing what we've always done to survive."

Networking is what they have always done, and they have not stopped. Athena Young and another BOSS student, Henrietta Walker, are organizing a support group for all the classes BOSS has graduated, a move that was precipitated by the troubles BOSS has encountered in implementing its microenterprise vision. About ten of the members of the first class, where perhaps the strongest bonds were created, began meeting regularly to try to provide a framework in which BOSS graduates and students could support one another, discuss their personal and professional problems, and perhaps begin to pool their resources to help each other or apply for grants to finance their projects. They were ready to go out on their own, with or without BOSS, and may still do so.

Young and Walker (whom Athena affectionately refers to as

"Mama Bear") are working hard to hold together the support group. "Henrietta is very people-oriented, very talkative. She can move in and adapt in many different circles much more quickly and fluently than I can," said Young. "Henrietta stays in touch with everybody. I don't know how she does it. I'm already feeling stretched really thin. I'm finding that I don't see my mother or my grandmother as much as I used to. I used to see Grandma three times a week; now it's down to once a week. My kids are complaining that I don't pay enough attention to them. I've really got to be careful."

The kind of overwork that Athena is experiencing is the result of too few people being involved in the work of sustaining community life. That is why it is important to bring in more people. The support group she and Henrietta are organizing should be very helpful to all of them. Thinking of the base communities in Latin America, I asked Athena whether she thought the BOSS support group would or should have a spiritual focus.

"I'm not connected with any church," Athena said. "My folks were all in the church, Baptist this, Baptist that. But I saw a lot of hypocrisy. Not among the people in the church so much as among the people who were the church leaders, and with the minister. I'm still plugged in by faith. I think that's what keeps the churches going, the faith of the people in them. When our BOSS support group gets going, if it's going to continue on for the other students who come out of the program in the future, it's going to have to have some kind of spirituality, some kind of spiritual base. It may not be the Bible specifically, but the spirituality will be here. In fact, among those of us who are starting the group, that spiritual bond already exists. Another thing—for the Sandtown project to work, there's going to have to be a spiritual awakening in the community. We're all going to have to get turned on to it."

The church is still the place where the "spiritual know-how," the vernacular community-building skills, primarily reside. For all its imperfections, no other institution survives that can provide that base. My wife has reminded me that churches are made up of people. "Your faith won't disappoint you, but the church as a structure may," she said. "It's especially hard for people who grow up in the church. They almost never continue in the church they grow up in, or else they take a long break." There are many for whom the church is still a home, however: churches in which social action, community empowerment, and spiritual renewal are intimately woven together in people's everyday lives. Following are some glimpses into a Muslim mosque in Upton, a BUILD member church in Sandtown, and the New Song interracial congregation, also in Sandtown.

Masjid Al-Haqq

Approaching the Masjid Al-Haqq, a "Black Muslim" mosque in Upton, on Wilson Avenue (renamed Islamic Way), I could hear the *muezzin* on a loudspeaker, calling the faithful to services, or *Juma*. It was a bright, sunny fall afternoon. As the services started, the sermon over the loudspeaker could be heard all around the immediate neighborhood. People on the streets seemed used to it, going about their business with the sermon in the background. Arabbers with their ponies and grocery carts stopped to sell fresh tomatoes and onions. People sat on their stoops, watching, listening.

"*Allah-u-Akbar*," the muezzin intoned. ("God is great.")

A tall, rangy brother with a walkie-talkie smiled and led me inside the masjid. He understood that I wanted to talk to the imam about community empowerment and community development in the Upton neighborhood. We took off our shoes and walked up the carpeted stairway, lined with older men selling books and scattered with young boys and girls in smocks and caftans, shawls and kufi hats. Inside, the brothers, lean and brown, faced the east corner of the masjid, looking comfortable in loose clothing, yet very disciplined, at attention. Their hands were workers' hands, rough and calloused. Their faces were determined, solemn. The women and children gathered on the opposite side, also facing east. They had beautiful, luminous brown skin, clear eyes, strong smiles, good, clean teeth. Babies and young children were passed around for hugs and care before the service and after.

The imam, William Shahid, a small, powerful man, was wearing a suit and a black kufi, and sported a gold-capped tooth. He was helpful and cooperative, like any good spiritual leader.

"*As salaam aleikum* [peace be with you]," he greeted me, clasping my hand firmly.

"*Wa-aleikum salaam* [and peace to you also]," I replied.

The imam told me of the elders in the mosque, sixty, even seventy years old, who had been Muslims for much of their lives and who had lived in Baltimore since they were born. Sister Shahidah, who joined in 1947. Charles Rashid, seventy years old, who joined in 1945, one of the founders of Islam in Baltimore. Louis Omar, a some-

what younger man who was an aide to Malcolm X and Louis Farrakhan in New York and then came to Baltimore. They would have
stories to tell. I arranged to return in about two weeks and begin
meeting people.

On my way out I met a young boy who was selling candy for a
dollar. I reached into my wallet but only had a ten. He had no
change. To get change we went downstairs, where members congre-
gated after the service and people sold books and food, and I immediately felt awash in the African vernacular. It was like being in one
of the old neighborhoods in Dakar, in Senegal, which is a Muslim
country in West Africa. The smells! The meals being fixed, as only
Muslims can. The bean pie! The books! The beautiful people!

When I returned to the masjid in two weeks and again attended
the *Juma*, I met several of the older members of the congregation.
Sister Jamillah, a beautiful old brown-skinned woman with a crinkly
smile and warm manner, told me I had a kind face and shared tales of
her trip to Mecca. "I made the *Hajj*," she told me proudly. "I've been
in Baltimore since 1941, when my folks came here from South Carolina, and I've been a Muslim since 1960. But I didn't do the *Hajj*
until 1986. I'll carry that experience with me the rest of my life. All
those people, facing east, all colors and ages and shapes and sizes. It
changed my whole life, my whole way of looking at things."

Waiting outside for *Juma* to start, I blended into the gathering
crowd. Men walked by and greeted me, shaking my hand. One of
them hugged me. Children poured out of two schoolbuses and lined
up in front of the masjid, laughing, talking. "They're from our
school," one of the brothers explained. "They just came from a field
trip to the Science Center. There are about seventy of them, grades K
through 8. Plus we have day care."

The school is not accredited, but they are working on that, and in
the meantime use the Montgomery County, Maryland, public school
curriculum. All the teachers (six, including the principal) have proper
teaching credentials. They are volunteers, but are given a stipend to
support themselves. Islam is stressed as part of the curriculum, but
the school is open to Muslim and non-Muslim children alike. Apparently, some of the children come from the Masjid Assafat, which is on
North Avenue. The imam later told me that they are looking for a
larger building for the school, and want to draw children from all four
of the masjids in Baltimore.

Inside, the *Juma* was quite an experience. Again, the women, girls, and infants separated to one side, while the men and boys old enough to walk took the other. This time I was able to observe the *Juma* from start to finish, and it was an impressive display of quiet discipline and communal prayer. There were several Arabs and one Caucasian in the congregation. The sermon, if you will, was on the necessity of aiding the poor and the unfortunate.

"That is our *deen*," the imam told the group. "It is our center, it is what we follow. It is who we are."

After the *Juma*, I talked with the imam for a while, and he introduced me to some more people. Then he said he would meet me downstairs later, so I went back down into the restaurant and lined up for some very good fried fish and string beans, yams, rice and gravy, bean pie, and punch. (I hadn't eaten breakfast or lunch, and it was about 2 p.m.) Shortly afterward, the imam joined me at the table.

"The masjid was founded in 1959, but the Nation of Islam community in Baltimore dates back to 1946," he said. "There were four different locations then. Now there are about a thousand people who come to the masjid, counting those who come every day, those who come every week, those who come once a month, those who come on big holidays like Ramadan. The usual *Juma* brings between two hundred and three hundred people. The masjid, packed, will hold five hundred."

In the 1960s and 1970s, like Black Muslim mosques all over the country, the masjid operated several businesses: it sold fish and newspapers and bean pies; it opened restaurants and clothing stores. People who worked for the masjid itself received a salary. The present imam was a schoolteacher for the masjid at that time, and he received a salary. But when Warith Muhammad (Elijah Muhammad's son) took over, he pronounced that the business of the Nation of Islam should not be making money or producing goods and services, but saving souls. (Like many other young African-Americans, I had been sharply disappointed when the Nation stopped those enterprises, which were a symbol of pride for everyone in the community. The imam's explanation clarified the objectives Warith Muhammad had been pursuing.) The businesses were sold to members of the masjid, who now operate them on their own, individually and in small groups. The masjid is now strictly a holy place, where the members come to focus themselves and receive spiritual guidance for their lives in the world.

Sharon Baptist Church

At the Sharon Baptist Church in Sandtown, similar tensions between the spiritual and the material worlds must be confronted. The Reverend Alfred Vaughn and Sharon Baptist Church are new members of the BUILD organization. Reverend Vaughn sketched out for me how the formation of smaller groups *within* Sharon Baptist was the key to the church's work.

"We reach out to senior citizens, helping them form their own peer groups. They talk about how to get medical benefits and social security, and arrange visits by government officials and experts to answer their questions. We also get young people in our church to "adopt" elders. Many of the elders have great gifts they can pass on. Many of them volunteer. They only need to feel that they are needed. It gives them new life. Whenever I go on a trip to preach in other churches, I always bring some of the elders with me. They find it stimulating, but so do I—I draw on my conversations with them as a source of ideas. They are great reservoirs of knowledge. I always sit them up front during services; they mothered and nurtured the church all their lives, they ought to be up front, so the younger people can see them, as an example."

Reverend Vaughn hopes that some of the church members who have moved away from Sandtown will move back, particularly into some of the housing for the elderly that is part of the Nehemiah Project. "We give school supplies to two thousand youngsters every August, and provide them with tutorial support throughout the school year. We've been particularly blessed in that respect because we have a number of retired schoolteachers in our church, many of whom retired early. They run our tutorial program. We have a Saturday church school which is much more than Bible study; it includes reading and writing, math skills, proper etiquette.

"There's no more aid to students in college, so we pay the tuition for a couple of young people in need. There's one young woman in her first year of law school whose tuition we are paying. We feel that will bring great dividends to our community. Our Men's Fellowship adopts one or two young men from the community, from a large family or a broken family, and supplements what their families can do for them—clothe them, take them to cultural events and baseball games, banquets, make them part of the male 'club.'"

Sharon Baptist takes its communion service out into the street beside the church on the third Sunday of every month. The church gets a permit from the city to seal off the block to traffic and holds its service on a large bandshell platform that is permanently affixed to the side of the church. "Each time we have communion outside the church, in the street, a dozen or so people from the community join the church," Reverend Vaughn says. "They know that the church also tries to meet them on the level of their daily struggle, and tries to help them. We are open to the community—for weddings, for funerals, to share joy and sorrow. No one has to guess whether they can have their meetings here. Members of the tenant council from Gilmor Homes [a block away] call upon us for the use of our meeting space," he said, very pleased. "We are blessed to be so close to the public housing project. It gives us so many opportunities to serve.

"When Jesus said, 'The poor you will always have with you,' he meant that you would always have an opportunity to *serve*. There would always be people who needed you. The historical mission of our church is to give our people a sense of their own personhood, to be the center of all our culture. But more and more, the church will have to learn to do things collectively for people, because government at all levels is withdrawing its support for our community. City, state, federal—the money isn't there any more.

"All the churches in Sandtown take that seriously. Right now, we're all working together through BUILD, a united arm of the church. Churches don't exist to have big bank accounts that don't help people. The renovation of people is more important than the physical look of a building. Give people the dignity, they will rise up and take care of the building. Before Jesus gave heavenly insights, he took care of the earthly things—fed the hungry, clothed the naked, gave sight to the blind. All the churches here, from storefront to cathedral, are faced with the same problem—the survival of black people. The godliness of our congregations is our power base. Real empowerment is being a vehicle for God to bring his kingdom to earth. God means for all of us to enjoy the bounty of the earth. The stronger should help the weaker."

The New Song Urban Ministry
The New Song Urban Ministry, located in Sandtown, is part of the evangelical wing of the Presbyterian Church in America, which seeks to build and nurture relationships across racial and economic barriers and to confront injustice. Convinced that hope and new opportunity can be rewoven into the fabric of communities like Sandtown-Win-

chester, New Song seeks to foster ministries that support the social, economic, and spiritual vibrancy of the neighborhood. To this end, it has embarked on programs such as health care and preventive health education, educational enrichment for children and youth, promotion of homeownership, emergency services, and youth leadership development. On the drawing board are programs involving legal aid services, transitional housing, and economic development.

The founders of New Song, two young white couples from the Baltimore suburbs, did a lot of reading and reflecting when they were in college and decided that they wanted to locate in a "community of need." When they began the process they were students or recent graduates. They had been involved in Christian youth work, Campus Life clubs, and the like. From the beginning, the goal of the New Song pilot group has been to apply the gospel holistically. Members feel development and empowerment are linked with evangelizing and that their health, housing, education, and youth work fleshes out the gospel that they follow; they do not see themselves as doing housing or social outreach just to evangelize people. New Song seeks "*shalom*" for everyone—not just enjoying complete peace in the hereafter, but also experiencing the great things of creation while one is alive.

New Song members like Allan Tibbels and Mark Gornik are constantly dealing with the fact that they have the very options that they are trying to create for others. Their task has been to convince people that despite their privileged backgrounds, they are serious about helping. In the beginning, New Song members talked to people in SWIA about housing development possibilities. SWIA became interested and began a partnership with New Song. The Association was open to having the New Song people move into the neighborhood and try out their ideas.

I first met the people from the New Song founding group, all white, serious young Christians, when they were working out of one of the apartments in a five-story building on North Stricker Street that they had renovated for the use of community residents. A young black man opened the door and asked me to wait for Allan Tibbels. The apartment was all exposed brick and renovated wood, pleasantly appointed in durable "Cargo" furniture. There seemed to be papers, newsletters, and computers everywhere. Tibbels soon appeared from another room, driving a very high-tech wheelchair. Like his colleagues, he is young, dedicated, and technically proficient, with a spiritual focus and a sense of humor.

The efforts of the New Song group are carried out under the umbrella of New Song Urban Ministries, "a ministry energized and encouraged by a faith community in which those who serve, those who are in need, and those who provide support have committed themselves to one another." Housing development is a key aspect of their ministry, and they have formed an affiliate of Habitat for Humanity International. Habitat principles focus on volunteer labor, donated materials, and a Christian approach. The homes are sold at cost, and the purchasers receive interest-free mortgage loans. Money for acquisition, and for construction or renovation, is raised by the Habitat affiliate, and the new owners pay them back over an extended period. The family provides sweat equity by working on the house for approximately two hundred fifty hours, and makes little or no down payment. The family lives in the house for at least ten years; if they sell before that, Habitat has the first right to purchase the house.

New Song is presently working on a small scale with three houses financed through Habitat, two sponsored by the New Song Church, and two by the city in conjunction with SWIA. The last-named project also involves a grant to train youth in housing renovation. All seven houses are being developed under the Habitat umbrella, and thus all are for homeownership. Some additional rental units are also planned, of which New Song will be the owner. New Song/Habitat's first house was occupied by a working mother with four children, who made about eight thousand dollars a year. She had been living in 500 square feet of substandard space. She was able to make a $145 down payment; she got a twenty-year mortgage; and the house was sold to her for $33,000. She pays $125 a month in principal and another $55 for taxes and fire insurance—a total of $183 a month for a three-bedroom rowhouse. As stated above, no interest is charged.

Early in 1992, New Song dedicated its headquarters, a four-story, two-hundred-year-old convent, originally housing the Sisters of Mercy, which had been abandoned for twenty years, boarded up, and occasionally inhabited by squatters. The dilapidated building was renovated through the financial donations of a broad range of people and institutions and with thousands of hours of labor donated by three hundred volunteers, including the pastor, church members, and members of the Sandtown community. The renovation itself impressed the people in the community with the changes that can be made in the physical—and spiritual—tenor of the neighborhood if people get inspired and work together. Habitat International does more new construction than rehabilitation, but rehab is key in Sandtown in order to preserve the neighborhood. It inspires neighborhood people when an old house is transformed; it helps overcome people's skepticism.

As Mark Gornik, pastor of the New Song Ministry, put it at the dedication, "Even in a city as segregated as Baltimore, people can cross racial and economic barriers to support a common cause." Dr. John Perkins, a black evangelist from Mississippi who was the keynote speaker, urged upscale professionals with a Christian spirit to move to neighborhoods like Sandtown and help them revive. "Jesus Christ did not commute to Earth," Perkins observed. Herman Gassaway, a community resident since his birth sixty-nine years before and a volunteer who helped restore the building, summed it up: "I think it's remarkable. It brings out something. I remember when it was a convent. It's good to see something happen in the community. We were so far down. We've come a long way."

I found myself, as an African-American, somewhat troubled about the New Song Church, and about how I was going to portray them in this book, if at all. Tibbels, in a subsequent interview, took exception to some of my early written impressions of the group that made them seem like a bunch of missionaries. I felt that they were interested in the poor of the community but not in the others who lived and worked there, the natural leadership. Their focus seemed imperialistic to me, despite their good intentions. Even if not all the clergy of Sandtown have taken the kinds of initiatives New Song has taken, that is no reason to ignore them. They need to reach out and make common cause with the other religious people in the community, I thought. They have much to learn and much to teach.

I decided to go back and talk with them some more, try to dig deeper, try to figure things out. I had watched New Song grow, become more rooted into the community over the year or so since the first interviews. I interviewed Tibbels again in early 1992, when New Song had already moved into their newly renovated brownstone on Gilmor Street, directly across from Gilmor Homes. They were running the church, Habitat, and New Song Urban Ministries out of the same building. Having reviewed the literature on liberation theology, it occurred to me to ask if they knew anything about it.

"Sure," Tibbels said. "We're very much aware of it. Mark Gornik, the pastor of New Song, traveled in Central America a few years ago, and saw those base communities up close. We respect the base community model, and we're following it to some extent, but our theology is very different. We're really fairly mainstream as far as our theology goes. It's just classic reformed Presbyterian theology. Calvin and Luther are very misunderstood," Tibbels said. "They gave their lives on behalf of the poor, and they lived very simply. We're just doing it instead of talking about it.

"Some of us have prayed and struggled over our ideas and convictions for ten or fifteen years. We come to Sandtown out of servanthood and out of repentance. We come to serve, because that is the example Jesus set for us, to live and work in partnership with the poor. Jesus didn't commute to Earth. At the same time, we come out of repentance. The living conditions of Sandtown have been caused to a significant extent by institutional racism, classism, things that we personally as suburban, middle-class whites have benefited from. We are complicit in that system. We're here to do our small part to make amends, but I should stress that we want to operate always in response to God's love for us, rather than trying to control what happens. That means that every moment is fraught with adventure and excitement, because every breath we take is by and in response to God's grace."

I reminded Tibbels of the struggle within liberation theology over the importance of indigenous culture, and the criticisms lodged against liberation theologians by some black American theologians in the early 1980s. Cornel West and James Cone, for example, were concerned that the Latin Americans were concerned only with class, and did not understand the significance of race in the North American context. "It must be hard to deal with that here in Sandtown," I observed. "It's not just a poor community, it's a black community, with traditional ways of doing things that still survive in many areas."

"We have a multicultural service," Tibbels said. "We try to create a space for people to worship in ways that fit with their traditions. And in our home Bible study groups, we stress empowerment, *shalom*, we call it, as well as spiritual development. Unlike liberation theology, we're not talking about socialism or leveling; when we say *shalom*, we mean parity, equality of opportunity, and access, access to housing and to a job that suits your talents and skills. There might be disagreements on approach in the Bible study group. We're nonviolent, for example. I'm not sure everyone around here is. But we take our direction from Martin Luther King, his ideas about non-violence and his ideas about inclusion."

I left Tibbels, still wondering how service, repentance, multi-culturalism, and empowerment work out when all mixed together, but very much convinced that New Song belonged in this book. Tibbels had suggested I talk to Gornik, the pastor of New Song, for theological details. "We disagree on some things," Allan said, "but he's the real theologian."

Gornik was hard to catch; he seemed to be everywhere at once. I finally took the liberty of telephoning him at home and told him about my conversation with Tibbels. I wanted to know about his travels in Central America, and what he thought of the base community model. As a young seminarian, Gornik began reading the work of Guillermo Cook, a Costa Rican liberation theologian who is a Protestant,[18] and wrote a paper about him. On the basis of that paper, Cook invited Gornik to visit Christian base communities in Central America. There, Gornik observed that the base communities were really ecumenical, not just Catholic. In fact, it appeared to him that the base communities were very Protestant in their focus on reforming the church itself. When Mark returned from Central America, he heard about the Reverend John Perkins, who had invited young seminarians to join him at his church in Mississippi for a year or so to help with the work of spiritual and community renovation among African-Americans there. Those who participated were inspired to begin similar projects in other parts of the country, coalescing into a movement called the Christian Community Development Association. "It's our perception that problems of race and class are hurting every denomination in the United States," Gornik said.

He observed, as has Harry Boyte, that the liberation theology model has to be decontextualized if it is to be applied in North America. Gornik felt that special caution had to be exercised in transferring the base community model to an urban black community in the United States. "There are some constants, and those have found their way into our work in Sandtown. In both cases, you're doing theology from the bottom up. Like the methods of Paolo Freire, there's a certain consciousness-raising that goes on simply through providing an intimate forum for people to raise questions about their social conditions as well as about their personal lives."

Gornik has also determined, from his observations of base communities in Central America, that too much emphasis on the political and economic order seemed to fragment the groups and burn them out. "People want spiritual nourishment. Many of them are not interested in abstractions. We've certainly found that here in Sandtown. The political and economic issues may become a very serious agenda item for our church and our home Bible study groups, but for now it's about building relationships, having fun, trying to be normal. Politics has to grow out of that, has to grow out of the community that's developing." Gornik amplified this point by stressing that he tries to stay "pretty nondirective" in the New Song home Bible study classes that are the closest analogues in their work to base communities. "It's really because we want to be a nonhierarchical church," he said.

BUILD

The Reverend Vernon Dobson, former head of the Ministerial Alliance and still a power in Baltimoreans United in Leadership Development, sat in his office in the rectory of Union Baptist Church. The office is on the first floor, and his windows face the street. Periodically, parishioners and neighborhood people peek through the window and wave at him, ask a question, a favor. Reverend Dobson is a large, kindly man with a craggy face and a gruff manner, like a stern but forgiving uncle. His speech easily rolls in and out of the rhythmic tones and metaphors of the vernacular sermons of the black church. On the wall behind his desk is a framed copy of the famous statement "Desiderata." As I read the words, perhaps for the hundredth time in my life, I noticed for the first time an inscription at the bottom: "Found, 1619, in the basement of Old St. Paul's Church, Baltimore."

It is BUILD's network of ministers like Vernon Dobson, rather than the organization itself or its respective congregations, that contains the elements of a base community. The ministers form a peer group, sharing experiences as they struggle with banks, corporations, and the city government. They are trying to raise consensus-oriented decision-making models for BUILD as a whole on the foundation of their peer relationships. Some of them are beginning to see the need to share power within their own churches, and between their churches and their immediately surrounding communities. In this respect, BUILD as a base community of ministers is beginning to see the need to challenge its members to apply to themselves the creed they propose to opponents.

"You must share your vision with people by making them partners in the process," Reverend Dobson said. "BUILD's original vision was to ultimately get people to participate in the power that was resident in each of them. Jesus said to all of us, Ye are lights of the world. IAF convinced us that this was best pursued in groups, with a critical mass. They had a professionalism about organizing that we veterans of the civil rights movement, with all our passion and people perspective, never had. We discovered that by organizing, we could release the captive not only in ourselves, but in our communities. But we mustn't forget that the ultimate reality is God. Any empowerment must lead you back to God. The impediments which we attack as members of a community organization—poor schools, lack of housing, poor medical care—are all impediments to being a child of God. BUILD is engaging institutionalized structures of power so that each person is free to exercise critical judgment and find their way back to God.

"We've done well in the larger arena, but we find that *within* our member churches, power is not being shared. We don't have justice *inside* the church. The clergy are mobilized to attack power inequities in society at large, but they're not prepared to give up any of the power that they wield inside their own churches. It's not just the churches, of course. No one in this country wants to share power, so there is struggle going on in families, in churches, in government, and in society at large. That's why there is a possibility of conflict between the ministers and the base communities that you're talking about, to the extent that they form inside the church. That's something we need to work on.

"We're beginning with the peer pressure that's exerted on the clergy who are members of BUILD. Leadership in BUILD is shared. People don't look to be quoted in the press or be interviewed on T.V. BUILD has had five directors, mostly women, who serve very short terms. It's not about office in BUILD. Each church has a voice, whether it has a hundred members or four thousand members. We also share power by being accountable to each other. The more we share power between clergy, because of the love ethic, the more these ministers are receptive to sharing power within their own congregations. We need to be opening up our own churches to the kind of leadership development we advocate for our communities in our contests with City Hall and the banks and businesses. But we still have a long way to go. There are impediments even to people of good will. We in BUILD have been spending a lot of time focusing on our relationships with business and government, and not enough on our relationships with each other and with our congregations and surrounding communities."

About two weeks after Reverend Dobson and I had that conversation, he invited me to meet with him and Gary Rodwell, the lead organizer for BUILD. We settled into the large meeting room at the rear of Union Baptist Church, both men taking a while to shake off telephone calls and questions from people who filed in and out, and get their papers and other paraphernalia straight. The two seem to be constantly engaged with some ongoing project.

"Five years ago, BUILD committed itself to a long-term plan that would enable us to *represent* the poor in the corridors of power," Reverend Dobson said simply. "Now, the situation in Sandtown provides us with a challenge. Can we organize a neighborhood so that its population *as a whole* is empowered? Right now," he said, "our live wires to the people of Sandtown are not hot to the touch. That's something that you've felt yourself, Harold, as you have been digging around up there, talking to people, surveying the situation. I know you have some ideas about further steps that could be taken, and I want you to explain them to Gary here."

I paused, gathering my thoughts, and experienced mild *deja vu*— a flashback to my student experiences as a community organizer, when I spent equal time in the library and in the community. I began by telling them that I had come to care about the many people I had met as I worked on this book, and had in some ways become part of the processes I had come to observe—so much so that at times, I did not know if I was writing the book or the book was writing me. At the same time, my role as a scribe continued; that is what brought me here, that is what I am good at, and I must be true to that, telling the story as I see it.

"I have an idea about how to root empowerment deeper into the community. The model is the Christian base communities of the liberation theology movement in Latin America. You start small Bible study groups, and facilitate discussion of what community is for the people involved, and what obstacles to community they think exist, always using the text of the Bible as a central resonating point for the discussion. Harry Boyte tells me that the liberation theology model has to be 'decontextualized,' because the base communities in Latin America grew up under very different conditions: a rural, agrarian society; stark class distinctions; a tightly woven social fabric. The question is, how to make the model relevant to a postindustrial society, whose economy is based on information rather than the tilling of land?"

"That's right," said Reverend Dobson. Rodwell nodded.

"I think the answer lies in the feeling of self-worth that develops when you participate in something like this," I continued. "It's like in the civil rights movement. Black people's feelings of self-worth were elevated, not just by white people's reactions, but by what they were doing themselves. They felt there could be no turning back. It's the same with this. People will start feeling more valuable, and they'll begin to question why they have to live in a context where people are shooting and killing each other, doing drugs, can't get a job, health care, or a decent place to live. At the same time, the reference to the Bible will provide a channel for people's anger, it will help them to treat each other with respect and love, and will help them approach their opponents with the strength of Christian love that Martin Luther King felt was so important.

"I would say, contact the ministers of all the churches in Sandtown, maybe start with a prayer breakfast, and explain the concept to them. Each of them could then have a prayer breakfast in their own church, and start a Bible study group that would use the Bible as a compass to manage discussion of what people want their community to be like, what obstacles stand in their way, and what they would like to do about it. They could meet maybe once a week to start, then go to once a month. Meanwhile, each member of the minister's Bible study class goes out into the community and starts their own Bible study group, meeting once a week, to do the same sort of thing. All the leaders of the dispersed study groups meet with the minister in Bible study format once a month, for reinforcement, direction, and inspiration.

"What do you think?" I asked them.

"I think it's exactly what we should be doing," Reverend Dobson said. "In fact, we've been talking about something like this for a while. Nehemiah was really a way to get things rolling in the community, so something like this could happen. That's why I wanted you to share your ideas with Gary."

"At IAF, we have the information and the know-how to do this," Rodwell said. "We haven't tried it yet, anywhere in the country. It would require lots of training, lots of facilitation, a really hands-on approach. We don't have the staff to do it now, but with sufficient resources we could develop the capacity. I think we'd have to develop some materials parallel to the Bible materials, some stuff out of democratic theory that says similar things, to bring in people in the community who are resistant to the idea of church. But eventually, they would be able to see that the Bible says the same thing, and there would then be a point of common ground with people who are already into the Bible. The overall thrust is very consistent with IAF policy since 1973, when we decided that churches should be the focal point of any community effort, because they were the only mediating institutions still intact in most communities."

"That's one of the things I'm saying in the book," I replied. "That the black church carries forward all the traditions and techniques of community-building."

"The problem is," Rodwell continued, "that the other players in Sandtown, the mayor and Enterprise, are under intense pressure to produce immediate results. The kind of relational process you're talking about doesn't show up as quickly as producing buildings. Right now, the community process they're initiating is all top-down. They want these task forces to come up with paradigms for community pride, economic development, you name it, and then go out and convince the people to go along. I would do it just the other way. Go to the people first, empower them, prepare them for dealing with the experts. That way you develop empowered people, and they are empowered not just in the context of the public spaces of the community, but in their families, in their jobs, and in their churches."

"It does take a long time," I said. "A lot of us have to accept that we may not see the results of this during our own lifetimes."

"That's what they say in the Bible," Reverend Dobson said. "All those who died in the faith, not having received the promise, their resurrection will be validated in us." He left and came back with a Bible, and leafed quickly to Hebrews 11:39–40.

> And these all, having received witness through faith, received not the promise,
> God having provided some better thing for us, that they without us should not be made perfect.[19]

"I agree," said Rodwell. "You have to educate people about the importance of the long term. You don't get a quick buck. At the same time, if you're a strategist, you need to spot short-term benefits, short-term victories, to keep things going."

"I think this is something BUILD will be interested in doing," Reverend Dobson said as the meeting came to a close. "We'll have to see how the other players take this."

Base Communities and Neighborhood Organizing

In a later discussion with Mark Gornik, I mentioned to him the idea of adapting the base community model to Sandtown by using home Bible study groups as satellites of Bible study groups taking place in community churches. As in my meeting with Vernon Dobson and Gary Rodwell, I had also recommended this strategy to Barbara Bostick of Mayor Schmoke's administration and to Pat Costigan of the Enterprise Foundation. Specifically, I suggested that they follow a "mini-VISTA" approach lasting at least a summer, and preferably a year. Organizers could be housed with families in the neighborhood and instructed to create linkages between groups in the community having leadership capacity and to facilitate the growth of smaller, informal peer groups for discussion, study, and civic action. The smaller groups would serve to root the process deeper into the neighborhood than is feasible for the formal leadership of established organizations. The organizers would each attend a different church (from cathedral to storefront), each spend part of the day at a "job" in one of the service agencies or one of the schools, and keep a journal. Project staff would meet with the organizers once a week to debrief them. (The training the organizers would need could come from the IAF and similar groups. An increase in funding for community organization would also be required.)

"That's a model that's crying out to be implemented here," said Gornik. "In a way, it's already being done informally in many of the churches in the community, through informal networking. Sandtown faces such a big problem, it has so many variations and dimensions, that one model just isn't adequate. Very few people even attend church in Sandtown. So many people who have come to us have no church history whatsoever. The youth have been almost completely lost. But I see renewal taking place everywhere. The storefront churches are very important for people who have been very wounded, who need a six-hour service to reach the spiritual intensity they need for the problems they face in their daily lives. The big churches like Bethel are important to bring in the strivers, the middle class and even the upper class, who can bring their skills and resources to bear on the needs of the community."

As he spoke, I thought about Masjid Al-Haqq and its combination of spirit and community, and about Sharon Baptist's outreach into Sandtown using peer groups, and about BUILD's organizing techniques.

"And you need New Songs," Gornik concluded. "Little churches that are doing community redevelopment. Maybe a lot of the renovation and renewal we're talking about can't be done by really large institutions."

I closed our conversation with the observation that I keep changing my mind about what is really going on in Sandtown. He laughed. "Join the club," he said.

And, in a way, that is the point. What is happening in Sandtown is a living, changing process that can only be communicated in snapshots. It is history being created as one observes and participates. These are the seeds of the New Community; such developments may well be occurring in similar communities all over the country—a life process, a process of struggle and renewal and pain and joy. As the "Desiderata" hanging behind Reverend Dobson's desk says, "Everywhere, life is full of heroism."

In many of these areas, social advocates as well as those for whom they advocate, fair-minded people trying to make the world better through their work in government, the church, and the neighborhood, are forming base communities for mutual guidance and support. They are trying to temper power with love, with spiritual discipline. As Dr. Martin Luther King said a quarter-century ago, "Power without love is reckless."

The Function of Base Communities

If organized protest activities are the leaves of a social movement, mediating institutions are its trunk and branches, and "free spaces" are its roots. In the experience of the black community, and certainly that of many other communities that retain their ethnicity, these "free spaces" are institutions steeped in the vernacular traditions of the ethnic group. In the black community, free spaces are found in barber shops and beauty parlors, Bible study classes, and musical groups from rappers and street-corner harmony to church choir and jazz quartet (think of how much black vernacular speech originates with black musicians). As Carol McGee Johnson of Harry Boyte's Project Public Life puts it, "A free space is a place where we come together to debate and discuss the public issues of the day with others like ourselves. Free spaces . . . allow us to connect our personal experiences to the larger public world in safer community environments. . . . Just as important, they help develop a keen sense of who we really represent, and why, when we enter the larger public world."[20]

Mediating institutions are of great importance to a social movement not only because they provide leverage and strength for organized protest, but because they exist close to, and grow directly out of, the "free spaces" of the vernacular community. In mediating institutions, vernacular speech, folkways, and ways of relating to one another are much more likely to be retained, while in organized protest much of our communication is couched in terms of demands made to outsiders, either in their language or in a "public" language. In Spanish, *a base* means more than just "among the lower orders" or even "the poor." It means also "at the foundation, the root." In other words, the vernacular underpinning of the entire culture. Organizers of basic Christian communities understood the importance of "indigenous" (i.e., vernacular) culture, not as "folklore," but as a base from which to create "new customs and values of liberation."[21] As one liberation theologian put it, "The power does not reside simply in the culture but in the forms of organization that our ancestors have handed over to us. If we exist today [as a people], it is because there is something in our traditions that has helped us continue living."[22]

It seems clear that to root development—social, economic, and even physical—into the black community, going deeper than the upper economic and social echelons, a more participatory and supportive forum of civic action will be necessary. An important reference point, if not the foundation, for such new forms is the remaining vernacular community, which has been neglected, even undermined, by the DuBoisian public sector strategies of Baltimore's civil rights and electoral activists. As these strategies increasingly neglected the black community's vernacular strength, they began to take on a hollow ring. DuBoisian tactics in the public sector must be balanced with Washingtonian, private-sector and voluntary-sector strategies of community-strengthening, institution-building, networking, and self-help. Mediating institutions, such as churches, schools, and community organizations, are essential to this task, but small base communities of one or two dozen people, spun off from mediating institutions or growing independently, are essential to counterbalance the tendency of mediating institutions to mirror the hierarchical character of the public and private bureaucracies with which they contend.

Chapter Nine
From Base Community to
New Community

If you suddenly became seriously ill and could no longer take care
of your own needs, who could you count on? . . . If the banks
suddenly collapsed and supermarkets closed, . . . who would you
turn to? Who would turn to you?

—Margo Adair, Green activist

THIS BOOK has been a discussion of attempts by African-Americans in
Baltimore (and their European-American allies) to renovate the community networks of Old West Baltimore: the vernacular techniques for
insuring that children are raised and educated properly, the food distribution systems linking black farmers to black city dwellers (still
alive among the Arabbers), the spiritual cohesion of the black church,
and the informal association of business owners and professionals, all
of which have been undermined. Politics cast exclusively in terms of
periodic elections has proven inadequate to the challenge of improving life, not only in these neighborhoods and settlements, but in those
in which most Americans live. The story of the struggle for participatory democracy and community empowerment in Baltimore's West
Side neighborhoods, an attempt to honor the best of the traditions of
both Booker T. Washington and W. E. B. DuBois, is offered as a
microcosm of a process that may be, or perhaps should be, occurring
in many other places in our country, in diverse and disparate communities, as many people seek to overcome their isolation from one another and, in some cases, rediscover their vernacular roots.

The Loss of Community

The suburbanization of the post–World War II era freed America's
white ethnics from many unwanted ties of family, neighborhood, and

culture—nosy neighbors, provincial values, the need to care for older relatives. These neo-ethnics are often now several generations removed from community life, which they abandoned to become upwardly mobile, middle-class, successful professionals. Their nuclear family units dot the suburban landscape, virtual strangers to one another, connected only by thin strands derived from mass media images and remote government officials. Their vernacular skills, in the economic and civic arenas as well as the cultural arena, have withered in the process.

Separated from the vernacular strengths of their old neighborhoods, white neo-ethnics, like black neo-ethnics, have become increasingly dependent on government for essentials of life that once were supplied by family and community. As government largess was withdrawn in the 1980s, these people's vulnerability became painfully apparent. Economic and political trends on both the national and international levels seriously undermined the ability and the inclination of the U.S. government to respond to the needs of many of its citizens. Blue-collar workers, particularly in construction and manufacturing, were hard hit by the recession of 1981–85, when five million such jobs were lost.[1] Autos, textiles, steel, and apparel, the traditional engines of U.S. prosperity, suffered greatly.[2] The recessions of the 1990s, in addition to maintaining previous levels of blue-collar unemployment, cut into the service industry as well, especially among professional and clerical workers in the finance, business service, and retail trades.[3] The middle class began to shrink, and the concentration of wealth at the highest economic echelons increased. Each additional percentage point of unemployment translated into an additional 3,000 incarcerations in state prisons, 4,000 commitments to state mental hospitals, 900 suicides, and 37,000 deaths (20,000 of those from heart attacks).[4] With individuals and families owing a staggering $3.3 trillion (an increase of 50 percent since 1980), a wave of bankruptcies was to be expected.[5] Six hundred thousand families declared bankruptcy in 1990 alone.[6]

In the post–Viet Nam era, the failure of nonparticipatory, representative democracy has produced a passive, media-oriented citizenry of angry, disaffected people, trying to hang on as their incomes and quality of life rapidly deteriorate. Green activist Margo Adair, a European-American, asked such alienated citizens the following questions:

If you suddenly became seriously ill and could no longer take care
of your own needs, who could you count on? Who would you rear-
range your life for if they got seriously ill? In either case, are institutions attractive alternatives?

If the banks suddenly collapsed and supermarkets closed, what
would you do? Who would you turn to? Who would turn to you?

In one positive legacy of the Reagan years, middle-class whites in
the suburbs began to perceive their extreme vulnerability to economic
and political reversals. As Adair observed in an interview in 1991:
"Schools shut down for lack of money. Public hospitals close their
doors. Ambulances shuffle the sick and wounded from one emergency
room to another. . . . Police fear walking the streets of drug-infested
neighborhoods. Health insurance is outside the grasp of many working people. . . . Every day brings a new environmental disaster."

Now that government is no longer prepared to meet people's
needs, where are the white neo-ethnics to turn? To the false community of "whites" or the "shadow interest" group of white suburbanites
pulled together by the Republican party?[7] Rediscovering their unique-
ness as Irish, Italians, Germans, and the like, middle-class whites
may well begin to celebrate their vernacular culture and tap its
strength. "If we want to succeed in creating fundamental social
change, it is imperative that we reclaim and restore community, the
ties and talk of daily life," said Adair. "This is essential for developing relationships that enable us to celebrate the joys and survive the
burdens of daily life with meaning, purpose, and humor." The alternative is for white neo-ethnics to become part of a fascist, false community, racist, repressive, and armed to the teeth.

The Limits of DuBoisian Strategies

Political parties seek to divide our society's various interests, rather
than integrate them into a coherent program.[8] As policy advocates,
they represent "shadow interests" that are unable to organize themselves at the level of the PACs and lobbyists. Shadow interests in the
Democratic party include the constituents for the New Politics of the
1960s and 1970s—environmentalists, members of racial minorities,
and women, as individuals and as members of diffuse "social movements" rather than as members of advocacy organizations.[9] The Republican party's shadow interests include working-class people who
feel threatened by the New Politics and many middle-class service

sector employees living in urban enclaves as well as exclusive suburbs. The latter, relatively affluent group seek to reduce their federal
tax burden so that they can spend their tax dollars at the local level,
in the exclusive communities in which they live. At the same time,
they seek to reduce their local tax burdens as well, so that they can
direct their money to private schools, private security, private recreational facilities, and a host of other services instead of paying for
public services to which less affluent people in their own communities
might have access.[10]

The use of primary elections has served to strengthen the hand of
demagogues who use ideology to mobilize and polarize these shadow
interests to bolster their own political fortunes. The consequent ideological cast to elections makes it difficult for successful candidates to
compromise or cooperate in order to translate their campaign promises into a workable program of government.[11] The result has led one
commentator to pronounce both parties "brain dead" insofar as policy
leadership is concerned. The Democrats before Clinton were unable
or unwilling to talk to the public about real issues such as industrial
decline and the maldistribution of wealth. They had no answer in
1988 to Bush's continuation of Reagan's "feel-good" politics of nor-
malization, aided and abetted by the media, with a level of negative
campaigning ("Willie Horton") that even Nixon would not have attempted. They failed to define liberalism in the contemporary context.[12]
Bush, on the other hand, with the aid of Lee Atwater, greatly advanced the continuing Republican campaign to identify Democratic
liberalism with crime, the black poor, sexual promiscuity, jobless-
ness, welfare fraud, and lack of patriotism.[13] Only the collapse of the
economy was able to temper this campaign.

Attempting to fill the vacuum left by the departure of government
from the sphere of social welfare are local civic organizations. The St.
Pius V Housing Development Committee, the Park Heights Development Corporation, BUILD, and similar groups act to assist those left
stranded by the government's failure to create the conditions for a
decent quality of life for all. This development has been applauded by
the same right-wing ideologues who engineered much of the state's
withdrawal from public support for the quality of life of most American citizens. After dispersing the democratic mass movements of the
1960s, defunding education and social services, and transferring
wealth from wage earners to business owners,[14] these ideologues now
promote a "New Paradigm" that calls for a complete devolution of

these responsibilities to the voluntary sector. For civic organizations to assume such responsibilities without access to the remaining resources of the federal, state, and local governments, however, would be foolhardy. The priorities these governments have established for the expenditure of whatever public revenues remain available still need to be debated.

No further retreat should be permitted from the regulatory "safety net"—minimum standards of environmental protection, civil rights, health care, and fair labor practices. But different approaches are needed to complement those that already exist. The civil rights movement, for example, while leaving in its wake a useful framework of government protection against racial discrimination, generally overlooked the problems of the black poor and working class and even contributed to such problems by encouraging the flight of the black middle-class from their old neighborhoods. This is not to say that the goals of the civil rights movement were incorrect—only insufficiently broad and deep. The alienation of individual members of one race or faith from individual members of others underpins larger, more obvious patterns like employment discrimination, *de facto* segregation, and the activities of hate groups. While cities like Baltimore continue with blue-ribbon meetings, litigation, legislation, and the projection of "integrated" images on video screens, it is also important to reach out to people at a personal level, to learn as well as to educate.

Some of the principal obstacles to the needed dialogue are simple mistrust and lack of self-esteem. Trust and confidence, undermined by racism for both whites and blacks, are essential to an individual's ability to choose community. Perceiving themselves as alienated from one another undercuts community groups—from tenant unions and residential associations to fraternal and church organizations—scattering and balkanizing them. Public officials often reinforce this fragmentation by providing just enough protection to "favored" groups to make them feel secure, but never enough to free them from dependence on government largess. Racism, especially, clouds our ability as individuals and as members of groups to develop autonomy, the proper balance between security and change, in a rapidly evolving world. How do we create and recreate the social, political, economic, spiritual, and physical space we need? To accomplish this task, we must be willing to struggle not only with the grave social and economic problems of racism, but also with a host of others, including sexism, human alienation, neocolonialism, inequitable allocation of resources within and between societies (for both consumption and development), environmental pollution, inadequate health care, drug abuse, population growth, and war. But this struggle cannot be carried on through a dialogue among the elite alone. The people as a whole must be involved.

We still very much need protest politics to contend with and shape the impact, particularly in terms of race and class, of large-scale institutions such as the market and the government. The logic of representative government leads us to place our faith in larger and more remote forms of government, where the illusion that everyone else is "just like us" can be sustained, and we can rationalize our deference to our representatives in matters of social life.[15] Such an illusion can be sustained because ethnic or vernacular culture at the local level has been relinquished by middle-class people, particularly suburbanites, in exchange for liberal, alienated noncommunity, cleared of threatening diversity but also devoid of subjectivity and communion. Obviously, a representative government managing society for a population who have in common only their self-definition as "white" constitutes a danger of which we should all be aware.

The Limits of Washingtonian Strategies

It remains clear that government alone cannot do the job, any more than citizens acting in concert can do the job alone. To meet their responsibilities for the future, American citizens must equip themselves with the skills and information and styles of civic work needed to face the challenges of a country with declining social investment and, in all likelihood, increasing social tension. Voluntary associations that seek to represent the interests of their constituents, or clients, or members, whether they are conceived as middle-class, working-class, working-poor, or poor, must reach out in earnest to their sources of legitimacy. This means reversing existing trends in many cases. Too often telephone calls have replaced door-to-door canvassing; letters (often duplicated or automated) have replaced telephone calls; media time or media coverage has replaced letters. Direct action campaigns such as BUILD's crusade against redlining have given way to lawyer-driven strategies using, for example, the Community Reinvestment Act; these strategies, while admirable, leave many citizens with no role to play.

Engagement with hierarchical institutions such as government

and the market can cause mediating institutions like community organizations, churches, and labor unions to develop institutional rigid-
ities, often hierarchical in nature, in response. Such bodies begin to
follow the "representative government" rather than the "participatory
democracy" model. Their leaders are elected; they use parliamentary,
rather than consensus-oriented, decision-making procedures, and
they tend to be captured by relatively high-status, upwardly mobile
people who have a very private sense of their own well-being. The
elitist tendencies of representative government thus reproduce themselves even at this level, where many community-based organizations
continue to operate in a quasi-electoral, representative mode. Leaders
are elected, power is centralized, and many neighborhood residents
do not participate effectively, if they do so at all.

To counter these tendencies, progressive Baltimoreans and their
counterparts in other U.S. cities need to encourage the development
of base communities at the neighborhood level. Base communities,
smaller, more flexible, and more intimate than even mediating institutions, are needed to sustain the spiritual and moral energy of citizens engaged in the public process. Base communities should also be
nourished at another level—within and between organizations involved in citizen action. In this variation, base communities develop
as individual members of various social and civic action organizations
come to share a common vision as a result of their work together. This
second type of base community is illustrated particularly by two of
Baltimore's social action organizations, the Maryland Alliance for the
Poor (MAP) and the Women Entrepreneurs of Baltimore (WEB).

MAP and WEB: Peer Groups of Social Activists

The Maryland Alliance for the Poor
The Maryland Alliance for the Poor (MAP) is a community of public
interest lobbyists who work at the state capital of Annapolis on behalf
of state residents who "lack one or more of the basic necessities of
decent human life." These lobbyists, and the organizations they represent as individuals, each focus on a single issue, such as affordable
housing, homelessness, residential energy, health care, public assistance, hunger, and self-sufficiency. The principal organizations active
in MAP, networked together by the community of their Annapolis advocates, are Action for the Homeless, Associated Catholic Charities, the

Baltimore Jewish Council, the Baltimore Urban League, Maryland Citizen Action, the Maryland Food Committee, the Maryland Low Income Housing Coalition, the Maryland State Conference of the NAACP, the Office of Social Development of the Archdiocese of Washington, Welfare Advocates, and the United Jewish Appeal. By joining together, they are able to present both a political united front and a comprehensive strategy to counter impoverishment and disempowerment. They can also more effectively demonstrate that all their issues are interrelated.

MAP's effectiveness grows out of the same sort of networking techniques used in base communities at the primary level. Its history illustrates how groups of citizen action organizations can be drawn together by the personal relationships of their most active members. Lynda Meade, director of social concerns of the Associated Catholic Charities, now a principal spokesperson for MAP, and Maryland State Delegate Howard "Pete" Rawlings (a Democrat whose district covers North and West Baltimore) were instrumental in bringing the group together. "We were always confronted with Solomon-like choices: fund anti-hunger efforts, but not affordable housing; increase assistance grants, but not the number of shelter beds," said Meade, in one of my first interviews in Baltimore. "We saw our agendas crumbling as the state's budget tightened in the mid-1980s. Then, in 1988, we decided to join together so that our respective issues would not compete with one another."

Rawlings, a civil rights activist, a founder of the state's black legislative caucus, and chair of the House of Delegates' Appropriations Committee, is directly linked into the Annapolis political process. Rawlings called a meeting of the lobbyists from the various coalitions that today make up MAP. At the meeting, he helped the lobbyists understand that they would do better working as a group than on their own. "We already formed a sort of 'community of advocates' that had been informally building for years," said Meade. "We joined together on various issues, lunched together, and socialized both in Annapolis and at home. For ninety days out of the year, the length of the legislative session, we practically lived together. When MAP was formed, we never even thought about guarantees. We trusted and respected each other, knew that each of us could deliver, each of us had the support of our organizations' boards."

This established pattern of informal collaboration and networking proved to be a strong base from which to proceed. According to MAP members, the agenda for the Alliance comes from the agenda of each member coalition. Each coalition responds to the agenda of its member organizations, which, in turn, respond to their members or constituents. How this agenda is created from the ground up, from each individual, to his or her organization, to the coalition level, and, finally, to the Alliance level, is a fascinating process. It is not linear, from bottom to top, but rather a recursive, holistic process. Staff lobbyists from the various coalitions meet to hammer out a proposed budget, representing (to some extent) their respective organizations or coalitions. They are prepared to "sell" their organizations on the need for a certain compromise or issue. Yet they are also fully aware of the parameters of their delegated authority—what types of issues or compromises or positions their organization is likely to accept, and which ones they are likely to reject. Key to the process is the staff lobbyist who has the confidence of his or her organization and/or coalition and is in a position to "commit" it at strategy meetings.

Ruth Crystal, a lobbyist for the Maryland Low Income Housing Coalition, is an attractive, friendly Jewish woman in her early forties. She is a veteran of the citizen action movements of the 1970s and 1980s, and a member of MAP. "There's a real sense of shared value among us," she said. "MAP members support each other *en masse* whenever any individual's particular issue comes up in committee. Members also know each other's issues, and whenever they run across a piece of information or a contact relevant to another member, they say to themselves, 'Oh, let me call so-and-so about this right away.' It's easy to get on the phone, because we're advocating for similar things and we know what each person in the group needs to get their work done."

Recent interventions in the area of public finance arose because that issue cuts across what each MAP organization is doing. "What do we all share in common?" had become a typical question at MAP meetings. They found that all their issues converged in the area of public finance and tax equity. I asked Crystal whether she knew of any similar groups. "They're few and far between," she said. "I'm a member of a dance collective that grew up in New England, and now reaches down to Baltimore. We're all dancers with our own companies, and we started collaborating, and then found that we shared a political vision, and ideas about childrearing and nutrition. Now we have a summer camp that all of us come to with our kids."

Women Entrepreneurs of Baltimore

Women Entrepreneurs of Baltimore (WEB) is a "second-generation" microenterprise project; that is, it was launched with little or no government assistance. WEB is another example of peer group networking among people who are not themselves facing dramatic decline in their quality of life, but who have organized to help others who are in distress. WEB started out with a much stronger emphasis on community networking than BOSS, its competitor. The WEB self-employment training proposal emphasized community-based support for trainees and graduates. From selection to training to business start-up and operation, the WEB project expected to rely on a strong network of community support: neighborhood sponsors, internships with existing small businesses, and a resource-sharing business incubator to strengthen the link between WEB trainees and graduates and their communities.

Denied the funding boost BOSS received, WEB was forced to begin its program in a more *ad hoc* fashion. Sondra Stafford, the WEB instructor, accepted everyone who signed up, called them together, and said, "You're a class." She developed a curriculum two weeks before classes started, and remained just two weeks ahead of her students. When classes ended in the summer, Stafford began reviewing the students' course evaluations as a guide to the program's future direction. Experiments revealed that mentor networks are better than individual mentors, since one person usually cannot respond to all the questions a budding microentrepreneur might have. WEB is considering teaching entrepreneurial skills through simulation rather than lectures, and perhaps even through starting a business for a student and teaching her and others in the class "by doing." In many ways, however, WEB staff feel that the results of the first effort speak for themselves: out of thirteen original participants, nine stayed in the program and turned in business plans. Four of that nine started businesses, all located in East Baltimore. One student, Natalie Towles, is trained as a baker and plans to start a business in Sandtown once the Nehemiah Project develops further. She is now sharing space in a delicatessen in Fells Point and exchanges a percentage of her baked goods for rental space. This arrangement also gives her an opportunity to build a customer base.

One of the most interesting things about WEB is the intensity of the relationships among the members of its board of directors, who are (with one or two exceptions) white, middle-class, professional women. "Networking is a strategy with us, not a tactic," said Dennis

Livingston, the one male board member. "Awilda [Marquez, the WEB director] recruited all of us to complement her vision of women helping each other in the informal economy, based on what she had seen during her work in Africa and Bangladesh."

Awilda Marquez is a lawyer with Piper & Marbury, a large and prestigious Baltimore firm. Of Puerto Rican descent, Marquez worked in the U.S. Foreign Service in the early 1980s. On assignment in Bangladesh, she observed the practices of the Grameen Bank, a pioneering microenterprise effort. The Grameen Bank introduced the circle lending concept, based on the concept of delegating authority to a group of borrowers for participant selection, credit delivery, and loan servicing functions. Candidates form "borrowers' circles," making themselves collectively responsible for the debts of each individual in the circle. Peer pressure thus replaces the role of collateral, large equity contributions, and proven track records as security for the loan. Grameen encouraged microentrepreneurs to join together to assist one another and achieve the benefits of economies of scale and specialization in the areas of supply, purchasing, and the procurement of insurance and health plans. On the political level, association presents an opportunity for microentrepreneurs to deal collectively with local authorities—for example, with respect to vendor licensing practices.

Convinced that such techniques could work in depressed inner-city communities like Sandtown, Marquez began organizing WEB soon after coming to Baltimore.[16] "Sometimes we met every Saturday," Livingston told me. "Employers of mine have threatened to fire me because I refused to work on Saturdays, but I came to Awilda's meetings anyway. The people all are trying to empower communities; some are focused on the women, others on economic structures, a whole variety of perspectives. But we all work together, drawing strength and inspiration and direction from each other. Each board member is a member of some other organization—government, corporations, community organizations. As a result of their involvement, their organizations have chipped in money, equipment, expertise. The possibilities provided by the kind of networking we're doing are endless."

The New Community: A Network of Base Communities

Base communities provide a networking focus, a source of spiritual and social direction, and a means of mutual support. For this reason

they may become important not just to the less fortunate, or even to
those who advocate on their behalf, like MAP and WEB, but to all of us
as we struggle for roots in a rapidly changing society. A "New Community" network, linking base communities at the neighborhood level
with similar communities of social and civic activists operating in and
around the "corridors of power," could do much to nourish and ener-
gize the movement for social justice, enhance participatory democracy
and community empowerment, and help to address some of our present social, economic, and political difficulties. In this book we have
observed many processes that move in this direction: individual networking, the group life of religious institutions, the intervention of
community-minded civil servants, politicians, and professionals, and
the work of community-based and social movement organizers. We
have looked at people and organizations that are building that kind of
autonomy, working on issues such as economic development, the provision of shelter, and the sharing of faith. Many of the individuals
involved are spiritually motivated; just as in Latin America, important
leadership in troubled U.S. communities like the neighborhoods of
Baltimore's West Side comes from religious institutions and from people with a spiritual vision who are committed to building social justice
in the here and now. The importance of a spiritual dimension that
emphasizes respect for and kindness to others, in theory as well as in
practice, should not be underestimated. Where people's sense of self-
esteem has been damaged along with their objective living conditions,
spiritual as well as material uplift is often necessary for them to sustain a sense of community.

How far along that path might a domestic "liberation theology"
take us? Part of the answer lies in the developments in BUILD, at
Bethel A.M.E. Zion Church, in the New Song Urban Ministry, St.
Pius V, Sharon Baptist, the Masjid Al-Haqq, and in the "base communities" that develop in their respective orbits. In each of these
cases, a desire to expand the boundaries of spiritual community has
led a congregation to confront the material poverty of the communities
in which they are located, and they have ventured forth into the arena
of social action. Reverend Dobson argued that base community organizing and the link-up of such small units should be orchestrated by
an institution that has a sense of history, ethics, and purpose, and
that the church is in the best position to play that role. No other
institution exists with its sweep of history and its ethical direction.
The government certainly cannot or will not do it. Multinational enter-

prises? Out of the question. "If it's not to be the church, that means an entirely new institution would have to be created. Do we have the time for that?" Dobson asked. Baltimore's Ministerial Alliance, of which Dobson is a member, has come to a conclusion: it is time to reassert the leadership of the church in Baltimore. The exclusive reliance on politicians elected from the black community is now seen to have been ill-advised. Even the civil rights movement made some wrong turns—the resulting loss of black institutions was never the objective.

"We have lost so much black historical reference, so much religious training, so many of the traditions that always made for excellence in education and achievement in the black community," Dobson told me. "Now it is time to get young preachers, people who don't have a congregation yet, to start doing some organizing, to help the institutional base of the black community move forward into the next century. That must not be lost. People in the black community need to learn how to participate again."

The balance between spiritual uplift and social action is a precarious one. As Frank Reid, pastor of Bethel, is fond of emphasizing, it is as easy for a congregation to concentrate so much on the secular that it becomes a community organization as it is for a congregation to concentrate so fully on the spiritual as to have no impact on the community of which it is a part. It is important for a spiritually directed group to strike a balance in their dealings in the community, to be spiritually inspirational without proselytizing, to be materially uplifting without worshiping the material world. In the final analysis, Reverend Dobson urges us to remember that the inner-city black community is not a "jungle."

"Middle-class people don't want to come here," he said. "They have their resources and they want to distance themselves from people who don't have what they have. But people here in Upton have some sense of respect for themselves and for others. A situation has been created in which they are not expected to participate in matters essential to daily life—in schools, in churches, in civic organizations, and at the workplace. This mindset has got to be changed. The church has got to take the lead, reach out to marginalized people, help them find the financial, political, and moral support that they need to realize their talent and their potential."

Peer groups inspired by the base communities of Latin America have the potential, in all countries, of bringing the general movement for participatory democracy and community empowerment alive. Such peer groups have the potential to evolve into a loose network I call the New Community, which exists independently of public or private bureaucracies. The New Community follows a pattern of mutual and other-regarding behavior, drawing from the vernacular but refined with modern democratic and humanistic concerns. It is created and re-created every day, in small cells, by the enlightened behavior of people in their relationships with their children, their families, their fellow religious devotees, their coworkers, and their fellow citizens.

Base communities can contribute to the processes of participatory democracy and community empowerment by enriching and texturing organizations, coalitions, and alliances that are actively aiding those injured by the government and the market and are also attempting to discipline government and market forces. This enrichment and texturing process has a number of focal points. One is to better equip individuals for participation in the work of voluntary organizations and their coalitions and alliances. This preparation is practical, theoretical, and spiritual. Another focal point is to create an economic network that can sustain members of these organizations and those whom they serve, so that an increasing proportion of the population will be able to exist without undue dependence on the public and private bureaucracies of the "system" Charles Reich describes. In this way the linear coalitions and alliances of voluntary organizations are complemented by a circular, woven network. The result is a useful tapestry of human civic, spiritual, and economic interaction that can balance the vagaries of both government and business. This tapestry is the essence of the New Community.

Base communities also have a major role to play in a truly thoroughgoing process of community empowerment. To fulfill this role, members of base communities have to link up to a larger network, so that they do not remain parochial. "To hammer out ways to work together on large projects that help to craft the environment, to create history. That's the reward," Boyte told me in a telephone conversation. "In this sense groups like BUILD have inherited the civil rights movement. Now they can deepen and extend it."

To accomplish these objectives, peer groups of Americans of all races—African, European, Native American, and Asian—should work through their churches, and through neighborhood and citywide associations, to create a social paradigm that can function in ways as yet unconceived by existing public and private bureaucracies. They can begin to influence the social parameters now set by such bureaucracies, interacting with the established order from an external and expanding vantage point. This new social paradigm is based not on conversion or conquest, but on respectful encounter, much aided by long experience in the facilitation of dialogue and the building of caring networks for organizing social life. To consider the movement for a New Community in relation to existing public and private bureaucracies, then, is to look at the evolving balance between declining hierarchical institutions and the increasing effectiveness and energy of the patterns of initiative, response, and respect (which we might call "custom") generated by base communities as they develop and link up. The movement toward a New Community is part of a trend toward a progressive sort of populism, built on relationships and structures close to the people, rather than upon media, electoral, and market manipulation. As one commentator has put it, it is time for "common sense talk about common sense ideas," to counter a different, reactionary populism based on racism and a general mean-spiritedness.[17]

Modern liberal democratic theorists contend that "popular government carries within itself a seed of totalitarian despotism that can be prevented from germinating only by the judicious application of a constitutional herbicide made up in equal doses of individual liberty, natural rights, private property, and market capitalism."[18] Yet, ironically, "the defense of the individual against the old tyrannies of hierarchy, tradition, status, superstition, and absolute political power has been sustained" by isolating individuals "not only from the abuses of power but from one another," creating an unbearable isolation that alienated individuals may seek to overcome through illegitimate, totalitarian communities.[19]

The social movements of the 1960s and 1970s were mass mobilizations aimed at securing adherence to their norms through nonviolent confrontation and force of example. Now, a wide variety of ordinary citizens must grapple with issues of civil rights, peace, women's rights, and the environment in much more intimate settings, employing techniques to humanize both themselves and their opponents. This dialogue, both quiet and strident, must take place in public schools, colleges, work settings, churches, and shopping centers. The language and terms of the discussion need to be accessible to the general population rather than so rarified as to make public policy, in real terms, a matter for the elite alone. During the American Revolution, such outreach took place in the form of plays, songs, and didactic literature on republican virtues. Political satire and epic poetry were found in abundance. Each of the Republic's one hundred or more newspapers published the full text of the proposed Constitution for discussion and debate in school, church, and tavern. Dialogue and open discussion are equally essential for the movement to build a New Community.

Clearly, the network, and the dialogue that creates it, must be increasingly inclusive. The interchange of ideas among geographically and otherwise diverse communities is as important to group vitality as exchanges of natural resources are to a self-sufficient economy. The process of exchange and interaction is presently hampered by racial and class segregation. Local government decisions made in the name of community autonomy have historically been some of the most important ways in which residential segregation has been perpetuated and more expansive notions of community thwarted. To achieve the heightened public discourse needed to advance people's images of themselves, we shall have to challenge such social dichotomies—a fact that underscores the limits of race and class as organizing social metaphors, even when used by progressive people. Both metaphors are based on mistrust of others, and while they may be useful—even essential—to mobilize people to resist social and economic oppression, they are inadequate bases upon which to build a different kind of society.

The continued struggle of social movements and neighborhood organizations to protect the legal and financial "safety net" in an era of declining federal presence must not, in the process, create insular, suspicious neighborhoods or social groupings, hostile to outsiders and quick to take offense.[20] The movement for a New Community must evolve toward a principled form of coalition politics that is mindful of, but struggles to transcend, social divisions like race, class, and ethnicity. American communities need to be linked by more than their relation to public or private bureaucracies. Only thus can "democracy" come to mean something more than rule by a majority of interest groups.

When acting in the political arena, New Community activists must somehow avoid being dragged into the prevailing interest-group competition over votes and politicians and money and power. The use of bureaucratic institutions and one-way media outreach must be continually reexamined and evaluated, as their employment can undercut the growth of the movement we describe. It is the formal role of civic action organizations to keep close watch on government, including the bureaucratic service-delivery system that can strangle neighborhoods and their people by, as John McKnight puts it, "exacerbating the very problems they're supposed to correct": the correctional institutions that train people in crime, hospitals that make people sicker, and "stupid-making" schools.

The focus of the civil rights movement was upon access to existing institutions of political power, and the electoral mobilizations of the 1970s and 1980s followed suit. But this politics of rights was insufficient to address the class-based economic problems of much of the black community, which required more than "piece of the pie" pluralism, "its rewards determined by negotiations with the federal government, the liberal wing of big business, and City Hall leaders and their machines."[21] James Jennings believes that only a transition to using electoral mobilization to challenge "structural and institutional arrangements that reflect and protect a system of wealth and power," seeking "change in the . . . status quo," can simultaneously respond to the "class, community, and race interests of black America."[22] His conclusion is that this transition would eventually demand a third party, because issues of economic and community empowerment are "too radical" for the Democratic party.[23]

Clearly, there remains a great need for government at all levels, especially the federal, to "set standards, evaluate and publicize local performance, work to insure equality between communities, and to insure integration and coordination of diverse community efforts."[24] However, while government is important for setting standards and presenting a framework for public debate, it should never (whether ministered through traditional or third-party politics) be allowed to displace community as the organizing metaphor for the social process that is going to take us into the future. It is of the utmost importance that base communities keep a low profile, render unto Caesar what is Caesar's, and, rather than attempt to become a part of the "representative" democratic system, supplement and chide that system instead. We need security and protection, we need a viable social network to tap and channel human creative energy, but we do not need hierarchy, repression, or exclusion. Where liberalism founders on the "disjunction between individual and sovereign," the New Community might conceivably expand as far as an uncorrupted drive for consensus around the several, mutual, and common needs of the participants can extend.

Both the government and the media have continuing, positive roles to play, engaging the civil community as a whole in conversation about poverty, disease, and environmental pollution as well as the continuing denial of civil rights to many of our people—all essential, quality-of-life issues. But the fundamental dialogue must be carried on in local communities. An emphasis on local, accessible avenues for individual involvement in governance points to active citizenship, rather than to judges or bureaucrats, as the path to social autonomy. The values of dignity and respect are to be found in human relationships rather than in government systems. It is by forming human networks, whether the people involved have government connections and backing or not, that individuals can begin to manage their own lives.

Local electoral platforms can and should articulate the need to legally restructure the governing machinery of the city by placing a premium on political participation, face-to-face discussion of public business, and the complete accountability of citizens who are elected to legislative councils or who serve on purely administrative bodies. Mediating institutions such as churches, community organizations, labor unions, public interest organizations, and social justice organizations, encouraged by their members who are working together in base communities, might begin sponsoring "neighborhood assemblies" in which a variety of such groups meet jointly at the neighborhood school or community recreation hall.[25] In these assemblies, public discussion of national as well as state and local issues could take place, a flexible, citizen-generated agenda be developed, and a system to ensure the accountability of local, state, and national elected officials created.[26] Such unofficial citizen assemblies, acting as a "shadow" or "parallel" local government, can exercise significant moral influence, overseeing the agenda and business of the official local government and challenging decisions not made in the public interest.[27]

Such networks are already being formed by people engaged in paragovernmental activities aimed at protecting their freedom and their quality of life. Their efforts are directed at problems such as the availability of adequate shelter and the organization of our use of physical space; the redevelopment of our economy to provide opportunity, diversity, creativity, and productiveness; and the enhancement of our society's spiritual and civic engagement and vitality in the face of media- and commercial-driven mass culture. Their efforts are laying the foundation for a revitalization of democratic community, at the state and local levels in particular. In Seattle, for example, a radio talk-show host and a newspaper columnist held town meetings of eight hundred to one thousand people to protest against the handling of the savings and loan bailout and question their congressional delegates regarding their positions on the issue.[28] Such actions may become more necessary as nonparticipatory democracy continues to repress rather than solve race, class, and gender divisions.

Base communities display an impressive diversity because of their origins in tribal, ethnic, neighborhood, labor, environmental, and gender groups. Their diversity is often grounded in vernacular or folkloric techniques for dispute resolution, for intergenerational relationships, and for the production of life-sustaining goods and services. This diversity, above all, is a tremendous asset, which, assisted by a mutual sharing of information, will aid in the growth of a New Community.[29] Satellite communications, audio tape, videotape, and relatively cheap means of duplication can open up vast networks of cross-group contact, making it possible for base communities all over the world to know about and learn from each other, and to work together. As such local base communities link up to respond to more global issues, their diversity of ethnic, cultural, and local contexts can provide a deep cultural, historical, and local grounding for such responses.

Jeffersonian republicans saw democracy not merely as "an annual exercise in choosing representatives, but also the population's actual participation in the governmental decisionmaking process," an opportunity for each individual to identify his or her particular good with the good of all.[30] Harry Boyte takes exception to the classic republicanism of Jefferson, supporting Jefferson's model of popular participation, but rejecting his conviction that citizens will necessarily identify their own good with the common good. Boyte sees modern Jeffersonians pursuing a moralized politics and exhorting citizens to put aside self-interest in favor of a common good which remains hypothetical, realizable only when citizens respect and trust each other.[31] Boyte seeks to emancipate citizen politics from its many historical shackles: the cynical manipulation we associate with special interests in the representative context, the civic virtue of romantic Jeffersonianism, and the protest language of polarized good and evil that emerged from the social movements of the 1960s. In their place, he advances a "dynamic conception of public action," in which citizens (through organized action) critique public policy, act directly to solve problems, develop pragmatic skills for dealing with experts and large institutions, and concede the moral ambiguity of politics in a diverse world in which one's values cannot simply be imposed but in which basic public goods are generated by a "turbulent political process."[32] This conception of citizen action constitutes a shift from "protest to participation in governance."[33]

Though shorn of is romantic attachment to civic virtue, what emerges in Boyte's work is still more Jeffersonian than Hamiltonian, more Anti-Federalist than Federalist. Boyte, like Jefferson, sees democratic government as a value, not merely because it promotes stability, the consent of the governed, or the accountability of leaders, but also because participation in the public realm is a means of developing the spirit, intellect, and civic awareness of the population at large. In this view, freedom, justice, equality, and autonomy are not values that the individual must protect from others and from the state, but rather a product of the intellectual and practical interaction by which all participate in shaping their social habitat.[34] In Boyte's view, community-based organizations are responsible for carrying on this kind of citizen debate. This is why Boyte, like other commentators, sees neighborhoods as sleeping giants, and their people, even the most disadvantaged, as having an immense untapped potential. Block associations, social clubs, civic groups, churches, and small businesses, providing counseling, social welfare services, and some limited housing and economic development, typically with very meager resources, are laboratories in which new ways of creating self and community are being explored and out of which models of more general application can be created.

The citizen action Boyte describes, based on the continued development of such voluntary associations at the neighborhood level, is a first step away from the "politics of elites and masses that masquerades for democracy in the West,"[35] a first step toward the kind of common action that Benjamin Barber hoped for in his book *Strong Democracy*: "Community that . . . displays . . . human interdependency without sacrificing individual identity and the freedom it secures," understanding individuals not as abstract persons but as citizens, so that commonality and equality rather than separateness are the defining traits of human society; a nonmonolithic "consensus that respects dissent"; and "a politics that recognizes conflict without enthroning permanent factions . . . , [but instead] aspires to transform conflict . . . . [with] a public language that will help reformulate private interests in terms susceptible to public accommodation."[36]

The "strong" democracy of Barber and Boyte is influenced by the civic republican tradition of Jefferson, but it is based on self-interest rather than affection. It promises a means of ordering society without alienation, atomization, or distancing, on the one hand, or sentimental romanticism about the virtues of the public at large, on the other. Rather, Barber and Boyte look to participation and reconciliation, directing society through reflective, critical choices based on reason, dialogue, and confrontation. Human community is to be created through a process of "genuine collective action . . . consciously and jointly shaping policy" and social life,[37] associating democracy with a civic culture of participation, citizenship, and political activity.[38]

It seems to me, however, that both Barber and Boyte have underestimated the spiritual and social damage that has been done by modern Federalism and its "humane" incarnation, the New Property. Increased citizen mobility, the growth of PACs, the influence of lobbyists, and the distortions of the mass media have fragmented the political system and increased its volatility. Our society at large is increasingly characterized by "high crime rates, public lying, private and public fraud, systematic inegalitarianism, economic chaos, exploitation, mean-spiritedness, commercialism, privatism, persistent racism, and the atrophying of public life in the neighborhoods as well as the central government."[39] Public skepticism about the rule of law or the need for civic participation is part of a larger loss of faith in the economic and governance system. Part of this skepticism is simply a function of the immense scale of U.S.-style representative democratic institutions, which create lonely and ineffectual citizens with little sense of connection to government—even though their contacts with it are on the increase.[40] Apathy, chaos, and greed have become the dominant forms of political participation in our culture, as representative party democracy gives way to the mass, "neodemocratic" politics of special interests, media-manipulated images, and fascist, *ersatz* populism.[41]

Observations from the West Side neighborhoods of Baltimore indicate that there remain many ways in which even the most polarized of us are connected rather than separate, though our interdependence is obscured by dichotomies of race and class. This interdependence is best revealed through the human processes of interrelation—conversation, collaboration, cooperation, and networking. Base communities are needed to make connections through informal exchange and bonding, connections that are more intimate than those made through contracts or hierarchical arrangements. Facilitators of the New Community movement, operating through a loose network of peer group "base communities," can enhance the communitarian processes, economic independence, spiritual balance, and political direction of more formal organizations of which they may be a part. Base community members can complement the work of neighborhood organizations, helping them to remain open and democratic, to develop boundaries instead of walls with respect to others, and to pursue issues that cause them to link positively with similar groups.[40] New Community facilitators might emerge from community-based organizations and share insights and techniques among themselves in peer groups like MAP and WEB. As members of base communities, facilitators would try to demonstrate a commitment to robust and continuous dialogue among autonomous individuals and between autonomous groups.[42] At the outset, and on a continuing basis, this dialogue must take place inside the base communities, in a context of intimacy, immediacy, and commitment, where the options of "exit, loyalty, and voice" are unavoidably at play,[43] where people learn to handle conflict by fighting gracefully and without choosing sides.[44]

Base communities are thus cells of a social movement, one which has a spiritual and communitarian emphasis and does not merely focus on civil rights, the environment, housing, war, or peace as disembodied "mega-issues" to be addressed only through government representatives. Too often, approaching such issues through representation to the exclusion of participation provides us with an excuse to run away from people we do not want to know, pursuing instead people who seem "just like us"—as long as we do not look very deep. A New Community network can help root us, help us comprehend and live out what it means to be an active member of a culture as well as of a polity or an economy. The movement for a New Community, operating in legal, media and political arenas as well as private and community ones, thus has the potential to take the civil community beyond labels like conservative and liberal to an arena of common ground and common survival that can transcend race, sex, religion, and economic class. As we look at the deterioration of the economic and political underpinnings of the post–New Deal era, we must begin to prepare ourselves to play a role in constituting the political and economic democracy that can and should mark our future. We must train ourselves to create instruments that can assert community values and heighten the integrity and comprehensiveness of public discourse.[45]

In Baltimore, one can see a level of sophistication, experience, and energy about issues of participatory democracy and community empowerment that matches that to be found in any other city in the country. To my way of thinking, that means that the citizens of Baltimore should be challenged to do more. This book has been an attempt to document and reflect on the development of new types of social action units, base communities, emerging from the crucible of citizen action that Boyte described in his *CommonWealth*. The base communities and peer groups germinating in Baltimore often have their roots in the vernacular black neighborhoods of Baltimore's Old West Side. These new social forms are emerging as people see the limitations of the New Property, of social protest, of electoral politics, and even of citizen action as Boyte conceives it. I chose black neighborhoods for study because that is the ethnic group with which I most closely identify; it is the community of which I feel most part. But the developments I chronicle in the African-American community are offered as examples of developments occurring in a broad and diverse array of communities, developments that are the constituent elements of a New Community.

It cannot be denied that the public and private sectors of the United States are in deep difficulty. The national economy continues to develop unevenly, with gross disparities between the vitality of different regions, and even between cities and suburbs. Upward redistribution of income and a decline in public support for human development is crippling the country's ability to regenerate a skilled, able workforce. Much of the U.S. trade deficit is a reflection of the nation's longstanding unwillingness to invest in its own productivity and quality of life—education, health care, overcoming crime and poverty, environmental protection, even industrial research and development. More and more we see an ugly and violent new reality emerging from depressed communities characterized by unemployment, low wages, menial work, high rents, crime, drugs, and alcoholism. This perception is starkly set off by the conspicuous consumption of the affluent. All these developments tend to alienate people from one another at the workplace, in the schools, and in their communities; cause them to stand in awe of the wealthy; and reinforce the elitism and estrangement of our representative form of government.

The need for a private- and voluntary-sector, vernacular complement to public-sector strategies of rights, benefits, and privileges has significance not just for the black ethnic group, but for most Americans. All over the country, a reliance on "rights" and electoral victories, to the exclusion of "responsibilities" and participatory democracy, has left our citizenry disaffected and alienated from one another. At a time in our national history when we will all need each other more than ever, this is a very serious problem that needs desperately to be addressed, and addressed quickly and effectively.

The social action peer groups now operating in Baltimore may well be precursors of a social form capable of absorbing some of the shock of the great changes in store for our nation. Communication between members of such base communities might help the larger, less intimate forms of association upon which we all depend work better together, not compromising their material and objective positions, but instead opening up more non-zero-sum solutions. New Community processes that create entrepreneurial, social, and political networks enhance such possibilities by building a culture of informally connected people, a context in which trust and trustworthiness can be built, risks taken, and sustaining relationships established. These processes, so different from protest or politics, yet still related to and intertwined with them, are a great national treasure, and could well serve to cushion us through fractious and difficult times ahead.

Notes

Prologue

1. Marvin Kaufman, "A Third Way in Economics," *Human Economy Newsletter* 12 (September 1991): 3.
2. Ivan Illich, *Gender* (New York: Pantheon, 1982), p. 68, n. 51.

Chapter One

1. Charles Reich, "The New Property," *Yale Law Journal* 73 (1964): 785–87.
2. Jules Lobel, "The Meaning of Democracy: Representative and Participatory Democracy in the New Nicaraguan Constitution," *University of Pittsburgh Law Review* 49 (1988): 830; Benjamin Barber, *Strong Democracy* (Berkeley: University of California Press, 1984), p. xv.
3. Barber, *Strong Democracy*, p. xiv.
4. Jacob E. Cooke, ed., *The Federalist* (Franklin Center, Pa.: Franklin Library, 1980), pp. 59–64; see also Barber, *Strong Democracy*, pp. 93–94.
5. Barber, *Strong Democracy*, p. 5.
6. Ibid., p. xiv.
7. Matthew Crenson, *Neighborhood Politics* (Cambridge: Harvard University Press, 1983), p. 17.
8. Ibid., citing Locke in n. 27.
9. Ibid., p. 10, citing de Tocqueville in n. 7.
10. Ibid., p. 17, citing Locke in n. 30.
11. Ibid., p. 12, on government's monopoly of the legitimate use of force, citing Max Weber at n. 11.
12. Ibid., p. 13, including citation at n. 16.
13. G. C. Loury, "Two Paths to Black Power: The Conflicting Visions of Booker T. Washington and W. E. B. Du Bois," Bradley Series lecture (American Enterprise Institute), delivered in Washington, D.C., November 13, 1991, p. 20.
14. From Abraham Chapman, ed., Black Voices: An Anthology of Afro-American Literature (New York: St. Martin's Press, 1970).

15. See generally Loury, "Two Paths."

16. Crenson, *Neighborhood Politics*, pp. 16–17.

17. Ibid., pp. 19–20.

18. David Lamoreaux with Gerson G. Eisenberg, "Baltimore Views the Great Depression, 1929–33," *Maryland Historical Magazine* 71 (1976): 430.

19. Ibid., p. 435.

20. Ibid., p. 442.

21. Frances Fox Piven and Richard A. Cloward, *Why Americans Don't Vote* (New York: Pantheon, 1988), pp. 156ff.

22. Charles Reich, "The Individual Sector," *Yale Law Journal* 100 (1991): 1413.

23. Charles Reich, "Beyond the New Property: An Ecological View of Due Process," *Brooklyn Law Review* 56 (1990): 734.

24. William Simon, "The Invention and Reinvention of Welfare Rights," *Maryland Law Review* 44 (1985): 34.

25. Ibid., 30–31.

26. See Robert Reich, "Partially Managed Trade," *New York Times*, April 1, 1990.

27. See Doris A. Graber, *Mass Media and American Politics* (Washington, D.C.: Congressional Quarterly Press, 1989), p. 77.

28. W. L. Bennett, *News: The Politics of Illusion* (New York: Longman, 1988), p. 27.

29. See Ibid., pp. 46–49.

30. Ibid., p. 60.

31. Kay Lawson and P. H. Merkl, *When Parties Fail: Emerging Alternative Organizations* (Princeton, NJ.: Princeton University Press, 1988), p. 303.

32. N. W. Polsby, *The American Election of 1988: Outcome, Process, and Aftermath* (Berkeley: Institute of Governmental Studies, University of California, 1989), p. 274.

33. Simon, "The Invention and Reinvention of Welfare Rights."

34. Ibid., p. 28 (conceding that the "social work" vision has "no sense of politics").

35. Ibid., p. 29.

36. This same process was operating during the Progressive era when, as a way of stemming "corruption," the power of the vernacular political machines was broken and hegemony established by "blue-ribbon" government characterized by professional administration and remoteness from the governed. See generally Richard Hofstadter, *The Age of Reform: From Bryan to FDR* (New York: Knopf, 1955).

37. Cf. Barber, *Strong Democracy*, p. 101.

38. This process of dispersal and deterioration is depicted in *Avalon,* a film made in Baltimore about several generations of a Jewish family in that city (Tri-Star Pictures, RCA Home Video, Burbank, California, 1991).

39. See Sara Evans and Harry Boyte, *Free Spaces* (New Harper & Row, 1986); Peter L. Berger and Richard J. Neuhaus, *To Empower People: The Role of Mediating Structures in Public Policy* (Washington, D.C.: American Enterprise Institute for Public Policy Research, 1977); Saul Alinsky, *Reveille for Radicals* (New York: Vintage, 1969).

40. Harold McDougall, "The New Property vs. the New Community," *University of San Francisco Law Review* 24 (1990): 399–420.

41. Compare Robert Cover, "The Supreme Court, 1982 Term—Foreward: Nomos and Narrative," *Harvard Law Review* 97 (1983): 4; Evans and Boyte, *Free Spaces.*

Chapter Two

1. S. H. Olson, *Baltimore: The Building of an American City* (Baltimore: Johns Hopkins University Press, 1980), pp. 95–96.

2. M. R. Della, "An Analysis of Baltimore's Population in the 1850s," *Maryland Historical Magazine* 68 (1973): 28.

3. L. G. Graham, *Baltimore: 19th Century Black Capital* (Washington, D.C.: University Press of America, 1982), p. 216–22.

4. Eugene Collier, "House Built on Rock: Union Baptist Church," *Negro History Bulletin* 47 (1984): 3.

5. P. E. Hogan, "Catholic Missionary Efforts for the Negro Before the Coming of the Josephites," Ph.D. diss., Catholic University of America, 1972, p. 23.

6. Ibid., pp. 26–27.

7. W. T. Smith, "Thomas Cole's War on Slavery," *Journal of the Interdenominational Theological Center* (1974): 44–54.

8. C. E. Lincoln and L. H. Mamiya, *The Black Church in the African-American Experience* (Durham: Duke University Press, 1990), p. 51.

9. James M. Wright, *The Free Negro in Baltimore* New York: Octagon, 1971, pp. 209–38.

10. Joseph Garonzik, "The Racial and Ethnic Makeup of Baltimore Neighborhoods, 1850–70," *Maryland Historical Magazine* 71 (1976): 395.

11. G. L. Browne, *Baltimore in the Nation: 1789–1861* (Chapel Hill: University of North Carolina Press, 1980), p. 191.

12. Olson, *Baltimore,* p. 118–20.

13. Della, "Analysis of Baltimore's Population," p. 23.

14. Olson, *Baltimore*, pp. 118–19.

15. Linda Shopes, Elizabeth Fee, and Linda Zeidman, *The Baltimore Book: New Views of Local History* (Philadelphia: Temple University Press, 1991).

16. Ibid., p. 5.

17. Ralph Clayton, *Black Baltimore, 1820–1870* (Bowie, Md.: Heritage Books, 1987), p. 7.

18. August Meier, *Negro Thought in America* 1880–1915: *Racial Ideologies in the Age of Booker T. Washington.* (Ann Arbor: University of Michigan Press, 1988), pp. 140–46.

19. Olson, *Baltimore*, pp. 185–86.

20. See generally Shopes, Fee, and Zeidman, *The Baltimore Book.*

21. Graham, *Black Capital*, p. 373.

22. Della, "Analysis of Baltimore's Population," p. 32.

23. Graham, *Black Capital*, p. 178.

24. Ibid., pp. 237–46.

25. Ibid., p. 237.

26. B. J. Fields, *Slavery and Freedom on the Middle Ground: Maryland During the Nineteenth Century* (New Haven: Yale University Press, 1985), p. 282.

27. S. E. Greene, "Black Republicans on the Baltimore City Council, 1890–1931," *Maryland Historical Magazine* 74 (1979): 203.

28. Garrett Power, "Apartheid Baltimore Style: The Residential Segregation Ordinances of 1910–1913," *Maryland Law Review* 42 (1983): 292, 298–300.

29. Ibid., pp. 292–96.

30. Association for the Improvement of the Condition of the Poor, *Housing Conditions in Baltimore* (Baltimore: Charity Organization Society, 1907).

31. Seymour Toll, *Zoned American* (New York: Grossman, 1969), p. 260.

32. Ibid., p. 262.

33. See generally Garrett Power, "The Unwisdom of Allowing City Growth to Work Out Its Own Destiny," *Maryland Law Review* 47 (1988): 651–52, 664–65.

34. Ibid., p. 660.

35. Ibid., p. 673; see also p. 674.

36. Robert Ryon, *Old West Baltimore* (Baltimore: Department of City Planning, 1989), p. 55.

37. Ibid., p. 54.

38. Division of Planning, *Upton Development Guide* (Baltimore: Department of Housing and Community Development, 1970), p. 5.

39. Ibid., p. 6.

40. Ibid.

41. Ryon, *Old West Baltimore*, p. 56.

42. Ibid., p. 58.

43. Hayward Farrar, "See What the *Afro* Says: The *Baltimore Afro-American*, 1892–1950," Ph.D. diss., University of Chicago, 1983.

Chapter Three

1. *Buchanan v. Warley*, 245 U.S. 60 (1917).

2. Garrett Power, "Apartheid Baltimore Style: The Residential Segregation Ordinances of 1910–1913," *Maryland Law Review* 42 (1983): 310–12.

3. Ibid., 314–15.

4. G. H. Callcott, *Maryland and America 1940–1980* (Baltimore: Johns Hopkins University Press, 1985), p. 145.

5. Ibid., p. 147.

6. Doug Birch, "Baltimore Upbringing Fueled Marshall's Outrage Against Racism," *Baltimore Morning Sun*, June 28, 1991.

7. *Meade v. Dennistone*, 173 Md. 295 (1938).

8. *Shelley v. Kraemer*, 334 U.S. 1 (1948).

9. Power, "Apartheid," p. 318.

10. T. J. Moore, *A Search for Equality: The National Urban League, 1910–1961* (University Park, Pa.: Penn State University Press, 1981), pp. 110, 168.

11. Ibid., p. 110.

12. Ibid., pp. 176–77.

13. Ibid., p. 177.

14. Ibid., p. 178.

15. Ibid.

16. Callcott, *Maryland and America*, p. 147.

17. Ibid., p. 154.

18. Denton Watson, "Frustrations That Overcame Marshall," *Baltimore Morning Sun*, July 1, 1991.

19. J. A. Argersinger, *Toward a New Deal in Baltimore: People and Government in the Great Depression* (Chapel Hill: University of North Carolina Press, 1988), p. 98.

20. Power, "Apartheid," p. 317.

21. S. H. Olson, *Baltimore: The Building of an American City* (Baltimore: Johns Hopkins University Press, 1980), p. 37.

22. See *Pinchback v. Armistead Homes Corp.*, 689 F. Supp. 541 (1988).

23. Baltimore Public Housing Authority, *Public Housing in Baltimore* (Baltimore: PHA, 1940), pp. 21, 31.

24. Callcott, *Maryland and America*, p. 148.

25. Ibid., p. 149.

26. Robert Ryon, *Old West Baltimore* (Baltimore: Department of City Planning, 1989), p. 64.

27. Ibid., p. 66.

28. Ibid., p. 62.

29. Callcott, *Maryland and America*, pp. 164–66.

30. Carl Schoettler, "Retired Police Commissioner Pommerlau Dies," *Baltimore Evening Sun*, January 20, 1992.

31. COINTELPRO was a domestic surveillance program of the FBI, hatched by J. Edgar Hoover, which allegedly dealt in harassment, intimidation, and violence. See Athan Theoharis, "Building a File: The Case Against the FBI," *Washington Post*, October 30, 1988; Saul Landau, "A Breath of Stale Air at the FBI; Was 'National Security' a Cover for Probing Central American Protestors?" *Washington Post*, February 7, 1988; Nat Hentoff, "Someone to Watch Over Us," *Washington Post*, June 19, 1984; Nat Hentoff, "When the FBI Creates Crimes," *Washington Post*, May 18, 1984.

Chapter Four

1. J. A. Argersinger, *Toward a New Deal in Baltimore: People and Government in the Great Depression* (Durham: University of North Carolina Press, 1988), pp. 175–76.

2. Ibid., p. 14.

3. Ibid., p. 80.

4. Ibid.

5. Robert Ryon, *Old West Baltimore* (Baltimore: Department of City Planning, 1989), p. 66.

6. Frances Fox Piven and Richard A. Cloward, *Why Americans Don't Vote* (New York: Pantheon, 1988), pp. 157–59.

7. Ibid., p. 123.

8. Ibid., pp. 153–55.

9. Sidney Blumenthal, *Pledging Allegiance: The Last Campaign of the Cold War* (New York: Harper Collins, 1990), pp. 60, 78–79.

10. Jack Germond and Jules Whitcover, *Wake Us When It's Over* (New York: Macmillan, 1985), p. 29.

11. Blumenthal, *Pledging Allegiance*, p. 79.

12. Paul Hawken, *Growing a Business* (New York: Simon & Schuster, 1987), p. 43.

13. Ibid., p. 44.

14. Ibid., p. 53.

15. S. H. Olson, *Baltimore: The Building of an American City* (Baltimore: Johns Hopkins University Press, 1980), p. 375.

16. Neil Pierce and Curtis W. Johnson, "The Neighborhoods: New Hope Glimmers for the Future," *Baltimore Morning Sun*, May 5, 1991.

17. Kenneth K. Wong and Paul E. Peterson, "Urban Response to Federal Program Flexibility: The Politics of Community Development Block Grants," *Urban Affairs Quarterly* 21 (1986): 305–6.

18. Pierce and Johnson, "The Neighborhoods."

19. Joan Jacobsen, "Park Heights Group Loses HUD Block Grant Money," *Baltimore Morning Sun*, October 11, 1991.

Chapter Five

1. Samuel Banks, "Black Empowerment and Self-Respect," *Baltimore Afro-American*, February 15, 1986, p. 2.

2. G. J. Fleming, *An All-Negro Ticket in Baltimore* (New York: Holt, Rinehart & Winston, 1960).

3. Ibid., p. 2.

4. G. J. Fleming, "Baltimore's Failure to Elect a Black Mayor in 1971," Joint Center for Political Studies Monograph (Washington, D.C.: Howard University, March 1972), pp. 3–7.

5. Ibid., pp. 25–26.

6. M. C. Evans, "19 Years After City Council Redistricting, City Hall Faces Racial Battles Again," *Baltimore Morning Sun*, October 22, 1990.

7. B. A. Franklin, "Key Blacks in Baltimore Support White Mayor," *New York Times*, August 7, 1983.

8. Ibid.

9. Urban League, "The State of Black Baltimore" (Baltimore: Urban League, 1987), p. 18 (quoting from the 1935 report).

10. Ibid., p. 13.

11. M. A. Fletcher, "Blacks May Need More Than Numbers to Gain Political Clubs," *Baltimore Evening Sun*, March 13, 1991.

12. Ibid.

13. Urban League, "State of Black Baltimore," p. 14.

14. Ibid., p. 15.

15. Evans, "19 Years."

16. Robert Barnes, "Schmoke Edges Mayor Burns in Baltimore Primary Race," *Washington Post* September 16, 1987.

17. Chris Harvey, "Schaefer's Political Links to Baltimore in Jeopardy," *Washington Times*, July 20, 1987.

18. "Holy Schmoke! A Star Debuts in Baltimore," *Time*, September 28, 1987, p. 25.

19. Ibid.

20. S. H. Olson, *Baltimore: The Building of an American City* (Baltimore: Johns Hopkins University Press, 1980), pp. 379–80.

21. Garrett Power, "Apartheid Baltimore Style: The Residential Segregation Ordinances of 1910–1913," *Maryland Law Review* 42 (1983): 320–21.

22. E. S. Bruchey, "The Development of Baltimore Business, 1880–1914, Part II," *Maryland Historical Magazine* 64, no. 2 (1969): 159–60.

23. Kurt Schmoke, "In Baltimore, Economic Ties That Bind," *Baltimore Evening Sun*, October 24, 1990.

24. Health and Welfare Council of the Baltimore Area, *Survey of Action Area Residents* (Baltimore: Health and Welfare Council, 1965), p. 56–64.

25. G. H. Callcott, *Maryland and America 1940–1980* (Baltimore: Johns Hopkins University Press, 1985), p. 169.

26. Ibid.

27. Ibid.

28. Alliance for the Chesapeake Bay, recruitment brochure (1990).

29. Ibid.

30. Olson, *Baltimore*, p. 382.

31. *S. Burlington County NAACP v. Township of Mount Laurel*, 67 N. J. 151 (1975).

32. Tom Keyser, "Race Summit Summons Different People, Opinions," *Baltimore Evening Sun*, November 30, 1990.

33. Tom Keyser, "Race Summit Offers Remedies," *Baltimore Evening Sun*, December 3, 1990.

34. "Interview with John B. Ferron," *Pride* (Baltimore), January–February 1991.

35. Bryan Moorhouse, "The Race Relations Summit," *Enterprise and Inner Harbor News*, December 6, 1990, p. 1.

36. Keyser, "Race Summit Offers Remedies."

37. There has been an exodus from the Baltimore public school system: the number of pupils declined from 193,000 in 1972 to just over 100,000 in 1985.

38. Keyser, "Race Summit Offers Remedies."

39. Wiley Hall, "Race Summit Takes First Step," *Baltimore Evening Sun*, December 4, 1990.

40. M. A. Fletcher, "Blacks May Need More Than Numbers to Gain: Political Clubs' Voting Patterns Affect Black Groups," *Baltimore Evening Sun*, March 13, 1991.

41. Terence Chalkley et al, "Man Overboard," *Baltimore City Paper*, July 12, 1991, p. 6.

42. Callcott, *Maryland and America*, p. 306.

43. Ibid.

44. Ibid., p. 313.

45. Ibid., p. 306.

46. Ibid., p. 313.

47. T. W. Waldron, "NAACP Studies Redistricting to Boost Black Candidates," *Baltimore Evening Sun*, October 28, 1991.

48. Jon Morgan, "Has Baltimore Lost Its Edge in the General Assembly?" *Baltimore Evening Sun*, April 26, 1991.

49. F. A. DeFilippo, "Regional Voters Tell Politicians to Tend to Their Own Backyards," *Baltimore Evening Sun*, November 29, 1990.

Chapter Six

1. James Bock, "Blacks Less Eager for Housing Integration," *Baltimore Morning Sun*, July 7, 1991.

2. B. S. Walker, "Life Sciences: Baltimore's Future?" *Baltimore Morning Sun*, May 24, 1991.

3. Robert Barnes, "Schmoke Edges Mayor Burns in Baltimore Primary Race," *Washington Post*, September 16, 1987.

4. Holly Sklar, "American Dreams, American Nightmares," *Z Magazine*, November 1990, p. 43.

5. J. H. Barton and B. S. Fisher, *International Trade and Investment* (Boston: Little, Brown, 1989), p. 25.

6. John Miller and Ramon Castellblanch, "Does Manufacturing Matter?" *Dollars & Sense*, October 1988, p. 9.

7. Erwin Chemerinsky, "The Question's Not Clear, but Party Government Is Not the Answer," *William and Mary Law Review* 30 (1989): 413.

8. Editorial, "Unforgiving Debts," *Dollars & Sense*, May 1990, p. 2.

9. John Miller, "The Speculative Bubble Bursts," *Dollars & Sense*, June 1991, p. 6.

10. Philip Moeller, "Economic Plans Sometimes Forget the Most Needy," *Baltimore Morning Sun*, March 27, 1991.

11. Ginger Thompson, "4th District, With Most Problems, Has Least Contested Primary," *Baltimore Morning Sun*, September 8, 1991, special tabloid section, p. 12.

12. Ibid.

13. Ginger Thompson, "Redistricting Yielded Its First Harvest for Black Politicians," *Baltimore Morning Sun*, September 14, 1991.

14. F. A. DeFilippo, "Election's Over—Now It's Schmoke's Move," *Baltimore Evening Sun*, September 19, 1991.

15. M. C. Evans, "Voter Registration No Longer Key Black Strategy," *Baltimore Morning Sun*, August 18, 1991.

16. Joan Jacobson, "Schmoke Criticized on Housing Policies," *Baltimore Evening Sun*, July 23, 1991.

17. Sandy Banisky, "Schmoke Begins Chapter 2," *Baltimore Morning Sun*, December 4, 1991.

18. Michael Ollove, "City Likes Schmoke Leadership, but Wonders Where It's Being Led," *Baltimore Morning Sun*, August 11, 1991.

19. G. H. Callcott, *Maryland and America 1940–1980* (Baltimore: Johns Hopkins University Press, 1985), p. 171.

20. J. Roll, "Schmoke Battles Great Expectations," *Montgomery County Journal*, July 11, 1991.

21. Terence Chalkley et al., "Man Overboard," *Baltimore City Paper*, July 12, 1991, p. 8.

22. F. A. DeFilippo, "Playing the Numbers Game," *Baltimore Evening Sun*, July 18, 1991.

23. B. D. Ayres, Jr., "In Baltimore, a New Style at City Hall," *New York Times*, April 14, 1988.

24. Ollove, "City Likes Schmoke Leadership."

25. M. A. Fletcher, "Schmoke Holds Re-Election Edge, But Swisher, Burns, Keep Up Election Heat," *Baltimore Morning Sun*, September 8, 1991, special tabloid section.

26. Editorial, "Re-Elect Schmoke," *Baltimore Evening Sun*, October 29, 1991.

27. T. W. Waldron, "State to Clean House at Jail, Bostick, 3 Others to Be Ousted in July 1 Takeover," *Baltimore Evening Sun*, June 19, 1991.

28. Paul D. Hanson, *The People Called: The Growth of Community in the Bible* (San Francisco: Harper & Row, 1986), pp. 469–70.

29. Ibid., p. 487.

30. Ibid., p. 468–69.

31. Cornel West, *Prophesy Deliverance! An Afro-American Revolutionary Christianity* (Philadelphia: Westminster Press, 1982), pp. 111–12.

32. Ibid., p. 112.

33. Ibid., pp. 117–18.

34. Ibid., p. 120.

35. Ibid., pp. 115–16.

36. Ibid., p. 121.

37. Diane Winston, "A Powerhouse in the Pulpit," *Baltimore Morning Sun* (Sunday magazine), June 30, 1991, p. 20.

38. See generally Harry Boyte, "Neither Intimates nor Innocents: Citizen Politics in the Public Sphere," *Civic Arts Review*, Summer 1991, p. 4.

39. Harry Boyte, *CommonWealth: A Return to Citizen Politics* (New York: Free Press, 1989), p. 139 (citing Peter Berger and John Neuhaus).

40. Wiley Hall, "Deliver or Stand Aside," *Baltimore Evening Sun*, June 25, 1991.

41. Kay Lawson and P. H. Merkl, eds., *When Parties Fail: Emerging Alternative Organizations* (Princeton, N.J.: Princeton University Press, 1988), p. 172.

42. Ibid.

43. Boyte, *CommonWealth*, p. 82.

44. Ibid., pp. 95–96.

45. Robert Fisher, *Let the People Decide: Neighborhood Organizing in America* (Boston: Twayne, 1984).

46. Boyte, "Neither Intimates nor Innocents," pp. 6–7.

47. Boyte, *CommonWealth*, p. 99.

48. Ibid., p. 119.

49. Ibid., p. 109.

Chapter Seven

1. Neil Pierce and Curtis W. Johnson, "The Neighborhoods: New York Glimmers for the Future," *Baltimore Morning Sun*, May 5, 1991.

2. Ibid.

3. Paul Hawken, *Growing a Business* (New York: Simon & Schuster, 1987), p. 47.

4. Ibid., pp. 48, 52.

5. Enterprise Foundation, "The Process of Neighborhood Transformation" (Baltimore: Enterprise Foundation, 1992); Enterprise Foundation, "The Community Planning Process" (Baltimore: Enterprise Foundation, 1992).

6. Enterprise Foundation, "Community Building in Partnership," draft report (Baltimore: Enterprise Foundation, 1992), p. 52.

Chapter Eight

1. Phillip Berryman, *Liberation Theology* (Philadelphia: Temple University Press, 1987), p. 68.

2. Carlos Mesters, "The Use of the Bible in Christian Communities of the Common People," in Sergio Torres and John Eagleson, eds., *The Challenge of Basic Christian Communities* (Maryknoll, N.Y.: Orbis, 1981), pp. 199–200.

3. Ibid., p. 200.

4. M. L. Vigil, *Don Lito of El Salvador* (Maryknoll, N.Y.: Orbis, 1982).

5. Pablo Galdamez, *Faith of a People* (Maryknoll, N.Y.: Orbis, 1986), p. 1.

6. Matthew Crenson, *Neighborhood Politics* (Cambridge: Harvard University Press, 1983), p. 300.

7. Ibid., p. 298.

8. Cf. ibid., pp. 148, 152.

9. Ibid., p. 284.

10. Ibid., pp. 189, 191, 192.

11. Sara Evans and Harry Boyte, *Free Spaces* (New York: Harper & Row, 1986), pp. 188, 192.

12. Gerald Frug, "The City as a Legal Concept," Harvard Law Review 93 (1980): 1059.

13. Crenson, *Neighborhood Politics*, pp. 123–24, 126–28, 154.

14. Ibid., p. 116.

15. Ibid., pp. 39, 43, 106.

16. Cf. ibid., pp. 300–301.

17. See ibid., p. 187.

18. See generally Guillermo Cook, *Expectations of the Poor* (Maryknoll, N.Y.: Orbis, 1985).

19. C. I. Scofield, ed., *The New Scofield Study Bible* (New York: Oxford University Press, 1967), p. 1323.

20. Carol McGee Johnson, "Citizen Politics: What's in It for Communities of Color?" *Colors*, January–February 1992, pp. 33–34.

21. Juanita Vasquez, Manuel Amboya, and Gregorio Vasquez, "Indigenous Mobilization and the Theology of Liberation," in Torres and Eagleson, *Challenge of Basic Christian Communities*, p. 43.

22. Ibid., p. 44.

Chapter Nine

1. John Miller and Ramon Castellblanch, "Does Manufacturing Matter?" *Dollars & Sense*, October 1988, p. 7.

2. Ibid., p. 6.

3. Karen Pennar and Mike McNamee, "The New Face of Recession; Fallout from the Excesses of the 80's Colors This Downturn," *Business Week*, December 24, 1990, pp. 58–64.

4. Catherine Lynde, "The Zero-Inflation Ploy," *Dollars & Sense*, September 1990, p. 8.

5. Editorial, "Unforgiving Debts," *Dollars & Sense*, May 1990, p. 2.

6. John Miller, "The Speculative Bubble Bursts," *Dollars & Sense*, June 1991, p. 8.

7. Jonathan Macey, "The Role of the Democratic and Republican Parties as Organizers of Shadow Interest Groups," *Michigan Law Review* 89 (1990): 1–29.

8. N. W. Polsby, *The American Election of 1988: Outcome, Process, and Aftermath* (Berkeley: Institute of Governmental Studies, University of California, 1989), p. 273.

9. Macey, "The Parties as Shadow Interest Groups."

10. Robert Reich, "Secession of the Successful," *New York Times*, January 20, 1991.

11. Polsby, *American Election of 1988*, p. 281.

12. Sidney Blumenthal, *Pledging Allegiance: The Last Campaign of the Cold War* (New York: Harper Collins, 1990), p. 311.

13. Thomas B. Edsall and Mary D. Edsall, "Race," *Atlantic Monthly*, May 1991, pp. 61, 73.

14. Ira Shor, *Culture Wars* (New York: Routledge and Kegan Paul, 1987), pp. 26–29.

15. Cf. Matthew Crenson, *Neighborhood Politics* (Cambridge: Harvard University Press, 1983), p. 170.

16. Randi Henderson, "She's the Boss," *Baltimore Morning Sun*, January 10, 1992.

17. Holly Sklar, "American Dreams, American Nightmares," *Z Magazine*, November 1990, p. 43.

18. Benjamin Barber, *Strong Democracy* (Berkeley: University of California Press, 1984), pp. 93–94.

19. Ibid., p. 101.

20. Crenson, *Neighborhood Politics*, p. 106.

21. James Jennings, "The Politics of Black Empowerment in Urban America: Reflections on Race, Class, and Community," in J. M. Kling and P. S. Posner, eds., *Dilemmas of Activism: Class, Community, and the Politics of Local Mobilization* (Philadelphia: Temple University Press, 1990), p. 129.

22. Ibid., p. 128.

23. Ibid., p. 131.

24. Barber, *Strong Democracy*, p. 259.

25. Ibid., pp. 268–69, 271.

26. Ibid., p. 270.

27. Ibid., p. 270.

28. Editorial, "Bucket Brigades and Bailouts," *Dollars & Sense*, April 1991, p. 22.

29. John B. Childs, "New World Order or Planetary Community?" *Z Magazine*, July/August 1991, pp. 98–99.

30. Jules Lobel, "The Meaning of Democracy: Representative and Participatory Democracy in the New Nicaraguan Constitution," *University of Pittsburgh Law Review* 49 (1988): 824 (citing Thomas Jefferson's letter to Major John Cartwright of June 5, 1824, reprinted in Hannah Arendt, *On Revolution* (London: Faber & Faber, 1963), p. 257. See also Jefferson's letter to Samuel Kercheval of July 12, 1816, reprinted in *The Works of Thomas Jefferson*, vol. 12, edited by Paul Ford (1904), p. 3.

31. Harry Boyte, "The Growth of Citizen Politics," *Kettering Review*, Fall 1991, pp. 67–68.

32. Ibid., pp. 69–76.

33. Ibid., p. 76.

34. Lobel, "Meaning of Democracy," pp. 877–78; Barber, *Strong Democracy*, p. xv.

35. Barber, *Strong Democracy*, p. 117.

36. Ibid., pp. 114–19.

37. Ibid., p. 8.

38. Ibid., p. 25.

39. Ibid., p. 110.

40. Paul Brietzke, "Administrative Law and Development: The American Model Evaluated," *Howard Law Journal* 26 (1983): 647–49, 695 (citing former President Julius Nyerere of Tanzania).

41. Barber, *Strong Democracy*, p. xiii.

42. M. S. Peck, *The Different Drum: Community-Making and Peace* (New York: Simon and Schuster, 1987).

43. A. O. Hirschman, *Exit, Loyalty, and Voice: Responses to Decline in Firms, Organizations, and States* (Cambridge: Harvard University Press, 1970).

44. Peck, *Different Drummer*.

45. Harry Boyte, *Community Is Possible* (New York: Harper & Row, 1984), pp. 217–18; Jesse Jackson, "Reconciliation for America: The Lion and the Lamb, the Powerful and the Poor," speech to the American Jewish Committee of Beverly Hills, reprinted in *Los Angeles Times*, May 20, 1989.

46. Gregory Alexander, "Dilemmas of Group Autonomy: Residential Associations and Community," *Cornell Law Review* 75 (1989): 1.

Bibliography

ACCION International. *An Operational Guide for Micro-Enterprise Projects.* Toronto: Calmeadow Foundation, 1988.

Ackerman, Bruce. "Law in an Activist State." *Yale Law Journal* 92 (1983): 1083.

Adair, Margo. "Culture and Communication." Manuscript. August 16, 1991.

———. "Materials for Facilitators." Manuscript. August 2, 1991.

———. *Working Inside Out: Tools for Change.* Berkeley, Calif.: Wingbow Press, 1984.

Albert, Michael, and Robin Hahnel. *Looking Forward: Participatory Economics in the Twenty-First Century.* Boston: South End Press, 1991.

Alexander, Gregory. "Dilemmas of Group Autonomy: Residential Associations and Community." *Cornell Law Review* 75 (1989): 1.

Alinsky, Saul. *Reveille for Radicals.* New York: Vintage, 1969.

Alliance for the Chesapeake Bay. Recruitment brochure. 1990. 6600 York Road, Suite 100, Baltimore, MD 21212.

Alperovitz Gar, and Jeff Faux. *Rebuilding America.* New York: Pantheon, 1984.

Anding, Timothy, et al. *City Venture Corporation: An Experiment in Urban Development Through Public/Private Partnership.* Minneapolis: Center for Urban and Regional Affairs Publication, 1990.

Argersinger, J. A. *Toward a New Deal in Baltimore: People and Government in the Great Depression.* Chapel Hill: University of North Carolina Press, 1988.

Arnold, J. L. "The Last of the Good Old Days, Politics in Baltimore, 1920–1950." *Maryland Historical Magazine* 71 (1976): 443–48.

Ashe, Jeff. *The PISCES II Experience: Local Efforts in Micro-Enterprise Development*, vol. 1. Washington, D.C.: Agency for International Development, 1985.

Association for the Improvement of the Condition of the Poor. *Housing Conditions in Baltimore.* Baltimore: Charity Organization Society, 1907.

Ayres, B. D., Jr. "In Baltimore, a New Style at City Hall." *New York Times*, April 14, 1988.

Bahro, Rudy. *Building the Green Movement.* Philadelphia: New Society Publishers, 1986.

Baltimore Public Housing Authority. *Public Housing in Baltimore*. Baltimore: PHA, 1940.

Banisky, Sandy. "Schmoke Begins Chapter 2." *Baltimore Morning Sun*, December 4, 1991.

Banks, Samuel. "Black Empowerment and Self-Respect." *Baltimore Afro-American*, February 15, 1986.

Barber, Benjamin. *Strong Democracy*. Berkeley: University of California Press, 1984.

Barnes, Robert. "Schmoke Edges Mayor Burns in Baltimore Primary Race." *Washington Post*, September 16, 1987.

Barton, J. H., and B. S. Fisher. *International Trade and Investment*. Boston: Little, Brown, 1989.

Bates, Timothy. "Black Economic Well-Being Since the 1950s." *Review of Black Political Economy* 12 (Spring 1984): 5–39.

Batra, Ravi. *Surviving the Great Depression of 1990*. New York: Simon and Schuster, 1988.

Beer, Jennifer E. *Peacemaking in Your Neighborhood*. Philadelphia: New Society Publishers, 1986.

Bell, Derrick. "The Republican Revival and Racial Politics." *Yale Law Journal* 97 (1988): 1609.

Benello, C. G. *From the Ground Up: Essays on Grassroots and Workplace Democracy*. Boston: South End Press, 1992.

Bennett, W. L. *News: The Politics of Illusion*. New York: Longman, 1988.

Berger, Peter L., and Richard Neuhaus. *To Empower People: The Role of Mediating Structures in Public Policy*. Washington, D.C.: American Enterprise Institute for Public Policy Research, 1977.

Berry, Wendell. "The Futility of Global Thinking." *Harper's Magazine*, September 1989, p. 19.

Berryman, Phillip. *Liberation Theology*. Philadelphia: Temple University Press, 1987.

Birch, Doug. "Baltimore Upbringing Fueled Marshall's Outrage Against Racism." *Baltimore Morning Sun*, June 28, 1991.

Bird, R. N. *Plan for Social Development: Park Heights Urban Renewal Area*. Baltimore: Department of City Planning, 1975.

Bloch, H. D. "Terence V. Powderly and Disguised Discrimination." *American Journal of Economics and Sociology* 33 (1974): 145–60.

Blumenthal, Sidney. *Pledging Allegiance: The Last Campaign of the Cold War*. New York: Harper Collins, 1990.

Bock, James. "Blacks Less Eager for Housing Integration." *Baltimore Morning Sun*, July 7, 1991.

Bookchin, Murray. *The Modern Crisis*. Philadelphia: New Society Publishers, 1986.

Boyte, Harry. *The Backyard Revolution: Understanding the New Citizen Movement*. Philadelphia: Temple University Press, 1980.

———. *CommonWealth: A Return to Citizen Politics*. New York: Free Press, 1989.

———. "The Growth of Citizen Politics." *Kettering Review*, Fall 1991, p. 67.

———. "Neither Intimates nor Innocents: Citizen Politics in the Public Sphere." *Civic Arts Review*, Summer 1991, p. 4.

Bratt, Rachel, Chester Hartman, and Ann Meyerson, eds. *Critical Perspectives on Housing*. Philadelphia: Temple University Press, 1986.

Brecher, Jeremy, and Tim Costello. "A Labor and Community Party?" *Z Magazine*, April 1990, p. 79.

Brietzke, Paul. "Administrative Law and Development: The American Model Evaluated." *Howard Law Journal* 26 (1983): 645.

Brown, Warren. "Port in a Storm." *Washington Post*, January 29, 1990.

Browne, G. L. *Baltimore in the Nation: 1789–1861*. Durham: University of North Carolina Press, 1980.

Bruchey, E. S. "The Development of Baltimore Business, 1880–1914, Part I." *Maryland Historical Magazine* vol. 64, no. 2 (1969): 18–42.

———. "The Development of Baltimore Business, 1880–1914, Part II." *Maryland Historical Magazine* vol. 64, no. 2 (1969): 144–60.

Bryant, John. "A Black Church in Baltimore." In Anthony Walker, ed., *See How They Grow*, pp. 39–46. (Glasgow, Scotland: Fount Publishers, 1979.

Buchanan v. Warley, 245 U.S. 60 (1917).

Callcott, G. H. *Maryland and America 1940–1980*. Baltimore: Johns Hopkins University Press, 1985.

Castells, Manuel. *The City and the Grassroots: A Cross-Cultural Theory of Urban Social Movements*. Berkeley: University of California Press, 1983.

Chalkley, Terence, et al. "Man Overboard." *Baltimore City Paper*, July 12, 1991, p. 6.

Chemerinsky, Erwin. "The Question's Not Clear, but Party Government Is Not the Answer." *William and Mary Law Review* 30 (1989): 411.

Childs, John B. "New World Order or Planetary Community?" *Z Magazine*, July/August 1991, pp. 98–99.

Chomsky, Noam. "The Tasks Ahead IV: Post-Cold War Cold War." *Z Magazine*, March 1990, pp. 8–13.

Clayton, Ralph. *Black Baltimore, 1820–1870*. Bowie, Md.: Heritage Books, 1987.

Clune, William. "A Political Model of Implementation." *Iowa Law Review* 69 (1983): 47.

Cohen, David, and Wendy Wolf. "Freeing Congress from the Special Interest State." *Harvard Law Journal on Legislation* 17 (1980): 253–93.

Collier, Eugene. "House Built on Rock: Union Baptist Church." *Negro History Bulletin* 47 (1984): 3.

Collins, Ronald K., and David M. Skover. "The Future of Liberal Legal Scholarship." *Michigan Law Review* 87 (1988); 189.

Cook, Guillermo. *Expectations of the Poor.* Maryknoll, N.Y.: Orbis, 1985.

Cooke, Jacob E., ed. *The Federalist.* Franklin Center, Pa.: Franklin Library, 1980.

Cover, Robert. "The Supreme Court, 1982 Term—Foreword: Nomos and Narrative," *Harvard Law Review* 97 (1983): 4.

Crenson, Matthew. *Neighborhood Politics.* Cambridge: Harvard University Press, 1983.

Crooks, J. B. *Politics and Progress: The Rise of Urban Progressivism in Baltimore 1895–1911.* Baton Rouge: Louisiana State University, Press, 1968.

———. "Politics and Reform: The Dimensions of Baltimore Progressivism." *Maryland Historical Magazine* 71, no. 3 (1976): 491.

Cutler, Phoebe. *The Public Landscape of the New Deal.* Hew Haven: Yale University Press, 1985.

Dahl, R. A. *Democracy and Its Critics.* New Haven: Yale University Press, 1989.

De Filippo, F. A. "Election's Over—Now It's Schmoke's Move." *Baltimore Evening Sun*, September 19, 1991.

———. "Playing the Numbers Game." *Baltimore Evening Sun*, July 18, 1991.

———. "Regional Voters Tell Politicians to Tend to Their Own Backyards." *Baltimore Evening Sun*, November 29, 1990.

Della, M. R. "An Analysis of Baltimore's Population in the 1850s." *Maryland Historical Magazine* 68 (1973): 20–35.

Division of Planning. *Harlem Park Neighborhood Information System.* Baltimore: Department of Housing and Community Development, 1983.

———. *Park Heights Neighborhood Information System.* Baltimore: Department of Housing and Community Development, 1982.

———. *Upton Development Guide.* Baltimore: Department of Housing and Community Development, 1970.

———. *Upton Neighborhood Information System.* Baltimore: Department of Housing and Community Development, 1983.

Downs, Anthony. "The Housing Challenge." *Brookings Review*, Winter 1988/89, p. 34.

Dreier, Peter. "Dreams and Nightmares." *The Nation*, August 21–28, 1982, p. 141.

Durr, W. T. "The Conscience of a City: A History of the Citizens' Planning and Housing Association and Efforts to Improve Housing for the Poor in Baltimore, Maryland, 1937–1954." Ph.D. diss., Johns Hopkins University, 1972.

Editorial. "Bucket Brigades & Bailouts." *Dollars & Sense*, April 1991, p. 22.

Editorial. "Re-Elect Schmoke." *Baltimore Evening Sun*, October 29, 1991.

Editorial. "Unforgiving Debts." *Dollars & Sense*, May 1990, p. 2.

Edsall Thomas B., and Mary D. Edsall. "Race." *Atlantic Monthly*, May 1991, p. 53.

Enterprise Foundation. "Community Building in Partnership." Draft report. Baltimore: Enterprise Foundation, 1992.

———. "The Community Planning Process." Baltimore: Enterprise Foundation, 1992.

———. "The Process of Neighborhood Transformation." Baltimore: Enterprise Foundation, 1992.

Evans, M. C. "19 Years After City Council Redistricting, City Hall Faces Racial Battles Again." *Baltimore Morning Sun*, October 22, 1990.

———. "Voter Registration No Longer Key Black Strategy." *Baltimore Morning Sun*, August 18, 1991.

Evans, Sara, and Harry Boyte. *Free Spaces*. New York: Harper & Row, 1986.

Fainstein, N. I., and S. S. Fainstein. *Urban Policy Under Capitalism*. Beverley Hills: Sage Publications, 1982.

Farrar, Hayward. "See What the *Afro* Says: The *Baltimore Afro-American*, 1892–1950." Ph.D. diss., University of Chicago, 1983.

Fields, B. J. *Slavery and Freedom on the Middle Ground: Maryland During the Nineteenth Century*. New Haven: Yale University Press, 1985.

Fisher, Louis. *The Politics of Shared Power*. Washington, D.C.: Congressional Quarterly Press, 1987.

Fisher, Robert. *Let the People Decide: Neighborhood Organizing in America*. Boston: Twayne, 1984.

Fleming, G. J. *An All-Negro Ticket in Baltimore*. New York: Holt, Rinehart & Winston, 1960.

———. "Baltimore's Failure to Elect a Black Mayor in 1971." Washington, D.C.: Joint Center for Political Studies Monograph, Howard University, 1972.

Fletcher, M. A. "Blacks May Need More Than Numbers to Gain: Political Clubs' Voting Patterns Affect Black Groups." *Baltimore Evening Sun*, March 13, 1991.

———. "Schmoke Holds Re-Election Edge, But Swisher, Burns, Keep Up Election Heat." *Baltimore Morning Sun*, September 8, 1991, special tabloid section, p. 1.

Foggie, C. H. "Retirement Notes in the Philadelphia and Baltimore Conference of the AME Zion Church." *AME Zion Quarterly*, July 1988, pp. 2–8.

Franklin, B. A. "Key Blacks in Baltimore Support White Mayor." *New York Times*, August 7, 1983.

Fromm, Erich. *To Have or To Be?* New York: Bantam, 1981.

Frug, Gerald. "The City as a Legal Concept." *Harvard Law Review* 93 (1980): 1059.

Galdamez, Pablo. *Faith of a People.* Maryknoll, N.Y.: Orbis, 1986.

Garonzik, Joseph. "The Racial and Ethnic Makeup of Baltimore Neighborhoods, 1850–70." *Maryland Historical Magazine* 71, no. 3 (1976): 392–402.

Garvey, Gerald. "The Post-Cold War International Order." Manuscript. Princeton, 1990.

Germond, Jack, and Jules Whitcover. *Wake Us When It's Over.* New York: Macmillan, 1985.

Gilderbloom, John I., and Richard P. Appelbaum. "Rethinking Rental Housing: A Progressive Strategy." *Journal of Housing* 45 (September–October 1988): 227.

Gill, Stephen, and David Law. *The Global Political Economy.* Baltimore: Johns Hopkins University Press, 1988.

Goldberg, Robert Marc. "Party Competition and Black Politics in Baltimore and Philadelphia." Ph.D. diss., Brandeis University, 1984.

Gooding-Williams, Robert. *Black Neoconservatives: A Critical Introduction.* London: Praxis International, 1987.

Gordon, David. "Do We Need to Be No. 1?" *Atlantic Monthly*, April 1986, p. 100.

Graber, Doris A. *Mass Media and American Politics.* Washington, D.C.: Congressional Quarterly Press, 1989.

Graham, L. G. *Baltimore: 19th Century Black Capital.* Washington, D.C.: University Press of America, 1982.

Greene, S. E. "Black Republicans on the Baltimore City Council, 1890–1931." *Maryland Historical Magazine* 74 (1979): 203–22.

Greene-Chappelle, S. E. *Baltimore: An Illustrated History* (Woodland Hills, Calif.: Windsor Publications, 1980.

Hall, Wiley. "Deliver or Stand Aside." *Baltimore Evening Sun*, June 25, 1991.

———. "Race Summit Takes First Step." *Baltimore Evening Sun*, December 4, 1990.

Hanson, Paul D. *The People Called: The Growth of Community in the Bible.* San Francisco: Harper & Row, 1986.

Hartman, Chester, ed. *America's Housing Crisis: What Is to Be Done?* Boston: Routledge and Kegan Paul, 1985.

Harvey, Chris. "Schaefer's Political Links to Baltimore in Jeopardy." *Washington Times*, July 20, 1987.

Hatch, R. D. *Beyond Opportunity: Jesse Jackson's Vision for America*. Philadelphia: Fortress Press, 1988.

Hawken, Paul. *Growing a Business*. New York: Simon & Schuster, 1987.

Health and Welfare Council of the Baltimore Area. *Survey of Action Area Residents*. Baltimore: Health and Welfare Council, 1965.

Henderson, Randi. "She's the Boss." *Baltimore Morning Sun*, January 10, 1992.

Hirschman, A. O. *Exit, Loyalty, and Voice: Responses to Decline in Firms, Organizations, and States* Cambridge: Harvard University Press, 1970.

Hofstadter, Richard. *The Age of Reform: From Bryan to FDR*. New York: Knopf, 1955.

Hogan, P. E. "Catholic Missionary Efforts for the Negro Before the Coming of the Josephites." Ph.D. diss., Catholic University of America.

Holmes, J. L. "What Shall We Be? A Study of the Political Thought of Three Black Americans." Ph.D. diss., Duke University, 1980.

"Holy Schmoke! A Star Debuts in Baltimore." *Time*, September 28, 1987, p. 25.

Hooks, Bell. "The Legacy of Malcolm X." *Z Magazine*, December 1990, p. 18.

Hwang, Hae-Sung. "Booker T. Washington and W. E. B. Du Bois: A Study in Race Leadership, 1985–1915." Ph.D. diss., University of Hawaii, 1988.

Illich, Ivan. *Gender*. New York: Pantheon, 1982.

Institute for Community Economics. *The Community Land Trust Handbook*. Emmaus, Pa.: Rodale Press, 1982.

"Interview with J. B. Ferron." *Pride* (Baltimore), January/February 1991.

Jacobs, Jane. *Cities and the Wealth of Nations: Principles of Economic Life*. New York: Vintage Books, 1984.

Jacobson, Joan. "Park Heights Group Loses HUD Block Grant Money." *Baltimore Morning Sun*, October 11, 1991.

———. "Schmoke Criticized on Housing Policies." *Baltimore Evening Sun*, July 23, 1991.

Jennings, James. "The Politics of Black Empowerment in Urban America: Reflections on Race, Class, and Community." In J. M. Kling and P. S. Posner, eds., *Dilemmas of Activism: Class, Community, and the Politics of Local Mobilization*, p. 113. Philadelphia: Temple University Press, 1990.

Johnson, C. M. "Citizens Politics: What's In It for Communities of Color?" *Colors*, January–February 1992, p. 28.

Johnson, L. T. *Sharing Possessions: Mandate and Symbol of Faith*. Philadelphia: Fortress Press, 1981.

Johnson, R. M. *The First Charity.* Washington, D.C.: Seven Locks Press, 1988.

Jones, V. L., et al. *An Action Plan for Improving Neighborhood Organizations and Community Self-Help in Baltimore.* Baltimore: Development Training Institute, 1989.

Kaufman, Marvin. "A Third Way in Economics." *Human Economy Newsletter* 12 (September 1991): 3.

Keyser, Tom. "Race Summit Offers Remedies," *Baltimore Evening Sun*, December 3, 1990.

————. "Race Summit Summons Different People, Opinions." *Baltimore Evening Sun*, November 30, 1990.

Kingdon, J. W. *Agendas, Alternatives, and Public Policies.* Boston: Little, Brown, 1984.

Lakey, George. *Powerful Peacemaking: A Strategy for a Living Revolution.* Philadelphia: New Society Publishers, 1987.

Lamoreaux, David, with Gerson G. Eisenberg. "Baltimore Views the Great Depression, 1929–33." *Maryland Historical Magazine* 71 (1976): 428–42.

Lawson, Kay, and P. H. Merkl, eds. *When Parties Fail: Emerging Alternative Organizations.* Princeton, N.J.: Princeton University Press, 1989.

Lincoln, C. Eric, and Lawrence Mamiya. *The Black Church in the African-American Experience.* Durham: Duke University Press, 1990.

Lippit, Victor. "Lippit Responds." *Dollars & Sense*, March 1990, p. 11.

Lobel, Jules. "The Meaning of Democracy: Representative and Participatory Democracy in the New Nicaraguan Constitution." *University of Pittsburgh Law Review* 49 (1988): 823.

Loury, G. C. "Two Paths to Black Power: The Conflicting Visions of Booker T. Washington and W. E. B. Du Bois." Bradley Series lecture (American Enterprise Institute), delivered in Washington, D.C., November 13, 1991.

Lynch, E. A. *Religion and Politics in Latin America: Liberation Theology and Christian Democracy.* New York: Praeger, 1991.

Lynde, Catherine. "The Zero-Inflation Ploy." *Dollars & Sense*, September 1990, p.8.

McCamant, Kathryn M., and Charles R. Durrett. *Cohousing.* Berkeley: Habitat Press, 1988.

McDougall, Harold. "The New Property vs. the New Community." *University of San Francisco Law Review* 24 (1990): 399–420.

MacEwan, Arthur. *Debt and Disorder.* New York: Monthly Review Press, 1990.

MacEwan, Arthur, and William Tabb, eds. *Instability and Change the World Economy.* New York: Monthly Review Press, 1989.

Macey, Jonathan. "The Role of the Democratic and Republican Parties as

Organizers of Shadow Interest Groups." *Michigan Law Review* 89 (1990): 1–29.

McWilliams, C. W. *The Idea of Fraternity in America*. Berkeley: University of California Press, 1973.

Meade v. Dennistone, 173 Md. 295 (1938).

Meier, August. *Negro Thought in America: 1880–1915: Racial Ideologies in the Age of Booker T. Washington*. Ann Arbor: University of Michigan Press, 1987.

Mesters, Carlos. "The Use of the Bible in Christian Communities of the Common People." In S. Torres and J. Eagleson, *The Challenge of Basic Christian Communities*, pp. 197–212. Maryknoll, N.Y.: Orbis, 1981.

Michelman, Frank. "Republican Property." Paper presented to Symposium on Law and Rhetoric at Northwestern University, June 2, 1986.

Miller, John. "The Speculative Bubble Bursts." *Dollars & Sense*, June 1991, pp. 6–7.

Miller, John, and Ramon Castellblanch. "Does Manufacturing Matter?" *Dollars & Sense*, October 1988, p. 6.

Mitchell, Constance. "Home, Sweet Home." *Black Enterprise*, June 1986, p. 291.

Moeller, Philip. "Economic Plans Sometimes Forget the Most Needy." *Baltimore Evening Sun*, March 27, 1991.

Moore, T. J. *A Search for Equality: The National Urban League, 1910–1961*. University Park, Pa.: Penn State University Press, 1981.

Morgan, Jon. "Has Baltimore Lost Its Edge in the General Assembly?" *Baltimore Evening Sun*, April 26, 1991.

Myers, W. S. *The Self-Reconstruction of Baltimore, 1864–1867*. Baltimore: Johns Hopkins University Press, 1909.

Nordinger, E. A. *On the Autonomy of the Democratic State*. Cambridge: Harvard University Press, 1983.

O'Keefe, Kevin. *Baltimore Politics, 1971–1986*. Washington, D.C.: Georgetown University Press, 1986.

Ollove, Michael. "City Likes Schmoke Leadership, But Wonders Where It's Being Led." *Baltimore Morning Sun*, August 11, 1991.

Olsen, F. E. "The Family and the Market: A Study of Ideology and Legal Reform." *Harvard Law Review* 96 (1983): 1497–1578.

Olson, S. H. *Baltimore: The Building of an American City*. Baltimore: Johns Hopkins University Press, 1980.

Orser, W. Edward. "Secondhand Suburbs: Black Pioneers in Baltimore's Edmondson Village, 1955–1980." *Journal of Urban History* 16, no. 3 (1990): 227–62.

Peck, M. S. *The Different Drum: Community-Making and Peace*. New York: Simon and Schuster, 1987.

Pennar, Karen, and Mike McNamee. "The New Face of Recession; Fallout from the Excesses of the 80's Colors This Downturn." *Business Week*, December 24, 1990, pp. 58–64.

Perin, Constance. *Belonging in America*. Madison: University of Wisconsin Press, 1988.

Perkins, John. *With Justice for All*. Grand Rapids, Mich: Eerdsmans, 1988.

Pierce, Neil, and Curtis W. Johnson. "The Neighborhoods: New Hope Glimmers for the Future." *Baltimore Morning Sun*, May 5, 1991.

Pinchback v. Armistead Homes Corp., 689 F. Supp. 541 (1988).

Piven, Frances Fox, and Richard A. Cloward. *Why Americans Don't Vote*. New York: Pantheon, 1988.

Polanyi, Michael. *The Tacit Dimension*. Garden City, N.Y.: Doubleday, 1966.

Polsby, N. W. *The American Election of 1988: Outcome, Process, and Aftermath*. Berkeley: Institute of Governmental Studies, University of California, 1989.

Power, Garrett. "Apartheid Baltimore Style: The Residential Segregation Ordinances of 1910–1913," *Maryland Law Review* 42 (1983): 290.

———. "Pyrrhic Victory: Daniel Goldman's Defeat of Zoning in the Maryland Court of Appeals." *Maryland Historical Magazine* 82 (1981): 282.

———. "The Unwisdom of Allowing City Growth to Work Out Its Own Destiny." *Maryland Law Review* 47 (1988): 626.

Regional Planning Council. *Baltimore SMSA, 1980: Household Populations*. Baltimore: Regional Planning Council, 1982.

Reich, Charles. "Beyond the New Property: An Ecological View of Due Process." *Brooklyn Law Review* 56 (1990): 731.

———. "The Individual Sector." *Yale Law Journal* 100 (1991): 1409.

———. "The New Property." *Yale Law Journal* 73 (1964): 733.

Reich, Robert. "Partially Managed Trade." *New York Times*, April 1, 1990.

———. "Secession of the Successful." *New York Times*, January 20, 1991.

Reichman, Rebecca. *The Dominican Association of Triciteros "San Jose Obero": A Case Study of Local Empowerment*. Cambridge, Mass.: ACCION International, 1984.

———. *Women's Participation in PROGRESSO: A Microenterprise Credit Program Reaching the Smallest Businesses of the Poor in Lima, Peru*. Cambridge, Mass.: ACCION International, 1984.

Rifkin, Jeremy. *Entropy: A New World View*. New York: Bantam, 1981.

Roll, J. "Schmoke Battles Great Expectations," *Montgomery County Journal*, July 11, 1991.

Rouse, Jim. "To Transform the Lives of the Poor." *Miami Herald*, September 5, 1991.

Rubenstein, J. M. "Relocation of Families for Public Improvement Projects: Lessons from Baltimore." *American Planning Association Journal* 54, no. 2 (Spring 1988): 185.

Ryon, Robert. *Old West Baltimore*. Baltimore: Department of City Planning, 1989.

Sale, Kirkpatrick. "Bioregional Green." *The Nation*, June 16, 1984, p. 724.

————. *Dwellers in the Land: The Bioregional Vision*. San Francisco: Sierra Club Books, 1985.

Sander, Richard H. "Individual Rights and Demographic Realities: The Problem of Fair Housing." *Northwestern University Law Review* 82 (1988): 874.

Schmoke, Kurt. "In Baltimore, Economic Ties That Bind." *Baltimore Evening Sun*, October 24, 1990.

Schoettler, Carl. "Retired Police Commissioner Pommerlau Dies." *Baltimore Evening Sun*, January 20, 1992.

Schorr, Lizbeth. *Within Our Reach: Breaking the Cycle of Disadvantage*. New York: Anchor/Doubleday, 1989.

Scofield, C. I., ed. *The New Scofield Study Bible*. New York: Oxford University Press, 1967.

Selznick, Philip. "The Idea of a Communitarian Morality." *California Law Review* 75 (1987): 445.

Shao, Stephen P. "1989–90 Economic Indicators for the Baltimore Region." Report for the Regional Planning Council, Mayor's Advisory Committee on Small Business. Baltimore: University of Baltimore Center for Public Policy, 1991.

Shelley v. Kraemer, 334 U.S. 1 (1948).

Shopes, Linda, Elizabeth Fee, and Linda Zeidman. *The Baltimore Book: New Views of Local History*. Philadelphia: Temple University Press, 1991.

Shor, Ira. *Culture Wars*. New York: Routledge and Kegan Paul, 1987.

Simon, William. "The Invention and Reinvention of Welfare Rights." *Maryland Law Review* 44 (1985): 1.

Sklar, Holly. "American Dreams, American Nightmares." *Z Magazine*, November 1990, p. 41.

Skotnes, Andor. "The Black Freedom Movement and the Worker's Movement in Baltimore, 1930–1939." Ph.D. diss., Rutgers University, 1991.

Smith, H. H. *Planning America's Communities: Paradise Found? Paradise Lost?* Chicago: Planner's Press, 1991.

Smith, W. T. "Thomas Cole's War on Slavery." *Journal of the Interdenominational Theological Center* 2 (1974): 44–54.

Steiner, Rudolph. *The Social Future*. Spring Valley, N.Y.: Anthroposophic Press, 1935.

Sullam, Brian. "Challengers Lay Jail Mix-Up to Schmoke." *Baltimore Morning Sun*, August 20, 1991.

Szanton, Peter L. *Baltimore 2000*. Baltimore: Morris Goldseker Foundation, 1986.

Taylor, Michael. *The Possibility of Cooperation*. New York: Cambridge University Press, 1987.

————. *Rationality and Revolution*. New York: Cambridge University Press, 1988.

Thompson, Ginger. "4th District, With Most Problems, Has Least Contested Primary." *Baltimore Morning Sun*, September 8, 1991.

————. "Redistricting Yielded Its First Harvest for Black Politicians." *Baltimore Morning Sun*, September 14, 1991.

Toffler, Alvin. *The Third Wave*. New York: Bantam Books, 1980.

Toll, Seymour. *Zoned American*. New York: Grossman, 1969.

Toll, William. "Rehabilitation and Revitalization: Black Perspectives on Race Relations." *Humboldt Journal of Social Relations* 10 (1982–83): 301–19.

Torres, Sergio, and John Eagleson, eds., *The Challenge of Basic Christian Communities*. Maryknoll, N.Y.: Orbis, 1981.

Unger, Roberto. *Knowledge and Politics*. New York: Free Press, 1975.

Urban League. "The State of Black Baltimore." Baltimore: Urban League, 1987.

Vasquez, Juanita, M. Amboya, and G. Vasquez. "Indigenous Mobilization and the Theology of Liberation." In Sergio Torres and John Eagleson, eds., *The Challenge of Basic Christian Communities*, pp. 38–45. Maryknoll, N.Y.: Orbis, 1981.

Vigil, M. L. *Don Lito of El Salvador*. Maryknoll, N.Y.: Orbis, 1981.

Wachtel, P. L. *The Poverty of Affluence: A Psychological Portrait of the American Way of Life*. Philadelphia: New Society Publishers, 1989.

Waldron, T. W. "NAACP Studies Redistricting to Boost Black Candidates." *Baltimore Evening Sun*, October 28, 1991. p. B4.

————. "State to Clean House at Jail, Bostick, 3 Others to Be Ousted in July 1 Takeover." *Baltimore Evening Sun*, June 14, 1991.

Walker, B. S. "Life Sciences: Baltimore's Future?" *Baltimore Morning Sun*, May 24, 1991.

Walker, P. K. "Business and Commerce in Baltimore on the Eve of Independence." *Maryland Historical Magazine* 71 (1976): 296–309.

Watson, Denton. "Frustrations That Overcame Marshall." *Baltimore Morning Sun*, July 1, 1991.

West, Cornel. *The Ethical Dimensions of Marxist Thought*. New York: Monthly Review Press, 1991.

————. *Prophesy Deliverance! An Afro-American Revolutionary Christianity*. Philadelphia: Westminster Press, 1982.

Winston, Diane. "A Powerhouse in the Pulpit." *Baltimore Morning Sun* (Sunday magazine), June 30, 1991, p. 20.

Wong, Kenneth K., and Paul E. Peterson. "Urban Response to Federal Program Flexibility: The Politics of Community Development Block Grants." *Urban Affairs Quarterly* 21 (1986): 293.

Wright, James M. *The Free Negro in Maryland, 1634–1860.* New York: Octagon, 1971.

Index